PENGUIN BO

AN ACCIDEN

Martin Bell was a staff member of BBC TV news from 1965 to his sudden and unplanned retirement in April 1997. Awarded the OBE in 1992, he was also voted Royal Television Society Reporter of the Year in 1977 and again in 1993 for his work in Bosnia, where he was wounded. He was elected to Parliament in May 1997 as an Independent but unsuccessfully contested the Brentwood and Ongar seat in the 2001 General Election. He is the author of *In Harm's Way*, which is also published by Penguin.

An Accidental MP

MARTIN BELL

PENGUIN BOOKS

PENGUIN BOOKS

Published by the Penguin Group
Penguin Books Ltd, 80 Strand, London WC2 ORL, England
Penguin Putnam Inc., 375 Hudson Street, New York, New York 10014, USA
Penguin Books Australia Ltd, Ringwood, Victoria, Australia
Penguin Books Canada Ltd, 10 Alcorn Avenue, Toronto, Ontario, Canada M4V 3B2
Penguin Books India (P) Ltd, 11, Community Centre,
Panchsheel Park, New Delhi – 110 017, India
Penguin Books (NZ) Ltd, Cnr Rosedale and Airborne Roads,
Albany, Auckland, New Zealand
Penguin Books (South Africa) (Pty) Ltd, 5 Watkins Street,
Denver Ext 4, Johannesburg 2094, South Africa

Penguin Books Ltd, Registered Offices: 80 Strand, London WC2 ORL, England

First published by Viking 2000
Revised edition published in Penguin Books 2001

1

'Sometimes' by Sheenagh Pugh reproduced on p.43
by kind permission of the author

The moral right of the author has been asserted

Set in Monotype Bembo
Printed in England by Clays Ltd, St Ives plc

For Fiona

'The unfortunate Independent Member has nothing to offer, but harsh refusal, or pitiful excuse, or despondent representation of a hopeless interest. Except from his private fortune, he has no way of making a single friend. In the House, he votes for ever in a dispirited minority. Can we conceive of a more discouraging post of duty than this?'

Edmund Burke, *Thoughts on the Cause of the Present Discontents*, 1770

Contents

1. The Death of News

The safety people presented their latest creation with the pride of master craftsmen. It was a flak jacket customized in a tasteful shade of off-white. It was the Rolls-Royce of flak jackets – or perhaps because of its weight the Sherman tank of flak jackets. It had pockets and flaps and Velcro straps, and exactly the sort of southerly protection that I had lacked when I was hit four years earlier. It featured a prominent BBC logo on the back, just in case my enemies needed target practice as I retreated. It also came equipped with two sizes of ceramic plate – smaller plates back and front for conditions of moderate danger and larger plates for conditions of extreme danger. The wearer was presumably supposed to put his finger to the wind on some blighted front line – and if somebody shot it off, remove the flak jacket with the remaining digits and insert the higher calibre protection. I didn't wish to seem ungrateful, for the BBC were pioneers on the issue of safety and took it seriously, but it occurred to me that at some point in my thirty-four years in their service – and probably some quite recent point – the lunatics had taken over the asylum.

From the time of the Greeks and the Romans armour has always been a compromise between protection and mobility. Safety lies not only in steel or chain-mail or ceramic plates, but in the speed of foot over open ground which they hinder. I seldom wore my old flak jacket except in front of the camera as a show of deference to the safety-conscious management. And I never wore the new one at all, although I carried it once on a trip to report the elections in Kashmir, where it was of limited value in a conflict where the weapons were rocks on one side and tear gas on the other.

Besides, the Bosnian war was in remission, and I clearly had more past than future as a war reporter. I had left that tragic and beautiful country for the last time in April 1996, seeking new challenges and failing to find them. A reporter as much as an actor can be typecast, and as much as an actor can be rested too. I discussed this at length with Kate Adie – there are few short discussions with Kate – whose career had passed into a similar sort of limbo. We remembered our Shakespeare:

> 'Perseverance, dear my lord,
> Keeps honour bright: to have done, is to hang
> Quite out of fashion, like a rusty mail
> In monumental mockery.'

At least that was one advantage of the new BBC body armour: being made of plastic, its mail would never rust in any kind of mockery but ours.

Kate was certainly more popular with her viewers than with her editors. So to some extent was I. We were facing the nemesis of minor celebrities, which was to be famous for being famous, and for nothing else. We had a good idea of what was happening to us: it was easier to take the reporter out of the war zone than the war zone out of the reporter. Except when we were calling each other, we sat beside silent telephones. To pass the time, we hit the celebrity circuit: we did charity lunches, literary dinners, Army Staff College seminars and students' unions – everything but weddings and barmitzvahs. We were yesterday's people, we concluded. In due course, and after the next purge, we would be air-brushed out of the BBC's equivalent of the Kremlin photograph. It had happened to Mark Tully in Delhi, an honourable man disgracefully treated, and we would be next in line.

We were supplanted by a new breed of correspondent more amenable to the instructions of head office; most of these were competent and reliable, but some were so inept under pressure, and so great a danger to themselves and to others, that they should not have been sent further afield than Bognor Regis. The watchword was quantity. At one point in Albania no fewer than eight of these lost souls were sent out to compete with each other, with results almost as violent as the events they were supposed to be reporting. Kosovo in 1999 was worse: the hostility between the Serbs and Albanians was matched in a minor key by the rivalry between the nineteen BBC journalists on the ground. Kate Adie, no stranger to intimidation, was accosted by a former colleague who threatened to rearrange her features so that she would never appear on television again. I remonstrated on her behalf, and was rewarded with an angry letter from that sad and obsolete character.

Towards the end of 1996 I did a little time and motion study. It told me that I had worked for eleven days in seven months. At that point without regret or hesitation I slipped a short note under the foreign editor's door thanking the BBC for thirty-four wonderful years and announcing my resignation.

Kate was appalled. 'You can't resign,' she said.

'I just have resigned,' I answered.

'Then you must retract it.'

'I'll do nothing of the sort. I refuse to be paid for not working.'

To those who know her, Kate has a gentler side than she shows to the viewing public, but that day it was in abeyance. She possesses the most eloquent body language of anyone I know. When you talk to her, or more usually when you listen to her, she does not sit down as most people do, but stands between you and the exit. She becomes Kate rampant. For this particular conversation, at a Balkan reunion in my London house, she had me backed up so far against the kitchen sink that I almost fell into it. She reproached me for defeatism. We should stand our ground and fight, she said, from inside the Corporation. And as the warrior queen of British television that was exactly what she did. A year and a half later, under the pressure of public opinion, the managers of BBC news were forced to rehabilitate her. A poll of *Radio Times* readers voted her the best TV and radio news reporter ever. She received nearly twice as many votes as the runner-up, whom modesty forbids me to name. And it was a sure sign of British resolve, during wars and rumours of wars in the Gulf, when she appeared with satellite dish in attendance on the bridge of HMS *Invincible*. Nor were her talents confined to British aircraft carriers; in a later crisis, she stormed her way on to the USS *Enterprise*. No war was worthy of its name without her.

I did not so much fight as capitulate. My resignation this time was not accepted (although four months later it was, and with alacrity). The BBC came back to me with an offer I could hardly refuse: a radio series on journalism and war, special assignments for the *Nine O'Clock News*, and a documentary about Kofi Annan, the new Secretary-General of the United Nations. Most reporters would have jumped at the chance. I accepted it reluctantly.

The problem was partly mine. I realized that my faith in journalism was shaken, like that of a true believer troubled by doubt: it put me in mind of the Roman priests described in Gibbon's *Decline and Fall*, who practised their religion with affected zeal and secret indignation. (The same Edward Gibbon MP, so prolific on paper, who sat in the House of Commons for eight years and never uttered a word.) My grandfather had been a journalist, the news editor of the London *Observer* in the 1930s. My father had been close to newspapers, as a columnist for the *Eastern Daily Press* for forty years, the creator of the *Times* crossword puzzle and its most notable compiler for half a century. I had been a reporter all my working life, starting with horse shows in Norfolk and ending with the war in Bosnia. In all that time there was a certain consensus among journalists themselves about what was news and what wasn't. They had a collective idea and folk memory of it. It was hard to define, but a bit like art – they knew it when they saw it. It lay somewhere on an axis between what they considered important and what they considered interesting. It might be important but not interesting (except to a few), like a shareholders' revolt; or interesting but not important, like a skate-boarding duck. In either case it competed for a place on the news agenda. The judgements were sometimes mistaken, but always confident. We thought we knew our business.

The same applied to foreign news. When I started in journalism, foreign news was the test of a serious newspaper, whether tabloid or broadsheet. It was essentially the unchanged world of Evelyn Waugh's *Scoop*, and there were scoops in Africa still. The Empire had gone, but the British bestrode the world of news imperially. Reuters and the BBC were its leading institutions. The television news agencies operated from London. The network news services, the BBC and ITN, competed fiercely and globally on a shared agenda. The popular papers had foreign correspondents, and photographers travelling with them. The *Daily Express* prided itself on being the first in and the last out of everywhere, and one of its most notable exclusives was filed from Prague by Dennis Blewett on telexed toilet paper. The *News Chronicle* had the great James Cameron roaming the world for it, until it folded, and as an undergraduate at the time I wept at its passing. The *Daily Mirror* took international issues as seriously as *The Times*, though it reported them differently. Donald Wise, an old soldier of the Suffolk Regiment and the *Mirror*'s man in Africa, famously began a dispatch from Luanda, at the beginning of the civil war, with a line about how an Angolan fell into his beer.

In the 1990s news and journalism died – that is, the news as we had understood it and the journalism as we had practised it. The economics of the marketplace made the decisions instead, and news was packaged and marketed as 'product'. It might as well have been soap flakes or HP sauce. It was whatever sold newspapers or raised the ratings – or, more usually, whatever stopped sales and ratings from declining. Kelvin MacKenzie, who promoted and embodied the changed state of news in his editorial rampage through the *Sun*, the *Mirror* and L!ve TV, defined the new agenda with an eloquent negative: 'Bosnia it ain't.' I try not to have enemies, but I do have opposites. I did not mourn the passing of the short-lived L!ve TV. Neither its topless darts nor its weather forecasts in Norwegian seemed to add to the sum of knowledge.

In TV documentaries the decline accelerated. Standards hit the floor and then went through it. Television, which used to be our window on the world, was now our basement. The classic TV documentaries of the 1990s were *Chippendales – the Secret Story* or

The History of Pornography. I wish I were inventing these. But television companies broadcast them, and harvested the ratings.

What followed was a general retreat from foreign news. The tabloids led the way, seldom taking note of the outside world except in their obsessions with football and royalty – and, just occasionally, Britons in trouble abroad. The broadsheets followed, trimming their coverage and cutting their foreign staff: audience research was telling them too that the foreign pages were the least read in the paper. One famous title considered abandoning its foreign bureaux altogether. The coverage given to Diana, Princess of Wales – and this was well before her death – did for our journalism what the O. J. Simpson case had done for the Americans': it marked the end of a tradition of self-respect. Nothing else mattered. There was no longer any principle remaining, but only profit and loss. To boost the bottom line, confessional chat shows hired actors and impostors and other mercenaries to tell lies about the sad and sombre margins of human relationships. That itself spoke well of our society, since there were not enough genuinely dysfunctional people in Britain to fill the schedule. But there was a dysfunctional television, and the scandal reflected it.

In TV news, ITN pioneered the change with an aggressive emphasis on domestic stories, seeking to turn itself into the *Daily Mail* of the airwaves. Apart from a hard-breaking news story that even the new journalism had to recognize – a war, an earthquake, or a spectacular famine – foreign news was no longer premier league. It was not even the first division; it was relegated to 'special reports' on Tuesdays and Thursdays only. In due course the BBC was trimming its sails to the same winds, turning its back on the outside world (though not to the same extent as its rival), and heading downmarket in the name of accessibility and 'news you can use'. The foreign news agenda, such as it was, turned increasingly on human interest stories: tearful orphans and fearless expatriates were especially in demand.

The strangest part of it was that both the network news services were haemorrhaging viewers at a record rate. By the mid 1990s their flagship programmes, the BBC's *Nine O'Clock News* and ITN's *News at Ten*, had lost half their viewers since their heyday in the 1960s and 1970s. The audience fragmented. Profits prevailed over programmes. Under the pressure of its advertisers, ITN was marginalized and driven out of prime time in the ITV schedule. After thirty years of public service *News at Ten* was quietly dispatched and laid to rest in March 1999, to the dismay of its journalists and the detriment of its viewers. I even attended its funeral, which ITN disguised as a celebration. Later that month, to its lasting shame and for the first time in its history, ITV had no prime time outlet for its coverage of a continental crisis, the cataclysm in Kosovo. When I publicly lamented the passing of *News at Ten*, I was denounced by one of the suits who ran the new order as 'the honourable member for the good old days'. Both networks' news services became minority viewing, and no longer the nation's bulletin boards. More to the point, they had also lost their nerve. Had the loss of nerve been the result of the loss of audience? Or – as I suspected – had the loss of audience been the result of the loss of nerve?

The loss of nerve took many forms: one of them was the imperative, in the new world order of broadcast news, not to upset people. I had met this in Bosnia, in our coverage of a deeply upsetting conflict. Images of suffering were not in good taste, but neither was the war. That was the way with the war that we saw, but not with the war that we showed. We were obliged to cut out the bloodshed from our coverage, to the extent that warfare came to seem almost benign, a spectacle without costs or casualties, and an acceptable way of settling differences. I felt this to be immoral, and won no popularity points with the BBC hierarchy by daring to say so.

'We should flinch less,' I wrote.

We should sometimes be willing to shock and to disturb. We should show the world more nearly as we find it, without the anaesthetic of good taste censorship. And if we do not, then perhaps we should ask ourselves whether we are merely being considerate, or indifferent. And in a world where genocide has returned in recent years to haunt three continents, we should remind ourselves that this crime against humanity requires accomplices – not only the hatred that makes it happen, but the indifference that lets it happen.[1]

A BBC reporter of the old school would have kept such heresies to himself. He would not, as I did, have voiced them openly and publicly in a speech in Chichester Cathedral; nor have echoed there the dismay of Eli Wiesel, the most eloquent survivor of an earlier and incomparable genocide: 'It is not because I cannot explain that you won't understand. It is because you won't understand that I cannot explain.'[2]

The timidity persisted and intensified. In August 1996 I was rushed out to Cyprus, after a re-ignition of the tension between the Greeks and the Turks. A crowd of Greek Cypriot demonstrators laid siege to a Turkish observation post on the Green Line near Famagusta. One of the Greeks climbed a flagpole to tear down the Turkish flag, and was shot dead by the Turks as he did so. The cameras were present, of course. The image that they showed was that of a man climbing up a flagpole and a man falling down a flagpole: that was all. It was the central point of the episode, and it brought the island to the verge of war. The BBC did not allow me to use it.

But I did use this incident and others in a series of radio broadcasts, called *The Truth Is Our Currency*, to reflect on the growing unreality of TV journalism. What should have been getting better was getting worse. Looking back on those broadcasts now, I realize that they already had a certain valedictory quality about them. They were a requiem for the golden age of news. It is a general tendency of retired hacks to believe that they lived and worked in a golden age. In my case, I have to insist that I really did. I made my escape before the mobile phone took over.

The new technology was a vast improvement on the old one. The new journalism was not. Our vaunted transmission systems, which enabled us in theory to pitch our dishes wherever the news broke, and which should have made it more vivid and authentic, were actually making it less so. Under the pressures of rolling deadlines and twenty-four-hour news, the reporters no longer made a fight of it, and seldom even reached the field of battle. They were withdrawn from the real world and driven back into their hotels and offices and editing rooms; they made indiscriminate use of 'soldiervision' – military video – without labelling it; they bestrode the rooftops of TV stations for hours on end to answer the tireless questions of distant and unknowing anchor people – Michael and Trevor if they were British, or Mort and Dan if they were American; they intercepted the news agencies' images and wove them seamlessly into apparently original reporting. They were not so much reporters as performers, like the cosmetic American anchor people of whom it was said that all you need is sincerity, and if you can fake that you've got it made. So important were appearances to them, that the men as well as the women packed make-up and hair spray for their travels to the war zones – or at least as close to the war zones as would offer the sufficient illusion of being there; a dispatch from 'the front' was as likely as not to be from the front of the press hotel in a well-provided capital. Their most favoured backdrop for war reports was nothing more conflictive than a palm tree. Virtual reality prevailed, and even the studio set was an illusion. The hell with it. It was not my kind of journalism, but a shadow of it and a sort of magic lantern show. I thought of it as 'newzak'.

The prize system further played to the worst in the news business. The honours bestowed annually and amid much fanfare, by the Royal Television Society and BAFTA among others, meant a great deal to the reporters and camera teams, and even more to the organizations which employed them. They were advertised in the public prints as evidence of excellence. I have an interest to declare here, for I received the odd bauble myself. Was I not voted the most promising newcomer of 1972? Did I not attend successive BAFTA award ceremonies, rubbing shoulders with the stars and marvelling at Emma Thompson's 'Oh gosh oh golly, I never expected this' routine? It was heady stuff for an ordinary working journalist. Yet the system carried within it, potentially at least, a virus of venality. The Royal Television Society's Journalist of the Year award went almost invariably to the reporter most shot at (I know this because I won it a couple of times), and offered an incentive to the young and ambitious to take risks and to cut corners, shading the truth. Rising reporters would be summoned before the management at some stage in their careers and gravely advised that it was time they won a prize; the unspoken postscript was that how they did it was up to them. And in deciding where to commit resources, a TV news editor was increasingly tempted to ask the question: never mind the merits of the story, do we think there's a prize in it?

Like other businesses, TV news no longer offered careers but only contracts. It had always been competitive, but now it was pervaded by a culture of ruthlessness, and a star system which applied to the journalists in the field as well as to the newsreaders in the studio. The star system had its own vocabulary: an ordinary reporter elbowed off a story by one of the big beasts of the jungle was described as having been 'monstered' or 'big-footed'. The fiercest competition, as with political parties, was not between organizations but within them. And the big names of the small screen were not necessarily the ones most beloved or respected by those who worked alongside them.

That was not all. In a few notorious cases there were reporters who stretched the truth until it snapped. These fabrications were well enough known in the business. They were few, but even a few were too many, and a source of shame to us all. One was a simulation of news footage in an attack on a UN helicopter. Another was a totally invented story about the victim of an earth-quake. A third was a reporter pretending to be in the thick of the action when he was many miles away from it. (Like the ITN correspondent who once signed off a story about Uganda, 'Sam Safari Suit, ITN, outside Kampala.' You bet he was outside Kampala. He was on the Kenyan border.) These were the corruptions of news. When the networks' managers were informed about them, the answer was that they didn't want to be told.

The BBC further distinguished itself by starving its comedy, its drama and even its regular news programmes, in order to spend £50 million on a rolling news service, *News 24*, that was virtually unwatched and unwatchable, because no one could receive it. We guessed that it was called *News 24* because it had only twenty-four viewers: it was unseen except by those who appeared on it, and their families. It was the most bewildering waste of money in the Corporation's seventy-five-year history. BBC Television's once dominant sports department was shedding its rights and contracts like autumn leaves. It could have saved the cricket, which it lost to Channel Four and Talk Radio, and the rugby which it lost to ITV, for a tiny fraction of the fortune wasted on that invisible news service. We had grown used to incompetence, but never before on such a spectacular scale, and justified in such impenetrable clouds of words. Farce shaded into tragedy. The management became more than ever the despair of the staff. The BBC was in the business of communication. Yet during my last five years as one of its reporters, I never received a corporate directive that I actually understood.

I was aware of a chapter closing. I had done all in TV news that I wished to do, and said all about it that I wished to say. I realize now, although I didn't at the time, that I had been too long inside the wire, and was looking for an escape. I regretted that, because of a hard and snow-bound tour of duty in Belgrade, I had not been told of an informal approach about the job of spokesman to Kofi Annan, the new UN Secretary-General. As it turned out he could not have been better served than he was by the eventual appointee, Fred Eckhard, a UN veteran whom I had known and respected in Bosnia.

My superstitions – and I am superstitious to a fault – also fore-shadowed a mysterious and unknowable career change. In the summer of 1995, with the Bosnian war still at its height, I sought refuge from it one night in the Writers' Club in Sarajevo, one of the very few hostelries still open. The gunfire subsided. An old man shuffled in, well dressed for those times, with a bunch of wild flowers for sale, which were chiefly white heather and whatever else he could gather in the hazardous open spaces. I paid him a ridiculous price for them – I think it was a hundred German marks – not because I sought any favours from him, nor even because he must have risked his life to pick them, but because he had an air about him of luminous wisdom and goodness. It was nothing definable, but his face shone with it. He looked like the ghost of a saint. He smiled benignly and murmured his thanks; and although I do not remember his exact words, they were to the effect that something extraordinary was going to happen in my life, even more extraordinary than had already happened, and very much for the better. It was a Balkan benediction. And with that he vanished, as if he had never existed. I wrote off the hundred marks. I could hardly submit an expense claim for them as 'hospitality to ghost'.

As for politics, I had not given it a moment's thought – except in two particular respects. One was that I had been the witness of a political and diplomatic catastrophe in Bosnia and had struggled to learn the lessons of it; I was unimpressed by Douglas Hurd's attempt to blame the journalists, as if things would have been better if the conflict had raged on and no one had known about it, but left it to the wisdom of the diplomats to resolve. In any case, both diplomats and wisdom had gone AWOL. He responded to our criticism by reminding us that no one had ever elected any of us to anything – or not yet, anyway. I remember one night sheltering in Sarajevo under small arms and cannon fire and idly wondering: suppose that someone one day did – would that make any difference? Possibly not – but the idea of making a difference mattered to me. So did the idea of honour. I believed that Britain's Balkan diplomacy, from the ill-fated and premature recognition of Croatia and Slovenia onwards, had lit the fuse to the powder kegs of Bosnia and Kosovo. It had been both unprincipled and dishonourable. It did not relate to the end of the twentieth century, but rather had been conducted as if it were Lord Palmerston's last croak – a defence of a national interest narrowly and discreditably defined. But, though the reporters took more risks than the diplomats, had the journalism been any more honourable? What moral high ground was there in our business? It was certainly not the hilltop on which I kept watch behind the Holiday Inn to count the explosions.

My other political thought was to lobby in vain to have some part in the BBC's coverage of the forthcoming general election, which seemed likely to be the most consequential for eighteen years. Elections were fought in military metaphors. I knew a thing or two about real campaigns, so why not let me loose on their political equivalents? I was quietly taken aside in a deep-carpeted office and told that this had ruffled certain feathers in high roosting places, and was anyway completely out of line: what could an old war reporter possibly have to contribute to the political battle ahead? (As it turned out, more than I could ever have dreamt of, but I didn't know that at the time.) My only duty would have been on election night itself, in which the BBC summoned all its hands on deck except the weathermen and the cast of *Blue Peter*. I was assigned to Edinburgh Pentlands to report the expected defeat of Malcolm Rifkind, the Foreign Secretary.

Instead I did something that changed my life. I went to an exhibition at the Royal Festival Hall. It was called, appropriately, 'The Edge of Madness'.

2. The Edge of Madness

'The Edge of Madness' was a line from General Ratko Mladic, the Bosnian Serb commander, who had threatened to bomb Sarajevo to that condition. It was the title chosen by Tom Stoddart for his exhibition of war photographs. He had been in the city in the worst of times, working for the *Sunday Times* in the summer of 1992. He had been injured at the same time that I was, but much more seriously. Running under fire and diving for cover outside the parliament building, he broke his ankle in six places and his shoulder. Undeterred, he returned to the war a year later, proving that a dodgy ankle and a titanium shoulder are no impediment to the practice of world-class photography.

The photographs were extraordinary: graphic, vivid and understated. Tom had omitted the combat and bloodshed, to provide a sharper focus on what remained: a portrait of people in warfare. He asked me to contribute an essay to the catalogue. In it I pointed out that my own overblown medium, television, could never have recorded the war as he did, or matched those frozen moments of fear and survival: '"The Edge of Madness" is a memorial to those times. It demands attention and rewards reflection. Its message is simple and serious. Lest we forget.'

I gave a short speech to open the exhibition, and supposed that my part was over. I should have known better, for Tom was wearing a suit. He is not at all the sartorial type, and I didn't know that he had one. It turned out that he was the official Labour Party photographer on board the Tony Blair battlebus in the campaign that had just begun. Tom has political connections. His partner in life was Kate Hoey, a prominent Labour MP who even then was marked out for promotion.

After the opening we adjourned upstairs to the People's Palace, the South Bank Centre's restaurant and crucible of intrigue. It was there, over the spring rolls and sweet and sour pork, that the conversation took a serious turn – and it wasn't about Sarajevo. Kate was eyeing me oddly. He whispered to her, and she turned to me.

'We think that you may be what we're looking for,' she said.

'I'm what?'

'It's about Neil Hamilton in Tatton. He'll be re-elected in spite of everything. We need someone to take him on.'

I took a layman's interest in politics. Being rather underemployed at the time, I had very little else to do. If the BBC had found me a small war somewhere, none of the rest of this story would have occurred. I was aware of the extraordinary circumstances in the Tatton constituency, and the attempts to dislodge its MP, Neil Hamilton, from the fourth safest Tory seat in the country. I was aware of the charges against him, some denied and some admitted, and of the headline accusing him of being a liar and a cheat. I was also aware that for more than a week the two opposition parties, having offered to stand down their own candidates, had been looking for an electable alternative – an independent acceptable to both of them and to the Tory rebels too. It had never occurred to me for a moment that I might be the chosen conscript: and if my service as a soldier had taught me anything, it was never to volunteer for anything.

A number of names had been suggested, Richard Branson's among them; but he was thought to be too close to Lady Thatcher to be acceptable to the Labour side. The best choice of all would have been Terry Waite, who actually came from the village of Styal in the constituency. He turned it down on the excellent grounds that he had already served one five-year term as a hostage and didn't want to serve another.

I could have steered the conversation to safer territory, then and there, with a Shermanesque declaration: 'No, not ever and not under any circumstances; if nominated I will not stand and if elected I will not serve.' But I didn't. I told Tom and Kate that I would think about it, and they might like to call me tomorrow. Part of me thought, this was dinner-table chat and nothing more would be heard of it. Another part thought, supposing it wasn't and that they were serious? Then I reflected that nearly all the regrets of my life had been not about the things I had done but about the things I had not done – the road not taken, the challenge not accepted. I had been banging on recently, with Bosnia in mind, about the need for principled journalism and principled diplomacy. Why not principled politics as well? Maybe there was a case to be made, every once in a while, for doing something breathtakingly foolhardy. Challenging Neil and Christine Hamilton, especially Christine, would be all that and more. I did not sleep well that night.

Next morning I convinced myself it had all been a dream, or rather a nightmare, and it would come to nothing. I set out to do something useful instead, and ordered a new car to replace the existing clunker. That evening the phone rang. It was Alastair Campbell, Tony Blair's spokesman. The Labour Party leader was keen on the idea, indeed his face had lit up at it, but what were my politics?

'Actually, I don't have any.'

'Did you ever?'

'At Cambridge, in the late fifties, I was Secretary of the Eastern Counties Young Liberals. We had twenty members, and the number went down every year. As a political force we were zero. I ended all that on joining the BBC in 1962.'

'But what do you vote?'

'Sadly, I don't. My record is appalling and I'm not proud of it. You see, I was always somewhere else when I should have been voting. In 1992, polling day was three days after the start of the Bosnian War. There was no provision for postal votes from the trenches of Sarajevo.'

'Skeletons in cupboards?'

'I'm looking, and I don't see any. The odd bone here and there perhaps – two marriages and two divorces, they're in *Who's Who* – but nothing really skeletal. I'll call you if I think of anything.'

He rang off, and a wave of alarm swept over me. I should have come up with some scandal, real or imagined; there might even be one out there which I had forgotten, and would loom out of the past to sand-bag me. I was passing the point of no return, and driven on by obstinacy.

Two more calls followed. One was from Dick Newby, a Vice-President of the Liberal Democrats. The other was from Paddy Ashdown himself, whom I had known from our times in Bosnia, where I had shown him graveyards and helped him deliver packages. His party were reluctant partners in the Tatton manoeuvre, and were more or less bounced into it by Labour. But he liked the idea of challenging Hamilton with a candidate whom he knew.

It was a closely held secret. Two days later I was driven north by Tim Clement-Jones, another of Paddy Ashdown's inner circle. I was to meet the constituency executives of both the Labour and Liberal Democrat parties. The difficulty was that they were hardly natural allies, especially in the north-west, where they fought each other tooth and nail, in Rochdale and Liverpool especially. They never co-operated, and neither would be seen anywhere near the other's meeting places. So it was that, like a parcel of used banknotes or an agent in an old spy movie, I was transferred between men in suits who were waiting for me in car parks. They knew each other, but barely a word passed between them. Labour took me over from the Lib Dems in the car park outside the public library in Wilmslow, and handed me back in the car park of Cotton's Hotel near Knutsford. I was faintly surprised that it didn't happen in monochrome. I was out of my depth in it. It needed Richard Burton or Orson Welles.

The mission was to persuade both local parties to stand their candidates down. They had every reason not to, and I was fully prepared for a political career which would have lasted two or three hours. Both had excellent candidates already in the field, Jon Kelly for Labour and Roger Barlow for the Liberal Democrats. This was by far the best chance they would ever have of wresting the seat from the Tories. But the arithmetic was discouraging. A recent boundary change favoured the Conservatives, by annexing the true-blue village of Alderley Edge and adding it to Tatton – a move resisted by its sitting MP, the redoubtable Nicholas Winterton. Whatever Neil Hamilton's other problems – and the *Guardian* was weighing in almost daily with damaging revelations – he was sitting serenely on a notional majority of more than 20,000.

The Liberal Democrats were reluctant. After a heated argument they voted by six to five to stand their candidate down, the candidate himself being one of the six. Tim Clement-Jones, who had been a long time in politics, called it the hardest meeting of his life. Labour were more easily persuaded. Central control was stronger there, and the will of Millbank prevailed. Jon Kelly, although disappointed, supported the decision. His partner did not. They would work for me in the weeks ahead with as much zeal as if Jon had been the candidate. Roger Barlow's troops were no less dedicated. The lure for both parties was the outside chance that just for once they might be on the winning side.

The Labour Party meeting was held in the upstairs eyrie of the White Bear in Knutsford, later to be demolished. Awaiting their decision, I was sipping an orange juice in the downstairs bar when one of the regulars came up to me with a conspiratorial look on his face. Two others asked for autographs. They wanted to know, but were too polite to ask directly, what brought a veteran of foreign wars to Knutsford.

'I suppose,' hinted the co-conspirator, 'that you're on some kind of secret assignment?'

'Why yes,' I answered, 'actually, I am.'

The story broke on the Press Association wire that evening. The political world went crazy. From a journalistic point of view, it was the first shock to disturb the still waters of an otherwise uneventful campaign. Tim Clement-Jones dropped me off, and I was totally on my own – part candidate and part fugitive. Being alone was necessary: an Independent, especially one only just announced, can have neither party nor staff nor advisers to help him. He is the loneliest soul on the entire political planet. I felt as A. P. Herbert had, when he first stood for Parliament as an Independent in Oxford in 1935: 'I wandered forlornly about the streets, wondering why I had got myself into this mess.'[1]

I was equally alone for the opening press conference, held the following day among a tumult of photographers at the Institution of Civil Engineers in Westminster. I had asked the BBC crew who had been shadowing me all morning if they could give me a lift down there. No, they said, they couldn't; I wasn't one of them any more, and they had been warned to keep their distance. I had the feeling that all the people I had ever known in journalism were there, not as friends and colleagues, but as antagonists and assassins if they had half a chance; for I had crossed the line between reporting the news and making it. I guessed that some would see that as a kind of betrayal. I remembered a line from Sir Thomas Wyatt, the Elizabethan poet and courtier: 'They flee from me, that sometime did me seek.'

I gave the first question to Robin Oakley, the BBC's Political Editor, for no other reason than that I was backing his tip, Antonin, for the re-run of the Grand National, postponed because of a bomb scare. Though the horse lost, the question was reasonably benign. Some of the others were not. They doubted my honesty. They took it for granted that because I had worked for so long as a foreign correspondent, during a famously liberal financial regime, I must have committed some acts of grand larceny in my expense accounts. I had surely stashed some loot away, perhaps in a Falkland Islands swimming pool or a Gulf War sun-house. I answered that, just the previous year, I had an expense claim queried for the very first time, after an innumerate taxi driver in New Delhi failed to provide a receipt. The old BBC would have trusted me. The new one did not. 'Tell Mr Bell,' sniffed the accompanying memo, 'that there may be no unreceipted expenses.' I offered the press my bank accounts and tax records. No one was even interested.

The news reports were fairly straightforward, but agreed that I seemed ill at ease. The reason for that was that I *was* ill at ease; and the misgivings would only multiply. That evening I packed a supply of shirts and white suits into a dark blue Globetrotter suitcase: I am a deeply superstitious character, and have had reason to be; both the suits and the suitcase are part of my ritual for surviving in dangerous places. Tatton would certainly qualify as one of those. I reflected that I would rather run the trench lines of Dobrinja in Miss Piggy, my faithful armoured Land Rover, than submit to such a press ordeal again. Driving north, I heard Christine Hamilton on the radio denouncing my 'flaming cheek' in daring to oppose her husband. I had the right to stand for the Monster Raving Loony Party in the Outer Hebrides if I wished to, but I knew that I had made my first mistake. I should have brought the flak jacket.

A word about the white suits is perhaps in order. They had no symbolism at all. I wore them because during the Gulf War, as an accredited and uniformed war reporter with the Queen's Royal Irish Hussars, I had been obliged to dig more blistering trenches than I wished to dig; and I vowed to cover the next conflicts as an unreconstructed civilian. These were in Slovenia and Croatia later the same year and turned out to be extraordinarily dangerous. Too many sharp-edged objects were flying through the air at a lethally high velocity. I was equipped with a couple of white suits at the time, I managed to avoid the incoming fire, and identified the suits with my daily good fortune. The white suits were a survival mechanism. I knew I was about to need them as never before.

Before leaving London, I looked up Tatton in the gazetteer. I couldn't find it. The reason was that it was neither a town nor a village, but a stately home and a park mainly inhabited by sheep and deer. But at its gates lay Knutsford, the constituency's political headquarters. The AA book guided me to a two-star hotel, the Longview, which had the advantage of being both in town and cheaper than Cotton's. Whatever else this was going to be, it would not be a rich man's campaign. Of the Longview's owners, Steve and Pauline West, I knew nothing; they might well have been Neil Hamilton's staunchest supporters. In fact they were admirably non-partisan, and we became the best of friends. Those unkind hacks such as John Sweeney of the *Observer* who saw Steve as

Knutsford's Basil Fawlty – and there was a slight superficial resemblance until he removed the moustache – were slanderously untruthful. With the possible exceptions of my daughter Melissa, David Soul and John Stalker, Steve and Pauline were the most important recruits of the campaign.

John Stalker, the former Deputy Chief Constable of Manchester, was Mr Integrity in the north-west. There was no one anywhere I would rather have had on my side. He came in, unbidden, off the street and offered his services, almost as soon as we were open for business in the cellar bar of the Longview, which Steve had provided as our first headquarters. It had a single telephone, and looked like a well-appointed bunker: all that it lacked was sand-bags.

Other early volunteers included David Geen, a former BBC producer who was, in his way, as eccentric as the candidate. He toiled heroically non-stop for the whole campaign, being driven at times close to tears and (I suspected) close to resignation. I was deeply relieved that he stayed with us. Colonel Bob Stewart was there as well, a true friend from our days in Bosnia together, and another certified good guy. He was joined by a number of serving soldiers of the Cheshire Regiment, in civilian clothes, who discreetly offered their support – and by three students of striking appearance, Sophie Solomon and Sophie and Antonia Harrison. They invariably wore black, and were compared by an inventive hack to the Women's Battalion of Death. They canvassed the youth and the wine bar vote, and projected a rather more fashionable image than the candidate whom they supported. They later became known as Bell's Belles.

Tuesday 8 April was the campaign's opening, and the first day of the rest of my life. Squadrons of journalists descended on us. Photographers and TV crews roamed and seethed. Satellite dishes mushroomed. I agreed to hold a news conference at 1 p.m. on Knutsford Heath, opposite the hotel. What I did not know was that Neil and Christine Hamilton, having found this out from the *Knutsford Guardian*, intended to be there too. Imagine the outrage, and the cries of 'media hijack', if I had done that to them.

I had lived through ambushes from Biafra to Bosnia, but never one like this. Since it was too late to turn back I plunged through the thickets of photographers and camera crews towards them. She was dressed in garish red and green and he in grey bounder's check – the Knutsford Heath equivalent of battlefield camouflage. I shook their hands and said I was pleased to meet them. It was my first – and I hope last – political untruth. I wished them elsewhere. Hamilton's agenda was to wreck my campaign there and then by having me accept that he was innocent until proven guilty. He was hiding behind the still unpublished Downey Report, and denying previously admitted wrongdoing. I, on the other hand, had nowhere at all to hide on the open heath.

'Do you accept that a man is innocent until proved guilty?' demanded Christine.

'I think there's a lot . . .' I began. But she wasn't on receive mode. She was on transmit.

'So you accept that my husband is innocent?' she shrilled.

'Look, I'm not going to be facing an ambush here.'

We prevaricated a bit until finally her husband found something to say for himself. 'I would just like you to say then that you are prepared to give me the benefit of the doubt on the allegations that have been made against me?'

'Absolutely, absolutely.'

It was a political elephant trap, and I fell right into it. What I meant to say of course, what I should have said – and was already saying to anyone who would listen, as the triumphant duo left the heath – was that I would give him the benefit of the doubt on the cash in brown envelopes, but not on the admitted wrongdoing: the free holidays, the misleading of the Deputy Prime Minister about his relationship with a lobbyist, and other breaches of trust. I was mortified. I had let so many people down. I felt I had lost the election there and then on the very first day in a blinding show of ineptitude. What I didn't know until very much later was that I had won it. People felt for the amateur having the sand kicked in his face. They found Neil Hamilton a hard man to admire. And as for Christine, the women especially didn't believe that a wife should do the talking for her husband.

The alarm bells rang in the headquarters of both the opposition parties. That night, for the record, I was obliged to read out a letter that repeated the charge sheet against Neil Hamilton. I could see it was necessary, but it was not my style. I had not liked attack-dog politics before, and I did not like it now. I am not the kind of man who can accost a relative stranger with an insult: 'Sir, you are a liar and a scoundrel.' The *Guardian* sent me its 'sleaze sleuths', David Leigh and Ed Vulliamy, so that I should be better briefed in the event of a formal debate; Neil Hamilton had lived through this, and I had not. Alastair Campbell wished me to challenge Hamilton to a rematch on the heath the next day. I refused. Alastair and I did not contact each other again for the rest of the campaign. From now on I would do it my way, avoiding the low road, emphasizing themes of trust and integrity, and leaving the voters to work it out for themselves. The negatives would be implicit in the positives. From that point on I made a resolution, so far as was humanly possible, not to practise the politics of disparagement.

The campaign was battered, but not blown out of the water. I needed more people to steady it, and set about recruiting them from the highways and byways, a bit like Yul Brynner in *The Magnificent Seven*. Like him, I ended up with an interesting assortment of gunslingers.

The election agent was Kate Jones, my high-octane publishing editor who happened to be on leave of absence from Penguin Books, where she specialized in disciplining the purple prose and bad jokes of her authors. She had sent me a fax offering to help – stuffing envelopes, she supposed. Then when she sent me another, I made her the agent. She knew little of election law, but she had the incentive to find out, and was a very fast learner. Kate's right-hand man was Anthony Crean, a Manchester barrister and Tom Cruise lookalike whose envious colleagues rewarded him by plastering his chambers with Hamilton posters. The press officer was Kate Edgley, an accomplished journalist. My minder and driver and Sancho Panza was Nigel Bateson, the mountainous South African who had been alongside me as cameraman in the Gulf and Bosnian wars. Another back-room volunteer, Bill Givens from Southport, added an air of tranquillity and did mysterious things with computers. The issues adviser was my nephew Oliver Kamm, a human encyclopaedia who was fortunately on gardening leave between one investment bank and another. He never needed to look anything up: he carried it all in his head. 'If you walked by him quietly,' said John Sweeney, 'you could hear the hum of deep thought like the buzzing you hear under an electricity pylon.' Sweeney was also part of the team, unofficial and self-appointed, and a never-failing source of daft ideas like riding across the constituency on a white horse. His job was to monster the Hamiltons.

Then there was my twenty-four-year-old daughter Melissa, 'of whom it could not be said that she was hideously deformed' (another Sweeneyism). She had been appalled by the débâcle on the heath and rushed from Brussels, where she worked for Reuters, to be at her father's side in his hour of need. She had studied politics for three years at Warwick University, but found it of little use in running a campaign. She became the team leader of Bell's Belles and pioneer of a newly invented wine bar strategy. She remained with her father to his great advantage. Neil Hamilton had his blonde lady beside him, and I had mine. There was nothing more to be said – except by the *Evening Standard*, which headlined 'The Butterfly Versus The Battle-axe'.

Melissa also watched the campaign pennies. She denied me the pleasure of the full English breakfast, complete with black pudding, which was one of the glories of the Longview Hotel. 'Dad, we can't afford it,' she said.

'I bet that even King Lear's daughters allowed him breakfast,' I muttered.

This wasn't yet a political machine, but it had the makings of a contraption. After a week we found a larger headquarters, the old electricity showroom on Princess Street. The dauntless Nigel Bateson slept on the floor to keep out the spies. We were joined by our two professionals, one from each of the parties that had stood down its candidate for us. I had no qualms about this. They were entitled to liaise with us, we badly needed their expertise – especially in the printing of posters and leaflets – and enough Conservatives were coming on board to give the campaign the all-party balance it needed. Robin Estridge, a valiant Tory from Alderley Edge, had led the defections from the Conservative Association, for which he was later congratulated by those who had reviled him at the time. Geoff Pullar, the former England cricketer, joined the first eleven. So did Gillian Irving, a former Tory office holder from Great Budworth, who put together the polling day battle plan. A dissident Conservative councillor, Laurence Hobday, bravely proposed my nomination. Richard Cussons, another Tory, prominently displayed brown envelopes in the window of his stationery shop in Knutsford. When the Conservatives later accused him of disloyalty, he explained with sweet reason that this was an outstanding example of the Thatcherite free market in action.

Labour's man in the back room was Alan Olive, an intense and determined veteran of many campaigns, with the logistical skills that we needed. The Liberal Democrats lent us Bill le Breton, a quieter character with a strategic grasp of how the thing was going. He was far too shrewd to share his optimism with us, but he had been through something like it before on the Isle of Wight. He later wrote, 'I knew how people reacted when the trust they have placed in an MP is shattered by corruption. They were crying out for a champion.'

There are difficulties inherent in any campaign, but especially one as improvised as ours. The Labour man was overheard on the telephone complaining that he wasn't too fond of the company he was keeping: 'The candidate is a Tory and the agent is a (expletive deleted) Trot.' He was wrong about both of us, but the remark said something about the prevailing tensions, and perhaps the conflicting agendas, in our headquarters. Not at the time, but very much later, I came to wonder whether Millbank would have preferred the campaign to crash in flames, still drawing attention to sleaze as the issue, but leaving Neil Hamilton in Parliament to embarrass his party. Somehow I didn't fancy the role of a kamikaze candidate.

The first walkabout – typically for our erratic crusade – was a simultaneous triumph and disaster. We chose the town centre of Wilmslow, which was Hamiltonian heartland. Making my first stumbling attempts at candidates' small talk, I counted the handshakes and noted the reactions. Twenty-five were in favour and three were against, one of them vociferously. I was aware of the TV networks' interest because I kept falling over their cables and cameras. Back in Knutsford, I watched the BBC's *One O'Clock News* with utter dismay. It included the one vociferous opponent, and no one else at all: not one other living soul. I asked myself, was I being unduly sensitive, now I had crossed the line from one world to the other? No, I concluded, in all my years in the BBC I had never been guilty of anything so blatant and one-sided. I had their numbers, so I rang them up and shouted at them. I had still been one of their reporters four days earlier. Could their standards have fallen through the floor quite so fast?

The BBC had already made it clear that, although I had unpaid leave of absence to stand as a candidate, my former job in news would no longer be available to me. If that was their attitude, I felt, after thirty-four sometimes dangerous years in their service, then I had no time for them either. I called a news conference – this time away from the hazards of the heath, in Knutsford's Little Theatre – and resigned on the spot. They accepted gratefully – though, to be fair to them, they later commuted it to early retirement. The resignation was more than a gesture. It sent a signal to the voters that there would be no going back.

The BBC behaves at its cringing worst in a general election, fending off blows that have not even yet been aimed at it. It pulled from the schedule a report I had done for Jill Dando's *Holiday* programme about tourism in Dubrovnik. Perhaps it wanted an equal opportunity for Neil Hamilton to sing the praises of the coast of Montenegro. My former employers never did understand the value of steadiness under fire.

All this time I was no more than a candidate-in-waiting. I had not been nominated, and the opposition parties in Tatton had not yet endorsed their executives' decision to stand down their own candidates. The Labour meeting was an emotional one, in a crowded school assembly hall addressed by John Prescott, the Party's Deputy Leader. Never before had Tatton merited the party's top brass on that scale. I had not met John Prescott before. I found him affable, a trifle reserved, and surprisingly nervous. He and Ian McCartney, fixer supreme and self-styled Socialist MP for Makerfield, were pacing apprehensively in an upper room, preparing their speeches as if this were the crux of the whole campaign. As Melissa and I watched these professionals in action, we realized what a lot we had to learn. I still don't know if John Prescott's heart was in it, but his rhetoric certainly was; the speech was a masterpiece, carefully scripted yet brilliantly extemporized, and hitting all the right notes. My own speech was shorter and less ambitious.

It said things about Neil Hamilton that I would not have ventured had the press been present. The motion to stand Jon Kelly down was carried by 144 votes to 11. Much thought was given to the presentation. We left separately, because I was not of their party.

The Liberal Democrats, to my great surprise, were easier. Having won over the executive by the narrowest of margins, we expected a repeat performance with the general membership. Liberal Democrats are world-class doubters and wonderers; if they were asked to form a government tomorrow they would look for the small print and ask abstruse and recondite questions about what exactly was meant by 'government'; but that evening they were unanimous about standing down their candidate, and putting their shoulders to the independent wheel. My only difficulty was outside the hall, in avoiding the attentions of Miss Moneypenny, a seven foot transvestite with platform shoes, plasterers' make-up and an overhanging superstructure. He or she – or it – also had political ambitions to be MP for Tatton. It was a popular objective in those days. Ten candidates shared it, and Miss Moneypenny was by no means the weirdest of them. There would have been eleven, had not the eleventh blown his deposit on the 2.15 at Newmarket.

The epidemic of strange behaviour also afflicted the Conservatives, at the moment of decision about whether to adopt Neil Hamilton as their candidate. If they had dropped him I should have folded my tent and left the three parties to fight it out as before. To the end, I could not believe that they would let him stand. Without Hamilton, Tatton was safe for them; with him, it was vulnerable. Why, I wondered, should they put at risk so safe a seat and damage their party's prospects everywhere else? Whatever had happened to their surest of instincts, which was to hold on to what they had? It made no sense. It still made no sense when at the Dixon Arms in Chelford the Tatton Conservative Association readopted Neil Hamilton by a margin of two thirds in favour, to one third against or abstaining.

I was pacing the Knutsford bunker at the time, and watching the box incredulously. 'A resounding victory,' declared the BBC's Nick Jones, a Corporation apparatchik.

'Doesn't seem resounding to me,' I grumped; and I noted that Hamilton had won a lower proportion of votes from his own party than I had from the two parties of which I was not a member.

And so began in earnest a campaign that left me professionally rather jealous of myself. Over the years I had covered more than twenty elections as a journalist, from Belfast to El Salvador, from Kuwait to Argentina and from South Africa to Canada, yet none so surreal and extra-terrestrial as the one in which I was a candidate. John Sweeney called it 'the strangest, most peculiar, most absurd, most hilarious political contest fought in a generation'. Just for once, he was understating it.

3. Planet Tatton

Neil Hamilton, in a rare moment when charity got the better of him, called me 'a nice enough man, but totally unsuited to politics'. I was clearly unsuited to his sort of politics, because I advanced towards the gunfire of the Tatton campaign without a lawyer. My former lawyer had sent me some papers from the back of his safe on his retirement a while back and I had not bothered to replace him. I saw no reason to. War reporters tend not to need lawyers, since they are rather more likely to be shot than sued. Parliamentary candidates on the other hand – especially if they are opposing the likes of Neil Hamilton – are seriously in need of a lawyer, if not several.

He came to the battlefield well armed. In Rupert Grey of Crockers he had not only an excellent lawyer but a close personal friend who stood by him loyally long after other so-called friends had deserted him. I, of course, was not a friend but an enemy (the category or idea of opponent did not exist for him), and I was hearing from Mr Grey on a daily basis. It was one of the minor mysteries of the campaign that Neil Hamilton managed to spend £250 on 'sorry you were out' cards. He was far too busy talking to his lawyer to have knocked on that many doors.

Two days into the campaign proper, Mr Grey opened fire with a three-page fax threatening legal action if we repeated any of the charges against Neil Hamilton that I had made in the open letter on the day of the Knutsford Heath ambush. These included the cases of admitted wrongdoing, which he set aside on the grounds that the court papers in which the admissions were made had been improperly published by the *Guardian*. Wrongdoing? What wrongdoing? There wasn't any. It was part of a monstrous conspiracy against him. 'I am the victim here,' Mr Hamilton said, and there were many people willing to believe him.

Had we complied with Mr Grey's demand, we might as well have given up and gone home, for we would have been left with no reason to campaign against so upright a defender of the public interest as the sitting MP for Tatton. For good measure, Neil Hamilton threatened to sue me anew when the election was over and the Downey Report had bleached his reputation whiter than snow. His lawyer wrote, 'If, as is confidently expected, the report clears our client of the charges of corruption, the damages he will be seeking will be very substantial indeed.' That raised the stakes and I knew it. The way the campaign was going, it would end with one or other of us facing ruin.

Neil Hamilton was living at the time entirely in a world of his own. He was a man with a dangerous combination of qualities. He was stubborn, single-minded, desperate and litigious. That was even without his wife. With her he was unstoppable. 'If you think we are going to chicken out three and a half weeks before polling day,' she scolded the reporters, 'you are all mad.'

In politics, you talk to the evening newspapers at breakfast time, because of their deadlines. Breakfast was therefore important, but seriously unrelaxing. My daily exchange with Melissa, over the scaled-down economy breakfast which was all she allowed, and after I had fired off some sound bites for the press, would go along these lines:

'What on earth have we got ourselves into?'

'Dad, I don't know.'

'How do we get ourselves out of it?'

'Don't know that either, Dad.'

'Well, at least we know one thing, which is why politics has got itself such a bad name.'

The legal manoeuvring upset me. This shouldn't be what politics was about. I held a news conference at which I handed out copies of the three-page fax. I urged Mr Hamilton to campaign more in the constituency and less in the courts, and to allow his lawyers to spend more time with their families. Let the people decide: if they really thought he was trustworthy, they should vote for him. 'Ladies and gentlemen,' I said, 'I do not respond well to being threatened; indeed, more accurately, I do not respond at all. I have in my time been threatened by some world-class intimidators, and I'm happy to say that Mr Hamilton is not in their league.'

Talk of trust always got Neil Hamilton going. He complained that it was the dirtiest election campaign he had ever known. Actually, it was the only campaign which he might just possibly lose. 'If you continue along the lines of your open letter,' he wrote, 'your emblem will not be a white suit but a whited sepulchre.' The scriptural reference baffled the hacks considerably.

He and his lawyers had another field day with the nominating process – and earned me my one and only mention in *Private Eye*'s 'Pseuds' Corner'. This was from my account of filing the nomination papers:

Bosnia was surely easier than this. Driving down the hill into Macclesfield with Nigel Bateson, my indestructible battle cameraman in Bosnia and the Gulf, we both concluded that it was much like driving down the Mount Igman road into Sarajevo under fire: much the same gradient but different dangers – and frankly, I would prefer the hazards I know.

Never mind the mockery of *Private Eye* – that was exactly how it felt.

The difficulty lay in the labelling. My advisers wished me to appear on the ballot paper as the 'Independent Anti-Corruption' candidate. The returning officer, Brian Longden, warned us that this would inevitably be challenged by Hamilton. What he refused to tell us was whether he would uphold the objection. He was a cautious man and a lawyer himself, possibly eyeing early retirement and anxious to stay out of trouble. Kate Jones thought him hostile: he was certainly nostalgic for the good old days of predictable three-party politics. In addition to his day job as Chief Executive of Macclesfield Borough Council, all that he had to do usually every four or five years as returning officer was to preside over two Tory landslides, one in Macclesfield and the other in Tatton.

Macclesfield would oblige again, but with ten candidates standing and the legal threats and objections flying, Tatton was already becoming a returning officer's nightmare. And those weren't all Mr Longden's problems: Miss Moneypenny, the seven foot transvestite, told him that she fancied him. He wasn't used to that, or to being addressed mincingly by a parliamentary candidate as 'Ducky'.

We retreated to Knutsford alarmed and careworn, unwilling to take the risk of being thrown off the ballot. We rushed round the constituency to our supporters from all parties with new nomination forms, these ones bearing the Independent label, and we filed them the next day. Neil Hamilton complained about that as well, but his objection was overruled. He would have objected if I had stood for the Flat Earth Party. His idea of a fair election was one in which he was offered no serious challenge.

If at that time you had been able to tour the country to assess the attempts of 3,724 candidates in 659 constituencies to secure a seat in the House of Commons, ours would have taken the all-comers' prize for the campaign in most disarray. It wasn't for a shortage of volunteers: more than 250 had already surged through the door. It wasn't for lack of all-party support, which was growing all the time. Nor was it for lack of a programme beyond the obvious demand for honest and open government. The manifesto was a centrist document, mildly eurosceptic, radical on some issues and conservative on others, and rooted in the same common ground as that of the mainstream parties. It sought no return to the excesses of Thatcherism, which included Neil Hamilton himself.

But the Hamiltons' evil eye was upon us. With two weeks to go until polling day, we still didn't have a single leaflet in the hands of a single voter. It wasn't our enemies but our friends who were beginning to do us damage. Sander Meredeen, a Labour Party activist from Nottingham, who had gone home in dismay after trying to help, wrote a letter to the *Guardian* which had a devastating effect on what remained of campaign morale.

I've just quit the campaign team after three days spent largely sitting around because there is no professional management, no clear lines of communication, no inspirational leadership ... I found a fumbling, stumbling team of volunteers expected to work without clear leadership ... Campaigns are not won by a candidate who stands around, looking lugubrious, like a little boy lost.

There was more to the same effect. (When it was all over Mr Meredeen sent me a most gracious letter: he shook us up, and may actually have achieved more through his protest than he did through his canvassing.)

Actually I didn't share the despair. I felt that the contraption, instead of lying in pieces on the floor, was beginning to come together. An air of unworldly amateurism suited us well, and helped to deflect attention from our two back-room professionals. I noted in my diary:

Either we are the Rolls-Royce of a political machine, mysteriously manufactured from nowhere out of nothing, and therefore the hirelings of sinister political forces, or else we are an amateur production and a bit of a shambles, led by a man of sublime political ignorance. The latter perception is not only the truth but the one that will do the less damage.

It was also gratifying to be attacked in the *Guardian*, the paper that should have supported us through good times and bad. Jonathan Freedland, its waspish columnist, observed: 'What is missing is technique ... the atmosphere is closer to that of a Blue Peter appeal than a guerilla campaign to oust a stubborn man from the fifth safest Tory seat in the country.' He got that wrong too: it was actually the fourth.

With ten days to go, I sensed that something was stirring out there that would confound the nay-sayers. Journalists on their flying visits, seeking relief from the blandness and regularity of the national campaign, felt it too. There was a buzz about the place. Volunteers flocked to it from all over the constituency, and all over the country.

An Accidental MP

The old electricity showroom had a new energy about it. It was swarming with canvassers coming and going, and with envelope stuffers working twelve-hour shifts at trestle tables. People walked for miles to save the cost of a postage stamp. Among the hundreds of letters from well-wishers plastering the walls was one from John le Carré and another with a biblical text which we posted in the window: 'And thou shalt take no gift: for the gift blindeth the wise, and perverteth the words of the righteous' (Exodus, 23.8). A letter of endorsement from Sir Alec Guinness was displayed alongside it: 'Every good wish for 1st May. Everyone I know is rooting for you.' Finally, it seemed, the force was with us. The posters and placards, in black and white UN-style lettering, had escaped from the lawyers' limbo and were starting to bloom in windows and gardens, like a benign contagion. I composed a stump speech which drew on G. K. Chesterton for its faith in the people of England, and on regimental values for its idea of conduct unbecoming a Member of Parliament. Cash in brown envelopes wasn't actually mentioned.

There was even a prayer appropriate to the occasion. It was written by Samuel Johnson in 1765, and entitled 'Engaging in Politicks with Hamilton'. It asked 'That no deceit may mislead me nor temptation corrupt me'.[1] The MP in question, William Gerard Hamilton, was known to his contemporaries as 'Single Speech Hamilton', because of the brilliance of his maiden speech, and scarcely heard of again.

I left the constituency once and once only, for Manchester United's training ground in Salford to receive the benediction of the club's manager, Alex Ferguson. In the north-west of England there was no one who counted for more, especially among the young; and the young were becoming involved. It hadn't been part of anyone's plan, but somehow we fired up the primary schools. The kids would come into the office in the morning with their drawings and poems, pick up lapel stickers, and go back and canvass their parents. The gates of the schools, where the mothers were waiting to collect their children, were also where they witnessed this little insurrection – and in many cases decided to be a part of it.

Never underestimate the power of the people to make the improbable happen. Most homes in Tatton received only one communication from the Conservatives – a glossy and colourful brochure which showed Neil Hamilton as the friend of the people and champion of meals on wheels. From us they were bombarded with between four and six leaflets printed in black and white. These are not only the colours of plain speaking, but since a third of our budget went on office space they were all that we could afford. We made the strategy up as we went along, but it was the foot-soldiering of the volunteers that made the difference. Many of these were new to politics, or had previously given up on it. The Tatton insurrection offered them something to believe in. A successful campaign is a process of ignition.

Sander Meredeen and Jonathan Freedland, I said to myself, you should come and see us now.

Among the many who did and who caught the mood was Simon Hoggart, the *Guardian*'s political columnist and sketchwriter, whom I knew well from our time in Washington. While I was canvassing in Great Budworth, as true blue a village as any in Tatton and where I was later to live, a veteran from the Second World War brought his car to a screeching halt outside the George and Dragon and thrust £50 for the campaign fund into my hand. After his day's inquiries Simon – as experienced a reporter of elections as any I know – said he'd never seen anything like it. He was accompanied not only by a photographer but by the *Guardian*'s cartoonist, Steve Bell. The cartoonist's eye noted that, in towns and villages which in a normal election were a sea of blue, Neil Hamilton's posters were to be seen on trees and hedges but nowhere else. Of course Hamilton still had his supporters, but theirs was a loyalty which dared not speak its name. I pointed out that unless the election rules had changed, trees and hedges didn't have a vote. Steve Bell coined a slogan for it: 'Trees for sleaze'. John Sweeney went around using it all day as if it were his own invention.

The Tories, it seemed, had gone to ground, leaving it to their people's reflexes, as well as an enduring respect for John Major, to deliver the vote as usual. No one came from outside to speak for Neil Hamilton, except two strange characters from *Living Marxism* magazine, drawn into the contest for a reason improbably connected with my reporting of the war in Bosnia. I was alleged to be building a political career on the misfortunes of the former Bosnian Serb President, Radovan Karadzic. Their editor had also taken exception to my theories of war zone reporting: to which I could only answer, that I had been there and he hadn't. Having sewn up the *Living Marxism* vote, Mr Hamilton canvassed very little in person: the abuse must have been terribly hard to take, and the indifference equally so. People would cross the street to avoid him, or disappear to the back of the shop. I began to understand the £250 worth of 'sorry you were out' cards. The window of his red brick citadel in Knutsford displayed a sign which asked 'Martin Who?' I was tempted to answer 'Neil How Much?' but guessed that the lawyers would not have approved.

The one break the Hamiltonians thought they had was when I mentioned that Michael Cole, Mohamed Al Fayed's spokesman, had once been a colleague of mine in the BBC. I made no secret of it. We had covered the 1973 Yom Kippur War together in Israel. In an immaculate safari suit, and with not a hair out of place, he had secured the first scoop there rather to my chagrin. If it was as clear a case of conspiracy as they thought, it was conspiracy from a long way away and across the sands of time and the Sinai Desert. In fact, Michael Cole did call me up one day from Harrods to ask if there was anything Mr Al Fayed could do to help. 'Nothing personal,' I said, 'but the best thing he can do to help is to stay away.'

There was a rumour that he had wished to land his helicopter on Knutsford Heath and distribute copies of the book *Sleaze*. Even I, a resolute anti-lawyer, could see some problems with that.

Most gratifying of all was the extent to which it was not a media-driven campaign. This was useful because Paul Johnson, the reactionary wordsmith who believed that Hamilton was the victim of a media conspiracy, had condemned me as the media conspiracy's candidate. (This filled me with self-doubt, not about the merits of the case, but about whether my beloved G. K. Chesterton was the Paul Johnson of his age.) Johnson was daft as a brush, but literate and fluent in a thousand-words-per-hour sort of way. He held me personally responsible for the Murdoch press, the excesses of the tabloids and the programmes of Channel Four – for none of which I had ever actually worked. The *Daily Telegraph* also disapproved; but since one of its own columnists, Boris Johnson, was standing for the Conservatives in Clwyd South, it was hardly in a position to object convincingly to journalists seeking election.

The media had nothing to do with it. This was a campaign to be won by pounding the pavements, the garden paths and shopping precincts – and so hard did I pound them that on the eve of the poll my shoes fell off my feet: my one half hour of rest that day was while I sat in my socks as the expert cobbler in Handforth got me back on the road. I wanted a clean break with my former profession, and no hint of a debt to TV's magic lantern.

I need not have worried. We had all the world's television in Tatton except our own. The Canadians, Americans, New Zealand-ers, Japanese, Australians, Dutch, Italians, Germans and French beat a path to the election's most colourful campaign – the French especially were wooed and won over by Melissa's command of their language (she is completely bilingual) – and for all of them, it was a contest that fulfilled their unshakeable faith in English eccentricity. Even the *Hindustan Times* came to see us. But the British networks, except in the documentary mode, were not among those present. There was no way under the Representation of the People Act that they could report a campaign with ten candidates in it. Paul Davies, an old friend and rival from ITN, confirmed this – ruefully, because it was too good a story to pass up. A BBC producer slipped me an internal memo that said, 'It is almost impossible to imagine circumstances in which Martin Bell may be interviewed.' That was especially gratifying. And I was secretly pleased that the BBC's *Nine O'Clock News* lost a third of its audience in the course of the election. When every story marched to the beat of party politics – an assertion and two denials, like a waltz without a melody – it was no wonder that the viewers were turned off. On Planet Tatton the mood music was more interesting and rising to a great crescendo; but that was our secret and we kept it to ourselves.

Not all the press, however, had gone away. To stand as an 'anti-corruption candidate', whether or not the label was on the ballot paper, was to invite the most intrusive scrutiny. The initial press conference at Westminster had merely whetted their appetites. This had nothing at all to do with Neil Hamilton, who in this sense fought a blameless campaign. But there were others seeking the dividend – whether financial or political – which would reward the front-page story bringing me down.

Anyone I had ever known was called up by these people and asked for the 'real story' on me – the personal or financial scandal which must be out there somewhere. They found the mother of my children in Tahiti, who refused to take their calls. They tried a friend in Washington, who gave them equally short shrift. They camped in another friend's driveway. They invaded the campus of the American college where my younger daughter Catherine was studying, and were duly escorted away by security guards. They went through the rubbish at my London home, and in vain did they put a ladder to an upstairs window. The house was guarded throughout the campaign by one of my Croatian minders, Sasa Schmidtbauer, who kept the intruders at bay. If this was journalism, I reflected, it was no more my kind of journalism than Neil Hamilton's politics were my kind of politics.

I don't deal easily with anger, since I have seen its effects too much in my other life. But I felt it inside myself, and launched a counter-attack against the unknown forces loitering in the murk. 'I urge these cowards and sleaze-merchants to desist, and especially to stay away from those of my friends and family who are so distant as to be beyond the reach of my protection.

'To Melissa and my staff I pledge that I shall redouble my efforts in this campaign, which will draw strength from the shady manoeuvrings of shady people.'

The worst ordeal of all was an interview with John Hellings of the *News of the World*: a half hour of purgatory in the back room of the old electricity showroom. He was persistent and quietly aggressive, not about my financial affairs in which he seemed sublimely uninterested, but about my private life. His focus was the break-up of my first marriage seventeen years earlier. I protested that it was none of his business. He answered that it was very much the business of his newspaper. I was tempted, in a fit of anger, to throw him off the premises. But caution prevailed, I gave him the outline of what had happened, and thus won the endorsement of the *News of the World*. I could have done without it at that price.

The *Mail on Sunday* travelled further, to Los Angeles. There it found my second wife, Rebecca, from whom I had been separated for nine years. The marriage had not ended well, for which I fully accepted my share of the blame, and I had no idea what she would say. She could not have been more gracious. Under the headline 'When the man in the white suit brought me tea in the morning', the paper reported her view that I was thoughtful and funny and would make a good MP. I wrote to her of my gratitude for her kindness. I now had the endorsement of two political parties and both my ex-wives. I supposed that this represented some kind of a record. Most of all I was relieved to have survived my trial by tabloids, at least so far. I had seen them bring so many others down. I knew they would be back, like birds of prey.

My spirits were lifted by the arrival of an unlikely ally – David Soul of planetary TV fame, the Hutch of *Starsky and Hutch*. We had been friends since he came to me for advice about an idea for a series featuring the adventures of a TV reporter in a war zone: there were no prizes for guessing who would be playing the TV reporter.

David is an old-fashioned South Dakota radical, with an abiding interest in politics and a matching sense of right and wrong. He volunteered to canvass for a day alongside John Stalker – a powerful team of cops both real and fictional – and stayed to the end. I could not have dislodged him and would not have wished to. He was a magical operator, schmoozing and smiling and proselytizing, knocking on the doors of houses to which he had been delivering the 'word on the street' for the best part of twenty years. There is an old Hollywood saying that you are famous when they can spell your name in Karachi: the same applies in Wilmslow and Alderley Edge. David was famous. He was also sharp. He disconcerted Neil Hamilton at a public meeting with a hard-edged question about public trust. Like me he was a natural independent and a tilter at windmills. On one occasion, at the Farmers Arms in Wilmslow, I swear that I saw him trade a kiss for a vote. On another, he had to produce his credit card to prove he really was Hutch, or had been. John Sweeney was with us at the time, and pretending to be Starsky.

In the final days, for the very first time, we sensed the chance of an upset. Our canvass returns put us at evens in Wilmslow, where Neil Hamilton was strongest. We were well ahead in Alderley Edge, whose Tories had not had him as their MP before and were reluctant to have him now. In Barnton, an admirable but unfashionable satellite of Northwich, the returns were running ten to one in our favour. With the place festooned in posters and white ribbons, polling day there was like a victory parade. A lady of a vintage to match my own kept me waiting on the doorstep while she went back into the house to assemble her teeth; she then rewarded me with a passionate kiss on the lips. Police reinforcements were sent to Rudheath to control the crowds at the polling stations.

As the polls closed I retreated with Melissa and Nigel Bateson to our hideaway in Knutsford. We had won or we had lost, and worrying about it wouldn't change a vote. 'Nor all thy tears wash out a word of it.' We tuned into television and the exit polls predicting a Labour landslide – but that belonged to another world and did not necessarily mean a thing in Tatton. Never in my life could I remember having felt quite so tired.

'I'm going to sleep, Melissa,' I said.

'Oh no, you're not. You've got a count to go to.'

She was quite insistent that the candidate had to show up.

The campaign team were well ahead of us at the Macclesfield Leisure Centre. They could see the votes being counted, and piling up higher on the trestle tables on one side than the other. They sent back deliberately ambiguous signals that all was not necessarily lost. We arrived at one in the morning through an ambush of cameras and cables and flashlights, amid great commotion on the floor and in the galleries, and noted with astonishment that some of those joining in the applause were the vote-counters themselves. Sweeney called them the accountants of democracy. It was the first time in my life that I had ever been cheered. Having no idea how to react, I studied my shoes. I remembered later what real politicians did – especially American ones: Walter Mondale was a master at it – they pretended to recognize friends in the crowd and waved at them.

There were three people whom I wished to avoid. Two of them were Neil and Christine Hamilton. The feeling was mutual. Christine always sidestepped me when she could, except once on Knutsford Heath. They were looking shattered. Nicholas Winterton, just re-elected as MP for Macclesfield, walked past them without a word. I might have felt some satisfaction, after all they had said and done in a brutal campaign; but their brokenness dismayed me.

Miss Moneypenny the Transformer, representing the Glamorous Party and a Birmingham nightclub, was not so easily eluded. She pursued me down a blind alley beside the counting tables, where she had me cornered. It is not usual for a parliamentary candidate, at the climax of the democratic process, to have to make small talk to a seven-foot transvestite with flashing nipples; but I did my best to rise to the occasion by standing on a chair. We thanked each other for a lively campaign which had enlisted the enthusiasm of the young, and wished each other well. At least I had it easier than Christine Hamilton, who also had no escape and with whom Miss Moneypenny insisted on discussing silk underwear, a subject of greater interest at that moment to the transvestite than to the candidate's wife.

At half past two in the morning Brian Longden, the returning officer, called us together at the foot of the platform. The figures he read out were beyond my dreams and Neil Hamilton's nightmares. I had 29,354 votes. He had 18,277. The other eight ranged between 73 and 295. Mr Longden remarked rather pointedly, with a glance in the direction of the blue rosettes, that it was not usual in these circumstances to ask for a recount.

All that remained was to get up on the platform and finish the business, so that we could go home. Hamilton called it 'a sad day for the people of Tatton'. I thought that offensive and graceless. It was, after all, the result and the climax of the process – not something done *to* the people of Tatton but something done *by* the people of Tatton. There is actually a word for it. It is called democracy. Neil Hamilton had a talent, just when you were feeling sorry for him, for persuading you not to bother: it was a waste of sympathy.

My own speech was shorter, addressed to all those people in the hall and the constituency who had put their faith in me, had dared to back the amateur and outsider, and to whom the contest in Tatton had not been the procession that it usually was, but a real democratic exercise.

I believe this is a proud moment for the people of Tatton, though I have to say a rather humbling one for me. I did not do this; you did it. It was not my victory; it was your victory. I believe you have lit a beacon which will shed light in some dark corners and illuminate the Mother of Parliaments itself . . .What you have accomplished here has been to me some kind of political miracle. I shall be, and shall remain, Independent. I shall take no party whip. I shall serve for one term only. I am deeply grateful to all of you, and may I repeat, just for the last time, a couple of lines from G. K. Chesterton that I used during the campaign:

Smile at us, pay us, pass us, but do not quite forget,
That we are the people of England and we have not spoken yet.[2]

You have spoken tonight magnificently, and I thank you from the bottom of my heart.

Then I went back to Knutsford, slept for two hours, and woke up to my surprise as a Member of Parliament. Oliver Kamm, the campaign's philosopher and think tank, had been up all night.

'Do you realize what you've just done?' he asked.

'I have no idea,' I answered, 'but I think that what we need is a cup of tea.'

'Politics,' said Václav Havel, 'can also be the art of the imposs-ible.'[3] Just to remember it by, I kept a few souvenirs of that campaign: a poster, a leaflet, a cartoon, a headline, a white rosette and a poem. It was the poem, sent by one of the thousands of well-wishers, that meant more to me than anything else. It summed the thing up so much better than words of mine. It was 'Sometimes', by Sheenagh Pugh.

> Sometimes things don't go, after all,
> from bad to worse. Some years, muscadel
> faces down frost; green thrives; the crops don't fail.
> Sometimes a man aims high, and all goes well.
>
> A people sometimes will step back from war:
> elect an honest man, decide they care
> enough, that they can't leave some stranger poor.
> Some men become what they were born for.
>
> Sometimes our best efforts do not go
> amiss; sometimes we do as we meant to.
> The sun will sometimes melt a field of sorrow
> that seemed hard frozen; may it happen for you.[4]

4. Where Do I Hang My Sword?

Frankly it would have been easier to lose. I knew that. At the back of my mind I had worked out a little concession speech which would have congratulated Neil Hamilton, paid tribute to my supporters of all parties who had run him close (for I guessed that the margin of defeat would have been small), and claimed some credit, in so safe a seat, for turning a procession into an election. It would also have been gracious, which his concession speech was not. I should then have headed south down the M6 with a smile on my face and not too worried about having lost two jobs in a month. Maybe a place could be found for a former war reporter and failed parliamentary candidate in the new Chancellor's 'Welfare to Work' programme.

But none of that happened. Instead my return to London was as much a journey into the unknown as the drive to Knutsford twenty-seven days earlier. If anything it was even more so. All I knew for sure was that I had just passed the biggest selection board of my life. I had a great deal to learn and very little time in which to learn it, and a great many people depended on me not to let them down.

My life was further complicated by a problem not faced by any other of the new MPs of the class of '97: my defeated opponent and his wife had taken to shadowing me. They were behind me on the grandstand at the Knutsford May Day festivities two days after the election. I held out my hand; he refused to shake it. They followed me to the Oxford Union three days later (Neil Hamilton was not a member, but he got in somehow). He was clearly unwell, and in what a psychiatrist might have described as a state of denial. I started to take a personal interest in anti-stalking legislation.

There were also some personal complications. About a year

earlier, when I came out of Bosnia for the last time and made a speech about it, I had met Fiona, who worked in the design department of an investment bank. She challenged some of the points I made, and I wished to know her better. I did so – and eventually married her. But at the time of my plunge into politics, on which she was distinctly under-consulted, we were no more than the best of friends. It took Fleet Street's finest ten days to find her, but they finally tracked her down to her cottage in Kent, from which I received an SOS late at night in my campaign bunker in Knutsford. Fiona is a sociable person except where the press are concerned; she would almost as soon face a firing squad as a photocall. On a later occasion, the day after our wedding, she was disguised with a large scarf and dark glasses, and hid from the pack of photographers behind a heap of farmyard manure – preferring its company to theirs. 'Odd things happen,' she noted, 'when you're married to Martin.' This time, she managed to slip out early in the morning to Gatwick, where she boarded the first flight to Malta and stayed there until the campaign was over. It was there that I called her at dawn on 2 May.

'I'm sorry to have to wake you with bad news,' I explained, 'but the bad news is that I won.'

'How much did you win by?'

'It was a landslide – 11,000.'

I announced it, she told me later, like a casualty figure.

My other anxiety concerned my daughter Melissa. She had left a well-paid job with Reuters in Brussels, on the day of the notorious ambush on the heath, to be with her father in his hour of need. The job was not retrievable. As it happened, she found another one with a financial news agency in London – and that wasn't all she found. One of the fellow campaign workers in Tatton was Peter Bracken, an ex-army major who took more than a narrowly political interest in her. I suspected there was something going on when Melissa stopped canvassing in Handforth one morning, pleading pressure of paperwork, to join him at our headquarters. 'But Melissa,' I remonstrated, 'you don't have any paperwork!'

They married a year later in the twelfth-century parish church of St Oswald at Lower Peover. And so it was that, as things turned out, I had to thank Neil Hamilton not only for a seat in Parliament but for a son-in-law, and in due course a grandson. They should perhaps have called him Neil. Instead they called him Max.

But at the time I was not in the mood to thank Neil Hamilton for anything. All I knew was that I was seriously unprepared for the task ahead. I was one of 260 new Members of Parliament. All the others belonged to a party, had been coached at seminars and candidates' schools, had pagers on their belts to instruct them, and were fulfilling presumably a lifetime's ambition. Both Labour and the Liberal Democrats won seats which were not on their target list. Planet Tatton, of course, remained in a world of its own.

So how do you get into Parliament? It's simple, really. You take the Northern Line to Embankment and then the Circle or District Line to Westminster. From there you walk to the far end of the great Gothic pile of rock facing you, and if the doorkeepers at Black Rod's Entrance know who you are they will let you in to be issued with a green-and-white-striped pass. This will allow you to get lost as many times as you please on your way to the Commons Chamber and your swearing-in. If you can find the post office you can also pick up the two thousand letters awaiting you, with more sacks full arriving every day. You even have your own coat-hanger in the Members' Cloak Room, with a neat pink ribbon attached to it; this solves the problem that has been troubling you since the moment of victory, of where to hang your sword. The House of Commons is that kind of place. What you do not have yet is an office, a secretary, or even the mistiest notion of what's going on.

Lacking a party, I urgently needed someone to make sense of it all – not a dignitary in eighteenth-century costume, a Black Rod or Deputy Principal Doorkeeper or Serjeant-at-Arms, but an experienced parliamentary secretary. As it happened, 128 of them were available, having worked for defeated Conservatives. As it also happened, new Labour MPs were discouraged from taking them on, on the rather absurd grounds that they were 'politically unsound'. So I was free to pick from the best of them, which I did.

Mary Price had worked for twelve years for Sir Hector Monro, MP for Dumfries and a Tory from the days before there were jokes about money in brown envelopes. He had retired at the General Election, and his chosen successor – Mary's prospective future employer – had been heavily defeated. So it was that I found her sitting in the Central Lobby, nervously clutching her first ever CV (she'd never needed one before), and sufficiently unemployed to consider working even for an Independent. I felt a twinge of guilt. I knew that the campaign in Tatton – especially the Neil and Christine show – had impacted heavily on Conservative fortunes elsewhere. Perhaps we had all played a part in putting Mary out of a job.

At least I could make amends. But first I gave her a copy of my book on the Bosnian war, and asked her to read it with a view to deciding whether she would actually be willing to work with me. She agreed to the risk next day. That may have been a reflection not so much on the quality of the book, as on her need to find employment.

We still had nowhere to work, except at a table in a shared and chaotic committee room; so I then went to see Simon Hughes, outgoing chief whip of the Liberal Democrats. This was not because of any hidden affiliations on my part, but because the office space of the smaller parties was looked after by the Lib Dems. My party of course was as small as a party gets (although at the same time the ninth largest in the House: it depended on how you looked at it). As a newcomer I was still a bit awestruck by the sheer grandeur of the place, and its air of being haunted by the ghosts of Gladstone and Churchill. Simon was not. 'It's all very fine to look at,' he said, 'but to work in it's a legislative slum.'

Either by luck, or because I had known Paddy Ashdown from the Bosnian war (he was the only one of the politicians visiting Bosnia who had the courage to drive down the Mount Igman road in an unarmoured vehicle), I was allocated an office of unusual charm, spacious and sunlit, not in the Palace of Westminster itself, but in Dean's Yard between the Abbey and the Choir School.

It was there that Mary and I started to climb the mail mountain. She was well suited to the task, since she had also once worked for Lord Hunt, the man who had planned and led the conquest of Everest. We were staggering under such piles of post as had other MPs, themselves overburdened, eyeing us with pity. It seemed that the election in Tatton had in some way caught the world's attention. One of my postal votes came from Vladivostok. A poetess in Calcutta sent a letter of congratulation. Another Martin Bell, from Macon in Georgia, was inspired to run as an Independent in its city council election. And a captain wrote to me from his merchant ship on the approach to Honolulu, 'Your victory almost turned me to religion.' Almost – but not quite: it was Michael Howard's parliamentary survival in Folkestone, he explained, that had prevented him from taking vows of holiness. Closer to home, an eleven-year-old wrote, 'I am pleased you are the MP of Knutsford, because my Mum and Dad voted for you and this is the first time my Mum and Dad got the vote right.' And at the Tatton Park Cottage Garden Show, which was my very first constituency engagement, a supporter told me that she had celebrated by planting her garden with honesty seeds.

Not all the letters were caught up in the euphoria of the moment. There was an angry minority out there who believed that Neil Hamilton had been badly treated, that the Downey Report would clear his name, and that I was part of a great conspiracy against him. Whenever some local councillor was caught with his hand in the till, or an MP was helping the police with their inquiries, I was invited to resign as MP for Tatton and stand as an Independent in that constituency. A Mr O'Keefe from Islington, who had supported three parties in his time, was especially upset that I belonged to none. I was further challenged to make my exit if, when the Downey Report was published, the former MP came out of it as white as the driven snow. This in fact I had already decided to do: but having read the transcripts of his cross-examination, I thought it a most unlikely turn of events.

The mail became so voluminous and complex it reached the

point that I realized I rather liked receiving bills. I knew what to do with a bill – pay it. But some of the letters, even the congratulatory ones, were almost unanswerable. For the sake of my sanity and survival, I began to consign more and more of them, especially those from outside the constituency, to the circular filing cabinet underneath my desk. Overnight the filing cabinet was cleared, and was available for the next day's surplus to be laid to rest in an equally permanent manner.

I realized that there were MPs who took a more leisurely view of things, and whose membership of the best club in town was hardly troubled by a constituent's letter from one week to the next. They seldom read the letters they received or signed the letters they sent. There was a new breed of constituency caseworker doing what the MPs used to do. I wouldn't go that far, but there had to be more to being an MP than writing as many letters in a month as I had ever written before in my entire life. There was surely some parliamentary business waiting to be done, and there was certainly a maiden speech to be delivered.

I am calm and equable in the face of known dangers. It is the unknown ones that scare me. A lifetime of addressing millions electronically did not prepare a man for the ordeal of a maiden speech before a handful of his colleagues in an otherwise deserted House of Commons. There was in my own case the additional difficulty of finding somewhere to sit. The Commons, unlike the Lords, does not allow for the category of cross-bencher. Its very furniture is confrontational, and requires you to show where you stand by where you sit: with the government or against it.

I received an early lesson in this when I joined an all-party group for the defence of the family farm.

'Are you Government or Opposition?' asked Lord Beaumont of Whitley, who bore a remarkable likeness to the Prophet Ezekiel and was chairman of the group.

'I'm neither,' I replied. 'I'm Independent.'

'I don't think it's possible to be neither,' he persisted. 'Are you on the Government side?'

'No, not really.'

'Then you must be Opposition.'

There are in fact six seats facing the Speaker, on either side of the aisle alongside the Serjeant-at-Arms. These were seats once taken by choristers in the days when there were serious prayers before parliamentary business. One of these would have been perfect for my independent purposes, and was where I sat when listening to debates. But they were technically outside the Bar of the House, which was no more than a white line on the carpet, and Members were not allowed to speak from them.

I wrote to the Leader of the House urging the suspension of this ridiculous, arcane and medieval rule – without result, because the pace of reform even in a reforming parliament was proving to be painfully slow. So for my maiden speech, and every intervention thereafter, I moved to the second row beyond the further shores of the Liberal Democrats and not so far from my old nemesis, Dr Ian Paisley (who proved to be most gracious, and even offered his help on meeting me again, twenty-seven years after he had stirred up his crowds against me in Armagh).

There are certain conventions for a maiden speech, as hard and fast as a battalion's Standing Orders. It must not be controversial. (It had not always been so, and I wished I could have matched the audacity of William Cobbett, who also entered the Commons late in life: 'Mr Speaker, it appears to me that since I have been sitting here I have heard a great deal of vain and unprofitable conversation.') The speech must speak well of the constituency from which the Member comes. And it must pay a proper tribute to the previous MP. I had no problem with the first two, especially the second, for Tatton is a beautiful corner of England, rich in its scenery and indeed in its history (King Canute and Highwayman Higgins being but two of its luminaries). But as for the third convention, the compliments due to the previous Member, this required some thought.

I spoke about land mines, mainly because other Members knew more about just about everything else than I did, but I knew more about land mines than they did. I liked the idea of people talking only about what they knew about, and felt it could be rather more widely applied. I spoke of the beauties of the Cheshire countryside, under threat from the second runway of Manchester airport. And then I spoke about Neil Hamilton. I paid tribute to the work that he had done for his constituents – a genuine tribute for he had indeed been an assiduous constituency MP, and this had been the real strength of his husband-and-wife team. I then thanked him for the effect he had had, whether deliberately or not, in reviving the spirit of democracy in Tatton.

Reaction to the speech was mixed. A surgeon wrote to me from Manchester that he hoped I didn't mind if he called it sanctimonious claptrap. Actually I did mind. I minded a lot. I felt that surgeons of all people should know better and care more about the hideous effects of land mines. On the other hand, a lady from Stoke-on-Trent said it was the only maiden speech she had ever heard worth listening to. The lesson of it all was to ignore the reviews and follow the motto of the old army commandos, which was to bash on regardless.

I made two mistakes that day, one of which I regretted before the other. My first mistake was to ignore another convention, which I had no one to advise me about, that after his maiden speech a Member stays in his place for the wind-up speeches at the end of the day. I failed to do that, and Gerald Howarth MP sent me a reproachful letter about it. I actually had a reason for rushing out: even as I was on my feet Mr Swampy's friends, the eco-warriors, were being forcibly evicted from their tunnels and tree-houses on the site of Manchester airport's second runway; it was in the constituency, and I had to be there.

My second mistake was to be insufficiently gracious about Neil Hamilton. I do not believe he was a bad man, only a weak one and a chancer – or, in his own words, 'a bit of a chump'. I doubt if the old Tory Party in the years BT (Before Thatcher) would have adopted him for any seat more winnable than Barnsley Central. I believed that his actions amounted to conduct unbecoming a

Member of Parliament, and had damaged his claim to serve for another term. That was quite apart from the issue of cash in brown envelopes, on which I had not campaigned because I did not think it provable. But still I should have found some kinder words than I did.

Gerald Howarth was of the same opinion, and intervened in the debate to say so. (It was most unusual for one MP to attack another's maiden speech, but I was coming to see that being MP for Tatton was not like being MP for anywhere else.) Howarth was Hamilton's last and closest friend in the House of Commons. He was MP for Aldershot, where he had succeeded Julian Critchley (two such different characters that it was amazing they shared the same planet, never mind the same constituency party). Neil Hamilton had Howarth at his side as he haunted the corridors of Westminster like the ghost of parliaments past. For the first few times that I spoke in the House, the Member for Aldershot routinely rose to object. Later he mellowed, or perhaps I did, and we eventually agreed a cease-fire in the Members' Smoking Room. We shared some military interests, for he was also the MP for the Parachute Regiment, and he even sought my support in the campaign to help Hamilton clear his name.

It was a strange episode and it caused me to reflect – not for the first time – that the story of my political career must have been devised by some mad computer, an unlikely conjunction of the planets, or an imp with a mischievous sense of humour; no writer of fiction could ever have made it up. Experience was teaching me not to disbelieve the unbelievable.

Sir Gordon Downey's long-awaited report on allegations against Neil Hamilton and twenty-four other MPs was published six weeks later. This was the report which had been blocked by the General Election, and Mr Hamilton had run his campaign on the claim that it would clear his name. It did nothing of the kind. The Parliamentary Commissioner wrote, 'The evidence that Mr Hamilton received cash payments directly from Mr Al Fayed in return for lobbying services is compelling; and I so conclude.'[1]

There followed an uproar which I did my best to avoid, being at the University of East Anglia at the time and receiving an honorary degree (which I did in my father's name: it should have been his, not mine). I did, however, feel that my campaign was vindicated and so was the judgement of 29,354 voters. Alan Barnes, Chairman of the Tatton Conservative Association, resigned – as he had promised to if the Downey Report found against the former MP. Mr Barnes was an honourable man, guilty perhaps of no more than an excess of loyalty in a cause that hardly justified it. There were many in the constituency who felt deeply hurt, and let down by someone they trusted. I made no injurious comment. There would have been no point in it, and it was not my style.

The Downey Report drew a line under the campaign and all its turbulence. I noticed a change in the character of the incoming mail. Quite absent were the accusations that I was a Labour Party pawn, and the demands for my departure. These letters were often in green ink, and concluded with what I call the 'polemical vocative': 'Mr Bell, you are a fraud and a hypocrite. The least you can do is resign.' In their place were some new concerns. Someone sent me a bar of soap and a message with it: 'I hope you don't let success go to your head. This is to help you to keep your hands clean – and a reminder of what happened to those who didn't.'

That wasn't the end of the matter. After a period of months – the length of the summer recess and more – it went to the Standards and Privileges Committee, the eleven MPs of all parties to whom the Parliamentary Commissioner reports. They could add to the report or subtract from it, endorse it or contradict it, or contribute some further judgements of their own. Mr Hamilton appeared before them in public to plead his innocence, but was not cross-examined. Neither was his principal accuser, Mr Mohamed Al Fayed.

Most of the meetings were private and confidential. They were also acrimonious. Parliament's new disciplinary procedures were working adequately in all the other cases – but in the Hamilton case, where matters of fact and the credibility of witnesses were in dispute, they were strained to breaking point. I was not at this time on the committee, and could not have been, for I was clearly an interested party. But what I believe happened was that a majority on the committee finally got tired of the whole affair – yesterday's man, yesterday's Parliament, yesterday's brown envelopes – and decided to limp to judgement.

Sensing this, Neil Hamilton did the last thing I ever expected him to do: he asked for my help. To the surprise of some, I agreed; I could hardly represent all my 64,000 constituents except one, my disgraced and defeated opponent. He came alone, of course. Christine Hamilton avoided me. She held me personally responsible for her husband's downfall, and even my gesture in buying her *Book of British Battleaxes* was not going to endear me to her. There was too much water under the bridge – or debris on the heath, perhaps. She confided to an interviewer that she had sometimes felt murderous, but never suicidal: it was only natural to wonder whom she had wished to murder. As for her husband, my guess is that his feelings were more mixed. He regarded me as a political nonentity, yet may have believed that I was in a special position to help him.

The meeting, which lasted for forty minutes, was calm and businesslike. The substance of it, of course, must remain confidential. But when it was over, I wrote a letter on Mr Hamilton's behalf to Robert Sheldon, Chairman of the Standards and Privileges Committee. It wasn't a hard thing to do. I actually shared some of my former opponent's publicly expressed concerns. Neil Hamilton was a difficult man to admire, but he surely had a case. The parliamentary inquiry, both by the commissioner and by the committee, did not have the status of a court of law. Its procedures, though painstaking, were less rigorous. Its purpose was to establish the facts. Yet the effect of its findings in the Hamilton case was close to that of a criminal conviction. The former MP, although a free man not charged with any criminal offence, was condemned – as he put it – to a 'life of penury and unemployment'. His party would not have him back; nor would the legal profession. Neither could he make a living by being lampooned on *Have I Got News For You.*

The committee's report was published on 6 November 1997. On the broader charge sheet against him – the free holidays, the undeclared gifts, the casual attitude to the rules of the House – it concluded unanimously: 'Mr Hamilton's conduct fell seriously and persistently below the standards which the House is entitled to expect of its Members. Had Mr Hamilton still been a Member we would have recommended a substantial period of suspension from the service of the House.' Yet on the specific charge, of receiving £20,000 in brown envelopes, of which Sir Gordon Downey had found compelling evidence, the committee demurred. 'There can be no absolute proof that such payments were, or were not, made.'[2]

The report then went to the floor of the House, unanimous only in so far as it was also ambiguous. Two of the three Conservatives on the committee, Quentin Davies and Ann Widdecombe (nobody's stooges, either of them), were deeply unhappy about it. Ann Widdecombe resigned. Both seethed with dismay as they failed to catch the Speaker's eye to express their dissent in public, although she called five members of the committee's majority. As Hamilton's own MP I wasn't called to speak either. The procedures of the place made me angry. I remember saying to myself, perhaps this was how Guy Fawkes felt.

As far as the House of Commons was concerned, that was the end of the Hamilton affair which had propelled me into it. I went outside in the evening drizzle to face not only the cameras and reporters, but Neil and Christine as well. She was extremely agitated. 'Go on,' she hissed to him, 'now's your chance. Put him on the spot!' He had not very much to put me on the spot about. Although I accepted the fairness of Sir Gordon's inquiry, I drew attention to the procedural inadequacies, the lack of a proper means of appeal, and Neil Hamilton's plight as a result. Simon Hoggart reported in the *Guardian* the following morning, 'Mr Bell is so painfully fair to everyone, he is probably saying even now that we shouldn't be too hasty in condemning Richard III.' He was right about that, and I wrote to his editor accordingly: 'How typical of the *Guardian* to join the clamour against the most maligned of English kings. There was a lot to be said for Richard III. It was the greatest of spin doctors, W. Shakespeare, plying his craft on behalf of the Tudors, who condemned him to live in infamy for ever.'

This exchange drew a friendly response from the Richard III Society, welcoming me as one of their own – and a letter of outrage from a follower of the Tudor orthodoxy. It was at that point that I began to suspect that there might be something in the national character which would doom my attempt to restore the cross-bench, and practise a politics of neither one party nor the other.

We are, it would seem, a disputatious people. We take sides. We enjoy our quarrels, whether York against Lancaster, Cavalier against Roundhead, or Labour against Conservative. Even Liverpool against Arsenal for that matter. Not for nothing are the front benches in the Commons set at two swords' lengths from each other. Not for nothing is it assumed that an MP possesses a sword and needs a place to hang it. And if we can't find a cause of war in our politics, we will find one in our history.

5. The People's Stooge

Becoming an MP is one thing. Being an MP is quite another. What I did not know, and could only learn by finding out, was whether there was a role for an Independent at Westminster. I hoped there was, but had no way of knowing. It was untrodden ground. No one had tried it since I was twelve years old. What I did know was that I could hardly build a four-year career on not being Neil Hamilton, and that expectations were set uncomfortably high. Most MPs are little known outside their own constituencies. Some are little known even inside their own constituencies. But I would find no refuge in obscurity; and if I failed, by whatever standards failure was judged, it would be a public and well-advertised fall from grace – painful to some (especially myself) and deeply satisfying to others. I imagined the political obituarists already sharpening their pencils. They had left me for dead once before. And to come out of it all merely as the MP with the highest dry cleaning bill would not be much of a distinction.

A measure of confusion prevailed for a while, not least inside the head of the new Member of Parliament for Tatton. Most of what had happened had been done to me rather than by me. I had expected my political career to last for a mere forty-eight hours, and now it was stretching out to the crack of doom or to the end of the new Parliament, whichever came first.

I was aware of a degree of turbulence in the constituency itself. A wave of recrimination swept through the Conservative Association, which had achieved pariah status by losing the party's fourth safest seat in the country, and doing great damage elsewhere. My new-found friends among the Tories at Westminster, surveying the casualties after the onslaught as if through the smoke of war, believed that Neil Hamilton had cost them fifty seats; with a few exceptions they hadn't esteemed him highly before, and certainly didn't now. He was history already. There were moves to have him expelled from the party. These came to nothing when it emerged that he had never actually been a member of it in the first place. That was the kind of party that it was then. His name was obscured by masking tape on the brass plaque outside the Knutsford headquarters. Certain other plaques that he had himself unveiled during his years as an MP and a government minister, at Wilmslow High School and elsewhere, were discreetly unscrewed from their walls. This seemed a mistake. Our history is our own and no one else's – both the bits that we are proud of and the bits that we are not – and how shall we ever learn from it if we deny it?

The local Tories declined to prolong the hostilities. To my surprise and relief they did not query my election expenses, which were scrupulously accounted and well inside the limit. They harboured few grudges, and we agreed an unspoken cease-fire. I never attacked them, and they let me get on with it. It was partly of their doing and greatly to their credit that, for the parliamentary term that followed, Tatton was spared the clamour of party warfare.

It was clearly no time for triumphalism – which was easy enough, because I didn't feel any. Nor would my supporters allow me to. 'Against Neil Hamilton,' one of them reminded me with brutal honesty, 'even a trained monkey would have won.' The brief euphoria of victory was superseded by its hangover – the dozens of urgent decisions clamouring to be taken. People and events conspired to prevent it from going to my head. In my first week as an MP I stopped at the traffic lights in St John's Wood on my way to my new place of work. I was feeling rather pleased with myself, for had I not just exchanged a declining career at the BBC and a down-market parking space in Shepherds Bush for a new lease of life and a parking palace at Westminster? A driver pulled up alongside me, and wound down his window with a quizzical look on his face.

'Excuse me asking,' he inquired, 'but aren't you Neil Hamilton?'

'No, I'm the other chap, the one who beat him.'

'Oh, that's all right then. And by the way, good luck.'

I needed it and received it. Since my new colleagues did not see me as a threat to the system, but rather as a curiosity and an anomaly and a bit of a lost soul, they showered me with advice from all quarters. Ivor Stanbrook, the former Tory MP for Orpington, sent me a copy of a useful little manual he had written, the fruits of his twenty-two years in the House, 'How to be an MP'. His counsel to new Members was to bide their time and keep their heads down for the first five years. But the first five years would probably be all the years I would have! Paul Flynn, the independent-minded Labour MP for Newport West, sent me his list of 'Backbenchers' Ten Commandments', containing the rather contrary advice to make as many waves as possible. His third commandment appealed to me especially: 'Seek novel remedies and challenge accepted wisdom.' So did his fifth: 'Never covet a second income, honours or a retirement job.'

I also sensed that I had the encouragement, from somewhere in the Elysian Fields, of my great predecessor, A. P. Herbert, the last elected Independent, who left the House in 1950 when the university seats were abolished. He represented Oxford University. According to his own account, he had also entered Parliament at three weeks' notice and as the result of a procession of accidents. He was a greater master of parliamentary procedure than I could ever hope to be, and had achieved more in his particular causes – especially reform of the divorce laws – than I could ever hope to achieve. He was an MP for fourteen years, exactly the same length of service as Neil Hamilton's; but there the resemblance ended. I felt him at my shoulder, watching over me. Indeed his account of those years, *Independent Member*, took the form of an address to his successor. 'I did not go into the House for fun,' he wrote, 'or professional gain: and I have no complaints about my parliamentary episode (I never thought of it as a career). Provided, that is, that something has been done worth doing, that some small mark has been left upon the sands.'[1] It was my own ambition of making a difference, more eloquently expressed.

On arrival at Westminster I received separate summonses from its two great ladies. During my first week I found myself by accident on the terrace – wherever I went it was by accident, terminally lost and on the way to somewhere else – where I was spotted by Madam Speaker from the splendour of her tower. She sent an emissary to usher me into the presence. She could not have been more warm and welcoming. I had the feeling that she had been taking a very personal interest in the election campaign in Tatton – even a proprietary interest. For the House of Commons was her House, and the disrepute into which some of its members had brought it had troubled her deeply.

From what she said later, and the Members she called to speak and those she did not, I sensed that – although scrupulously fair – she had a preference for independent-minded MPs rather than those of the robotic tendency who seemed hardly able to ask a question unless their pagers framed it for them. The only significant time during my first year when I tried to catch her eye but failed was during the debate on Neil Hamilton himself. He was by then my constituent, I felt that he had not been treated in all fairness by the Standards and Privileges Committee, and I wished to stand up and say so. She would not allow it. Her resignation, announced in July 2000, was a source of great sadness to me, and a loss to the House. It did not feel the same without her. I felt bereaved.

The other summons was from Lady Castle, eighty-six years old and still as sharp as a knife and as bright as a button. We took tea and scones among the peers and baronesses. We must have looked a very odd couple, she having been in politics for sixty years and I for just six weeks. The very heart and soul of Old Labour, she was still relishing the standing ovation she had received at the previous party conference. She was at odds with New Labour's lighter ideological accoutrements and some of its controlling personalities, whom she dismissed as 'those bastards'. She distilled the wisdom of her long career into a single phrase. 'Young man,' she said (thus winning me over completely), 'whatever else you do, you must never be afraid to stand alone.'

I found this consoling, since I saw no prospect of standing in any other way. As the first elected Independent for forty-seven years I felt like a mariner at sea without a compass or chart, or even a destination, except the rather minimal ambition of surviving without disgrace. I could have sought the protection of an established party, but I would have let down a great many people, including myself, if I had done so. At a joint appearance one morning on David Frost's TV emporium, Tory MP Alan Duncan assured me that before the parliamentary term was over I would have to show my true colours – as Conservative, Labour or Liberal Democrat. He felt that I must be concealing some secret allegiance. I replied that there was another category: none of the above. (Actually, since arriving at the Commons I had rather got to like the Scottish Nationalists, on purely personal grounds. They seemed a decent lot, with a saving sense of humour, and not too consumed by the ubiquitous political plague of self-importance. But how could I, only quarter Scottish, represent Tatton as a Scottish Nationalist? We had our exiles, but I doubt if it would have gone down too well in Alderley Edge. Besides, I believe in the Union. Alex Salmond, the party's leader, assured me that would not be a problem.)

For a few short months, the number of Independents in parliament doubled. That is, we were two instead of one – hardly a mighty political force, but not negligible either. Peter Temple-Morris, elected as Conservative MP for Leominster, grew increasingly disenchanted with his party's euroscepticism and was pushed before he could jump. He crossed the floor of the House, to the great delight of one side and derision of the other, and did not pause on the cross-bench before joining his new friends on the Labour benches. Technically he sat as an Independent, and we enjoyed a most convivial lunch at which I pleaded with him to remain Independent, even offering to campaign for him, and we worked out what our policy would be if ever we could agree one.

He even conceded to me the 'party leadership'. After that he went all the way over and took the Labour whip. Peter is a delightful man, but politically gregarious and the sort who might find fulfilment in a peerage or an ambassadorship. He prefers the comfort of a big party around him.

I, on the other hand, do not. Parties are the bedrock of stable government, essential to its functioning, and I admire the agility of those who feel able to stay inside them – even if it means from time to time speaking and voting for things they don't believe in. Such people would either avoid the critical division bell by heading out on an urgent fact-finding mission to Bangladesh, or confide their doubts to me in confessional places, like the corridors and the Smoking Room. They would lower their voices to a whisper, lest they be overheard by the whips. Or the party exiled them to the cities and shires, for the Gulag of 'constituency weeks' (later discontinued), in the course of which they were forbidden to show their faces at Westminster. A. P. Herbert once remarked, 'I do not think I could have endured a month in Parliament under the conditions which guide and bind your "party man".'[2] I admired his stamina. My limit would have been two weeks.

My own ideal party is quite small – actually, with a membership in single figures. The single figure is one. With two you would get a disagreement; with three, a faction fight; and with four, a schism. This is just a personal preference, held with equal strength during my thirty-four years in journalism. I tended to work beyond the rim of the civilized world, in war zones and other unquiet places outside the reach of editors with preconceived notions. I had an unwritten pact to this effect with Mark Damazer, who was Head of Most Things at BBC News and whose editorial meetings turned into soliloquies because no one dared to challenge his Rolls-Royce mind. I would have done so, but was elsewhere. The principle was the same in journalism as in politics. The centre always sought to impose control. An editor trying to rewrite a correspondent's dispatch and a whip trying to ventriloquize a back-bencher's question were embarked on parallel enterprises.

The nightmares collided one day when I agreed to be interviewed from Manchester by David Frost, who was inquiring about the private lives of politicians. David and I grew up together in the same small town in Suffolk, and I drove him in my mini-van to the first transmission of *That Was The Week That Was*, but there are limits even to a friendship so long established. With ten minutes to go, the disembodied voice of one of his producers echoed down the line warning me that I wasn't allowed to mention Peter Mandelson's sexual preferences, which were at that time much in the news.

'Actually, I hadn't intended to discuss them because they don't interest me, but since you mention them you may be provoking me to do so.'

'You really mean that?'

'Let's put it this way. I didn't work freely for the BBC for all those years, in order to be messed about by it when I left it.'

I watched and waited for a while. I observed the wisdom of the old soldier's saying, that time spent in reconnaissance is seldom wasted. Again I followed the advice of A. P. Herbert, 'You should sit quiet for a time, and study carefully how things are said and done.'[3] In the House itself I attended debates of little interest to me or my constituents, to get the feel of the place. I marvelled at the length and emptiness of many of the speeches – the council chamber number-crunching on one side and the sub-Churchillian rhetoric on the other. Of course, there were exceptions: Kenneth Clarke on the economy, Tam Dalyell on devolution; Oona King, surely the brightest of the new intake, on the world beyond our borders; and Dennis Skinner on whatever it was to which he applied his well-aimed Bolsover boot. There were others who earned their mention in dispatches – Tony Benn, Bob Marshall-Andrews, Paul Flynn, Gerry Bermingham, Richard Shepherd, Paul Keetch – the unincorporated league of the independent-minded. But as for those who merely made up the numbers, it seemed that the more they spoke the less they said.

Sometimes I was left-wing and sometimes I was right-wing. Sometimes I was in the front line with the progressives and sometimes in the last ditch with the diehards. It depended on the issue, on the advice I was receiving from a variety of sources and on my own convictions. I am a democrat, a radical, a libertarian and a Blairite – Eric Blair, that is, not Tony – an Orwellian minus the socialism. I am neither of the right nor the left, nor even on all issues of the centre. I am opposed to change for change's sake, and also to tyrannies and Utopias and New Jerusalems. I am suspicious of grand ideas – whether a greater Serbia, a united Ireland or a Marxist-Leninist Mozambique – which are then promoted through the barrel of a gun and cause great mischief and misery. I have seen that mischief and misery for myself in those places and others. Instead, I am an ameliorist. *Ameliorism for ever* is hardly a slogan to set the prairie on fire, but as an idea it has merit. It challenges the scepticism of the philosophical conservatives with the belief that modest but significant improvements are possible and necessary, especially for the poor and the underprivileged. Such improvements are also needed most urgently in our democratic practices, which have been corrupted by the parties through such self-serving devices as the electoral college, the closed-list voting system, the appointment of party creatures to the House of Lords, and other levers of power and patronage. The Tatton experience convinced me that people are entitled, at the very least, to MPs of whom they need not feel ashamed.

I also believe that there are problems which can be managed rather than solved, and not every grievance merits its own crusade. The best can be the enemy of the good. Not all good things are compatible with each other, and no party or government can deliver the perfect society. As Isaiah Berlin puts it, 'The very idea of the perfect world in which all things are realized is incomprehensible, is in fact conceptually incoherent. And if this is so, then the very notion of the ideal world, for which no sacrifice can be too great, vanishes from view.'[4]

Then there were the issues of the moment, on which I could hardly be accused of opportunism. With the exception of Arts Council funding for the D'Oyly Carte Opera Company, few of them were crowd-pleasers or vote-winners. I earned some opprobrium by campaigning with the help of Ludovic Kennedy for two Scots Guardsmen, Jim Fisher and Mark Wright, convicted and imprisoned in Northern Ireland as common murderers. I dismayed many people by my opposition to the ban on fox hunting. (An anti-hunting rally outside Parliament, where I was set upon by a person with purple hair, was the first time I had been spat at in public since I was a young reporter in East Belfast and accused of filming a riot that wasn't happening.) I enraged many more and was targeted by the gay and lesbian lobby after voting against the proposal to lower the age of consent for homosexuals. Gwyneth Dunwoody, the admirable veteran Labour back-bencher from Nantwich and Crewe, was right behind me that day as I disappeared into the 'no' lobby. 'I think I'll follow you,' she said. I may have been wrong, but I could see the strength of the arguments on both sides, and was influenced by my own experience and the opinions of my constituents.

In finding a role for an Independent I wasn't so much looking for an opportunity as waiting for one. It came seven months into the new administration, when the calm weather of Labour's honeymoon blew up into a storm. This was the Bernie Ecclestone affair. It had to do with campaign financing, and the extraordinary arms race in election spending to which both major parties were committed, each political superpower blaming the other. They had spent more than £25 million apiece on the 1997 General Election, although in retrospect Labour would still have won if they'd spent a tenth of that, and ten times as much would not have bought it for the Tories. Such war chests were without precedent in British politics, and could not be filled by the usual methods of fund-raising. There weren't enough rubber chickens out there for the rubber chicken dinners, or loyalists with the will to consume them for the greater good of the party. Both parties were thus in the market for big contributors and principled benefactors (that's code for our moneybags) rather than fat cats (code for their moneybags). Even the traditionally penurious Liberal Democrats were no back-markers in fund-raising.

Among the benefactors was Bernie Ecclestone, the impresario of Formula One motor racing. Although of no known political persuasion, the previous January he had given a million pounds to the Labour Party. Then in September, with Labour in office, he met Mr Blair in Downing Street to put the case for Formula One to be exempted from the banning of tobacco advertising in sports events. It was a Europe-wide ban, and he had received equal access in other European capitals. A month later the Labour government announced an adjustment of its policy, along lines which accommodated the interests of the motor racing industry.

There may have been no connection at all between the donation and the political change of course. With their hands on their hearts, or at least their pagers, the Labour loyalists insisted there had not been. But it was handled ineptly, and the policy switch was difficult to defend by a government which had been swept into office on a wave of public disgust with Tory sleaze.

It should have been an easy opportunity for the Conservatives, still a demoralized Opposition, at the next Prime Minister's Question Time. They were presented with a shot at an open goal, but they couldn't score from it. Their difficulty was that they too had solicited donations from big-name contributors. All were anonymous, some were foreigners and of dubious reputation. The Asil Nadir affair was well remembered. As for the Labour side, the closing of ranks at the first sign of trouble meant that a critical back-bencher's question would be heavily penalized.

Here, I thought, was a chance for an Independent. So it was that with thirty seconds to go I managed to catch the Speaker's eye for my first parliamentary question to the Prime Minister. 'Does the Prime Minister agree with me that the perception of wrongdoing can be almost as damaging to public confidence as the wrongdoing itself? Or have we slain one dragon only to have another take its place with a red rose in its mouth?'

The question, which was parried rather than answered by Mr Blair (who never quite worked out if I was friend or foe), had more impact than most. Simon Hoggart of the *Guardian*, who surfeited regularly on sporting metaphors, described it as 'The ref scoring on the rebound'. I was reproached by a few New Labourites for my ingratitude: had not the party stood down its candidate for me? 'You seem rather popular with the Tories,' one of them remarked accusingly. But some of the older Labour Members, who belonged to a less sycophantic tradition, rather liked it, and were kind enough to tell me so. A veteran listed it among his five best questions. I received a few angry letters from government supporters, but a gratifying silence from those Tories who had earlier accused me of being a Labour stooge. Now, I supposed, I would be called a Tory stooge; and in due course that happened too. The only kind of stooge which I would admit to being was a people's stooge. What better definition could there be of a Member of Parliament?

Months later, in the division lobby where I first encountered Peter Mandelson, I told him how pleased I was to meet him, especially as I had once been described as his puppet. 'Some puppet!' he said, and moved off rather sharply. He was not yet a secretary of state, but still at the height of his influence as the *éminence grise* of Downing Street and the New Labour project.

I heard it mooted, months later, that this whole episode gave an entirely new meaning to 'cash for questions'. It was even suggested that the 'scandal' of my campaign legal fees having been paid by Labour and the Liberal Democrats, reported in the *Daily Mirror* the following January, had been leaked by someone in the Labour Party angered by my disrespect in asking the question at all. 'Mr Bell should have been more sensible, shouldn't he?' said this party source. 'Tony Blair was in a little bit of trouble and we didn't need to hear cutting remarks from Martin Bell.' I was pleased while I was driving across Derbyshire the following week to receive the personal assurance of Alastair Campbell, the Prime Minister's spokesman and confidant, that the story had not come from them, and that they had no interest in damaging me politically. And of course I believed him. But it was possible that it had originated, without his knowledge, from someone lower down the party's hierarchy.

In that case, since I paid the legal fees back with my own money, it could indeed have been an expensive question. It had not been a short one either, and I worked it out at £208 a word.

If that was what it took to be accepted as a true Independent, then I reckoned it cheap at the price. The touching part about it was that my supporters in the country, dismayed by the apparent attempt to 'get' me, started sending in money to pay off the bills themselves. I urged them not to, and thus embarked on what I believe to be something unusual in British politics: a fund-lowering campaign. But we still ended up with £832 in a separate account, to be held against any further legal challenge, and distributed to charities at the end of the parliamentary term.

Actually I believe that I did the Prime Minister a favour. He was always at his best, and quick on his feet, answering real questions from real people. My next one suggested a sort of whips' cease-fire, in which Members should feel free to ask the questions they wished to ask, rather than those they were prompted and programmed by others to ask. As Prime Minister's Question Time developed it seemed to me, and to others, not so much a showpiece of democracy as a disgrace to it. Just when you thought that it couldn't get worse, it did. Whenever I heard the phrase 'May I congratulate my Right Honourable friend . . .' I would lower my head into my hands, dreading the sludge of sycophancy to follow. These 'greasers' questions' were too much for some of the Right Honourable friend's cabinet colleagues. Clare Short for one drew a proper distinction between loyalty and servility. The questions from behind her, she said, sometimes made her cringe. And in Andrew Mackinlay, the Member for Thurrock, I found a kindred spirit. 'I didn't work for twenty years to become a Labour MP,' he said, 'in order to be a cipher when I got here.'

For a while I went AWOL – reluctant to attend Prime Minister's Question Time, because it damaged my faith in democracy. And when I turned up I would sometimes leave early, in utter despair and dismay.

It surely does the Prime Minister no service, in any government, to hear only from the queue for office – back-benchers eager for preferment and indifferent to inconvenient truths. Something like that happened to Lady Thatcher, and ultimately undermined her. It suits a General Secretary of the Party or President for Life in the Great Hall of the People, but not a British Prime Minister. Independent thinking on the back benches – and, within limits, constructive criticism – will serve our own leaders better.

This is what happened with the Bernie Ecclestone affair. Mr Blair responded with a political innovation – a Prime Ministerial apology, live on television, at least for the handling of the episode. That was the mark of an original political mind. Of more lasting benefit, he then set up the Neill Inquiry into the funding of election campaigns. After the excesses of the 1997 election, there was clearly a need for a measure of restraint and a set of rules that would work. Either that, or our democratic system of government would be for sale to the highest bidder.

Again the Independent lobbed in his two penn'orth. In my own evidence to the inquiry I suggested an upper limit of £2 million per party per national campaign, with a further limit of £50,000 on individual contributions and all donors above £5,000 to be named. This, I argued, would put an end to the corruption and the perception of corruption, which were already threatening to reach American proportions. It would be a pretty cheap government that could be bought for £50,000. Democracy could only be strengthened by having a party's campaign brought back within the reach of its own supporters to fund it. Beyond that lay the dangerous road to the buying and selling of influence.

If there were ever to be an Independent Party, which the law now proscribes, one of its principles would have to be the return of politics to the people in whose name it is practised: not the big contributors or the interest groups or the lobbies in so many causes, but the 'little people' who are canvassed every four or five years and then completely taken for granted. The party or movement which can enlist their idealism will have their support and deserve it. An anonymous constituent kindly wrote to me, 'You are catching on. Please continue on these lines. One of the little people.'

I ventured to point out to Lord Neill's Inquiry the sort of results that could be achieved by attempting this new kind of politics. It reduces fund-raising to a formality. In Tatton, we imposed a £100 limit on individual contributions, yet still raised twice as much money as we were allowed to spend on the campaign. An eight-year-old from Mr Hague's constituency sent £1 of his pocket money. 'My dad and me have full support for you,' he wrote. 'I give you some of my saved up money. Good luck.' Two pensioners sent their pension increase of £1.30 each. A Gulf War veteran even offered his medals (an offer declined). People didn't have to be pressured to do this. Rather the reverse: in the first week I returned regretfully to their senders two cheques for £4,500, being very substantially over our self-imposed limit. But politics can and should be fun. People like to give to a cause or a candidate in whom they believe. If we can find the causes and candidates – and even the parties – for them to respond to, then we can reverse the drift into apathy, and re-ignite the idealism of the young. Just twice in my life I saw it happen. It was like a Prague Spring in the heart of Cheshire, and again in the heart of Essex.

Because of the resonances of Tatton, and a certain dissatisfaction with the party system, I found myself under growing pressures in Parliament, much in demand and falsely perceived as a sort of MP at large. I was urged to champion causes I had hardly heard of: to back Utopian schemes for world government, to endorse the re-launch of *Penthouse* magazine ('reinventing pornography isn't easy', wrote its editor plaintively), and to verify the existence of unidentified flying objects. I was even invited to attend something called an 'Intergalactic Sparkle' – 'a mass meditation and an attempt to commune with aliens or whatever unknown forces exist in our vast universe'.

Harder to resist were some well-known forces from our own universe – people writing to me from all over the country urging me to start a national party or movement of independents. One wrote: 'Oh for dozens of Independent MPs, to save us from the excesses of party politics.' And another: 'I rather like the idea of "men in white suits" in each constituency replacing the party apparatchiks at the next election.' I hated to disappoint them, but I had to. A party of independents is a contradiction in terms, like a convocation of hermits. And James Goldsmith with all his millions had not been able to establish his Referendum Party as anything more than a spoiling force in a single General Election. The Independent revival, such as it was, might be a short-lived phenomenon, or it might not. The times were changing; and for as long as it lasted, I could reasonably claim to represent something that no other MP stood for, and that remained true to its character however defectively I did it.

'Anything worth doing,' said Chesterton, 'is worth doing badly.'

6. 'Mr White'

You know that you're in trouble when they make a movie about you.

I had not been an MP for long before I received a call from a TV production company asking if I would like a walk-on part in a forthcoming production, to be shown on Channel Four at the end of the year, called *Mr White Goes to Westminster*. It would tell the story of a world-weary and unfashionable TV reporter persuaded to stand for Parliament against a sitting Tory whose career was clouded by allegations of sleaze. It was of course a completely implausible scenario. Against all the odds, including his opponent's formidable wife, the challenger won the election and unexpectedly entered Parliament. Any resemblance to the real world would be denied by the TV company's lawyers, although they might have had a hard time explaining why the actors chosen to play the Tory and his wife were Neil and Christine Hamilton lookalikes. The title role was taken by Bill Patterson, who somehow managed to appear even more crumpled and despondent than the original. His bravura performance reminded me of the vain attempts of my campaign staff in Tatton to persuade me to smile, just once or twice for the cameras, if I could remember how. Never in my entire life, I grumbled at them, had I had less to smile about.

The part I was asked to play on TV was that of a minor celebrity handing a hamburger-shaped trophy to my alter ego, the fictional Mr White, at an authentically gruesome television awards ceremony. I declined the offer, and the cameo role went instead to John Humphrys, a former colleague who had turned interviewing into a performing art. Mr White's story was so similar to mine, at almost every point in the campaign, that I felt it necessary not to confuse people, more than they would already be confused, about where the reality ended and the fable took over. This was all the more necessary because the Tatton-style campaign merely set the scene, before the first commercial break.

What happened then, on Mr White's arrival at Westminster, was that the script embroiled him in all sorts of misadventures which had not – so far at least – happened to me. He grew quickly disillusioned with Parliament, was driven to drink and had an affair with a new Labour MP who unwisely lent him money to promote his Private Member's Bill. This was another point where the narrative parted company with reality: there are hidden costs to being an MP, like having to buy enough raffle tickets to paper the walls of the Palace of Westminster, but paying for Private Member's Bills is not one of them.

The programme was a deft political satire, but I watched it with alarm as well as amusement, as the hapless Mr White was hounded by the press – their hero one day and their villain the next. 'Mr Clean Is Mr Mucky', screamed one of their headlines. I was concerned that it might be prophetic, for I was aware that in the nature of things, I was a prime target for the tabloids: nothing personal, but the public disgrace of the MP for Tatton would be a prize worth having. I knew that the 'anti-sleaze' label would come to haunt me. I abominated that 'S' word anyway: it was too vague and made no distinction between the personal and the financial. I surely had no wish to be tainted with it. One of my minor ambitions was to stay off the front page of the *Daily Mail*, or any page of the *News of the World*, for the duration of the parliamentary term.

I picked the wrong newspapers. I had forgotten the *Daily Mirror*. Within a month of *Mr White Goes to Westminster* the *Mirror* ran a front-page splash apparently lifted straight out of it. 'Martin Bell And The Secret £9,400', the headline proclaimed. 'Warning Bells For Mr Clean.'

The *Mirror*'s reporter had called me three days earlier. They had information, he said – and managed to sound both conspiratorial and menacing in saying it – that the legal fees incurred in my election campaign had been paid for by the Labour and Liberal

Democrat parties which had stood down their candidates for me. I knew nothing of it, I told him, but would look into it and call him back.

I was on the telephone at once to Piers Coleman, the lawyer who had advised us.

'Tell me they didn't pay it,' I pleaded.

'I'm afraid I've got bad news for you,' he answered, 'they did pay it.'

'How much?'

'Nine thousand four hundred pounds, split down the middle between them.'

The *Mirror* had got the figure right, because I gave it to them as soon as Piers Coleman told me. Their story hinted at a £5,000 fine, and a re-run of the election. It was hard to decide which would be the more disagreeable fate of the two.

There was a part of me that couldn't see the scandal of it. I had been seeking to unseat no ordinary MP, but the litigious Neil Hamilton with his lawyer at his side. The constant threats of legal action were his principal campaign weapon and his best hope of re-election. They had been dealt with by my back-room team, who had no reason to keep me posted about how they did it, while I was out on the doorsteps canvassing voters. Besides, the two opposition parties surely had a right to ensure that the Independent they were supporting was not blown out of the water by Mr Hamilton's first broadside. Nor was there any precedent for legal advice being included as a campaign expense. Neil Hamilton himself employed a lawyer, but made no mention of it in the accounts he submitted later to the returning officer. I was entering a nightmare world of distorting mirrors, including a distorting *Daily Mirror*. Should I now take legal advice on the legal advice? And who should pay for that?

Part of me knew that I was in deep trouble – so deep that it might bring my term of office to a swift and spectacular end. When a tabloid goes for you, it does so with more than a passing headline, and its campaign will run for days. There will be follow-ups and side-bars and companion pieces (the *Mirror* found a compliant expert in electoral law to demand my resignation). Editorials will thunder. Columnists and cartoonists will echo the party line. You will be lucky not to have the sports pages going for you too, for betraying the British tradition of fair play; or the star-gazer, for being doomed to failure from birth by an unfortunate conjunction of the planets.

At dawn on the day of the *Mirror*'s 'scoop' the journalists were parked on my doorstep in multitudes. I told them to wait for a news conference in the constituency at noon. I would confront the dragon there, in the knowledge that one of us would slay the other. So once again I headed up the M1 into the unknown, alone and even a bit afraid, as I had at the start of the campaign: just another of those everyday nightmares that go with being a politician without a party. For an Independent MP, the great unanswered questions of politics are, 'What have I done that I have forgotten, and what kind of trouble have I got myself into now?' When they hold the funeral rites for my career, they should scatter the ashes at the Watford Gap service station.

In Tatton the journalists were also thick on the ground – as many as for the battle of Knutsford Heath. The satellite dishes were back as well, a sure sign of a public figure in trouble. Some of my friends in the press – and I had them both from my past life and my present one – assured me that they had been asking around in the town, and couldn't find a single one of my constituents who saw it as much of a scandal. The *Daily Mirror* thought otherwise of course. Their reporter, a black-clad hooligan of uncertain provenance, who had apparently been trying to learn his trade at a school of intimidation, lunged at me brandishing a copy of his paper, for the benefit of his photographer, as if I were the guilty man exposed.

'These are serious charges, Mr Bell,' he menaced. 'You'd better have some answers to them.'

'Then I suggest you listen.'

My office in Knutsford, above the old election headquarters, must have had five times as many people in it as the fire regulations allowed. The hooligan ranted on for a while, but the questioning of the others was fair and reasonable. I told them what I had known, and what I had not known, and why there was no reason that I should have known it, and my personal opinion that it was a small storm in a small teacup. If they wished to think me naive they were free to do so, but I doubted whether naivety was an indictable offence. Certainly Neil Hamilton had never been accused of it. The audience included by invitation Peter McDowell, the Conservatives' agent in Tatton, who had shared the misery of defeat the year before. He had now seen the press pack in full cry against two successive MPs; and of the two, Mr Hamilton's had been by far the greater ordeal. I no longer regarded Mr McDowell as an adversary. 'It shouldn't happen to anyone,' he said. The *Daily Mirror* front page later adorned the walls of the toilet in his Conservative headquarters.

The episode diminished my respect for journalism. I noted in my diary for that day, 'I hate my ex-profession for its airs and graces, its lies and distortions.'

At that point I did something that no prudent and professional MP should do, for it invites a write-in campaign by well-organized opponents: I threw myself on the mercy of my constituents. I asked them, not for their support, but for their opinion on whether or not I had betrayed their trust. If they believed that I had, then I would 'consider my position'. My only regret afterwards was not political but stylistic – that I had resorted to such a tired old phrase from the political dictionary. What I should have said more plainly was that I would resign. I am a democrat, and believe that MPs should not cling to office against the wishes of their constituents.

I also decided to pay back personally the £9,400 to the Labour and Liberal Democrat parties. Whether or not I had an obligation to do so, I felt it would be a useful way to draw a line under the episode, and even in a crude sort of way to pay for my independence. I do not usually have that kind of money lying around in my bank account, but as it happened, it was almost exactly the size of the windfall that I had received the previous year when the

Halifax Building Society turned itself into a bank. Typically I had been among the 2 per cent of members who had voted against the conversion, because I believed it would enrich the directors at the expense of the borrowers; but I was sufficiently flexible – or perhaps hypocritical would be a better word – to accept the money when they sent it. Now I knew what to do with it.

Strangely enough, the hard part was to get the parties to take it. The Liberal Democrats were initially reluctant, and the Labour Party's cheque mysteriously went missing at the first attempt, falling into a black hole between the offices of the treasurer in Walworth Road and the director of finance in Millbank. Maybe they weren't as efficient as I thought they were, or maybe it was just small change to them. I remember thinking, I bet they cashed Bernie Ecclestone's million more efficiently than my meagre £4,700.

All that remained then was to find out whether the people of Tatton thought I should still have a job. I did not have long to wait. Out in the street an old lady came rushing up to me. 'Don't you dare leave us!' she demanded. That week I received 700 letters in favour and only seven against. The sentiments of the majority ranged from '*nil illegitimi carborundum*' to 'we are not going to allow you to give us up' to 'we the people of England are behind you'. Most gratifying of all, many were from former supporters of Neil Hamilton, who believed I was the victim of some kind of a Labour Party stitch-up. They included a magistrate, Major Sydney Hulme MBE, who had given me the benefit of the fiercest doorstep diatribe of the entire election campaign. It had been so withering, and had so dispirited me, that I had actually stopped canvassing for the evening because of it. And now he was a supporter. The *Wilmslow Express Advertiser* even carried the headline, 'Bell's Our Man, Pledge Tories'. And so far as I could tell, Labour and the Liberal Democrats weren't alienated, either. It must have been beginner's luck. Thanks to the *Daily Mirror*, I was poorer financially, but richer in friends and experience.

That weekend, I fulfilled a long-standing commitment to deliver a sermon, the first and probably the last of my career, in Knutsford's ancient Unitarian Chapel. I didn't have a biblical text, but after all that had happened I certainly had a theme: 'the uses of adversity'. I remember it as the only time I had ever had any control over the length of a church service. When it was over, one of the congregation delivered her verdict: 'That was very nice,' she said. 'Can we have the other half next week?'

And they handed me a petition of support with all their names on it.

No more was heard from the *Daily Mirror*. The scandal they had exposed left me in a stronger position at its end than at its beginning. I am no expert, but I believe this is unusual in politics. At the same time, it made me rather wary of the tabloids, and left me wondering what else anyone had done on my behalf, or I had done and forgotten. If they doubt your honesty long enough, you can end up doubting it yourself. I kept in my head a sort of parliamentary 'days to do' chart, like the calendars that used to be cherished by national servicemen, on which I ticked off the months that I had managed to survive without scandal: I expected to be demobbed after forty-nine months, and wished for an honourable discharge. Like a soldier hiding in the ranks I sought a measure of obscurity, in so far as it was consistent with the white suit; and above all, what I didn't want from anyone was a knock on the door in the small hours of the morning – which of course was what happened next.

In January 1999 it was the *Mail on Sunday*. The reporter was apologetic. It was about my stepdaughter, he explained. I drove him to Knutsford, and over a coffee in the patisserie on King Street, he laid out the whole sad story.

Jessica Sobel was the daughter of my second wife, Rebecca, by her first marriage. When I used to tell people that I was my second wife's fourth husband, I noticed that their eyes would glaze over. Jessica was a bright, attractive girl, more than a touch insecure and seriously in need of loving care. After my marriage to her mother ended, she continued to stay with me in Washington during university vacations until the BBC posted me to Berlin at the beginning of 1990. She then moved back to the West Coast. What the *Mail on Sunday* had uncovered was a truly tragic story of what sounded like a descent into some kind of a Hollywood hell: drugs, prostitution and bit parts in pornographic movies all featured in it. She had written a book about her experiences, *Once More With Feeling*, under the name of 'Jewel'. In her interview for the *Mail on Sunday* she had spoken kindly and wistfully about me, as the father she never had. Her real father had apparently committed suicide in mysterious circumstances at his California home the year before. She believed that he had been murdered.

'So what do you think of that?' asked the reporter.

'Give me time. Give me just a little time and I'll tell you.' I was actually in a state of shock. My own family life, although eventful, had been quieter. I had heard nothing from Jessica for many years and had no knowledge of the events that had befallen her. I couldn't think what to say, except perhaps that her story – a personal tragedy, sad and simple – hardly seemed to merit the three-page splash that the *Mail* were planning to devote to it. The headline alone took up nearly a page: 'The Secret Life of Vice Martin Bell's Stepdaughter Has Hidden From The Man She Loves Like A Real Father'. If Jessica's stepfather had been someone else, would they have bothered to print a word of it? What it called for in my view, which differed from theirs, was a time of private sympathy and public silence.

I wrote to Jessica immediately, to express my sympathy and to tell her that I felt for her, and that I hoped that writing the book had helped her draw a line under that part of her life. I tore up the first attempt and redrafted it because, although words had been my business, they failed me now – and I found it a very difficult letter to write. I thought that she wanted to hear from me, because the *Mail* had told me so, and given me her address. I hoped for an answer to the letter but didn't receive one. That was because she sold it. She had auctioned it in a bidding war between the *Sun* and the *Daily Mirror*. 'I needed the cash,' she said.

The bidding war was won by the *Mirror*. I knew that, because they called me rather tentatively some weeks later to inform me that they were flying Jessica to London; and would I like to meet her? What I did not know, and did not discover till later, was that she was also being paid to make the trip: as well as the letter, she had sold her story a second time over. I suppose I should have been angry, but I was merely sad that her life had come to this, and the ordeal of it was clearly not yet over. A sceptical friend suggested that next time I wrote to her I should send something less saleable, like a Christmas card.

Of course I wanted to see her. We had not met for eight years, and we had so much to catch up on – easier to talk about on my side than on hers. What I didn't want to do was to have the *Mirror's* minders and snappers all around, as they whisked us from her secret hotel to an uncomfortable photo session in Green Park. The pictures looked artificially posed, as indeed they had been. Only after the *Mirror* had finished its business did I have half an hour with her privately in the hotel, and then some more time on the terrace of the House of Commons. The story as she told it was even grimmer than the one that the *Mail on Sunday* had outlined, with details that they fortunately had not known about. I gave her a copy of my book, and asked for one of hers when she could send it. We took refuge in the memory of happier times in Washington. That evening, when I resumed my MP's duties, Melissa took over – still under the eye of a *Daily Mirror* enforcer – as comforter and friend. We both decided, as predatory photographers circled, that life in the goldfish bowl was not to our taste.

We were saved by the Prime Minister. He chose to give the *Mirror* an 'exclusive interview' on the same day, which took the Jessica story off the front page and reduced it to manageable pro- portions in the following day's paper; but that still left more than enough of it. And for once I had to respect the *Daily Mail*, which had not been part of the bidding war, for catching my discomfiture with accuracy: 'His lucky white suit always kept him safe from mortal peril. But even after swapping the world's trouble spots for politics it hasn't stopped Martin Bell from falling victim to the odd ambush. He has on occasion found himself at the centre of events, not of his own making, that left Mr Clean's trademark jacket looking a little crumpled.' I accept fair comment when I see it.

The worst part of the tabloid treatment was not the personal affront, but the collateral damage done to people beyond the victim's reach or responsibility. I had seen it with others, Jack Straw included, and now was in the firing line myself. Having dealt comprehensively with my former stepdaughter, the news sleuths started in at some time later on my father-in-law. There had been a problem burying two of the herd of Friesians on his farm near Ashford. 'Dead Cows Dumped By MP Bell's Father-in-law', proclaimed the breathless headline. It was the *Mirror* again, of course. My brush with the tabloids left me bruised and saddened, and a little introspective. I had to ask myself, what kind of journalism was this? Where did its horizons end? What were the limits of reference beyond which no one would be bothered – a distant aunt, a second cousin twice removed, or even further? And more to the point, had I myself ever practised it? The answer came back, 'Well, hardly ever,' and it may be that I was due for some retribution.

We have all done things we are ashamed of, and this was mine. It happened in 1985, while I was still Washington Correspondent. I was ordered by the BBC to O'Hare airport in Chicago, to charter a smaller plane and fly with a camera crew to the town of Industry, Illinois. The mission there was to follow up a tabloid story – the *Mirror*'s, as it happened – naming the half-sister of a minor member of the royal family, whose Austrian father was alleged to have fought for the Nazis in the Second World War. (BBC News was at the time under new management, and going through something of a tabloid phase itself.) Industry is a very small town, and I found her easily enough. When I knocked on her door, she was not only reluctant to be interviewed – quite understandably – but was courageously protected from our intrusions by her elderly husband who was, himself, dying of cancer. I prayed that the satellite transmission from Chicago would fail (of course it didn't), and I vowed that I would rather bury the dead than be that kind of journalist. Even journalists are capable, sometimes, of a sense of shame.

Then there is the special case of the Murdoch press. I used to regard it as a regrettable fact of life, like the weather, until my attitude was changed by a remark by Rupert Murdoch at the Annual General Meeting of his News International in September 1997. Asked if he had any regrets about his newspapers' purchase of the grainy photographs of Princess Diana and Dodi Al Fayed in the back of a boat just before her death, he answered that his only regret was that he paid too much for them. I found this such an affront to common decency that I have not bought one of his papers since – nor shall I. So I was hardly surprised when one of them, the *Sunday Times*, included me in its category of 'Enemies of the People'. I took that as a kind of commendation.

As to whether it helps, in being an MP, to have been any kind of journalist, I am not so sure. Most of it is common sense, and knowing what to avoid, such as guest appearances on *Have I Got News For You*, or going for night-time walks on Clapham Common. Anyone can learn it. It is useful to be open and candid, and never to hide anything, but rather to get the worst out first, as I did with the business of the legal fees; if you do not, you will die the death by a thousand cuts. The sword of truth is a dangerous weapon. If it is the sword of anything less than the truth, it will slay whoever wields it.

Luck also plays its part: in politics as in sport you can take the field with the utmost confidence, yet still be stretchered off. It is useful to know which sections of the media not to bother with (like the BBC's £50 million extravagance, *News 24*, which at that time lacked a measurable audience). It is useful to be able to compress your thoughts into sound-bite size – the two or three sentences which are the most a reporter has space for, either in broadcasting or in print. It is useful to know the hacks themselves, who can be trusted and who should be treated with caution. (A friend of mine actually keeps a list of the ill-intentioned ones.) It is useful to know which radio and TV interviewer used to fiddle his expenses on an industrial scale, or which one dumped his girlfriend in Nicaragua, and to let him know that you remember it, so that he should at least be civil in his questioning. It is useful to contribute a column to the local newspaper, discursive and as non-political as possible. On a UNICEF mission to Burundi I was the *Knutsford Guardian*'s first foreign correspondent, unpaid of course; and from the War Crimes Tribunal in The Hague I filed as a roving columnist for my other newspaper, the *Manchester Evening News*. It is above all useful to understand the impermanence of it all. Today's news is gone tomorrow, and electronically it vanishes into the ether. In its printed form it is just waste paper: it doesn't even get to wrap the fish and chips any more, since the fish and chip industry cleaned up its act.

My mailbag at the time was overflowing with letters on everything from the Alderley Edge bypass to the Gulf crisis of the moment, from unidentified flying objects to car boot sales, from fur farming to fisheries policy. Non-constituents would write to me and add a postscript: 'Sorry to burden you with this, but who else is there?' But on the family episodes involving Jessica I received no more than a couple of letters, both of them sympathetic. People rightly judged that they were personal matters, although sad ones, and were happy to leave it at that.

I also realized that I shared a common failing of journalists – even and perhaps especially ex-journalists – of being far too sensitive to what was written about me. Politicians have the hides of oxen, and need them. Journalists do not. Indeed, they are notorious sewers – I'm sorry, I mean suers. When it comes to criticism, they are very much better at handing it out than taking it. But journalists and politicians are different kinds of people. Journalists have rivals and politicians have enemies – another reason why crossing the line between them is a difficult thing to do. It is useful to know that too, and to understand the destructive power of ridicule. The Hamiltons didn't. Journalism knows no armistice, and two years after their fall from grace they were still being pursued by Fleet Street's hounds of hell: a flamboyant evening out with Oxford University's Conservatives drew extensive coverage in the *Sun* and the *Evening Standard* headline, 'Sleazy Does It'.

Instead of complaining about my own much gentler treatment at the hands of the tabloids, I should have been grateful to the *Mail on Sunday*, the *Daily Mirror* and the rest of them, for their public and political services: they had knocked me into shape, taught me a few survival techniques, and done for me as an MP what basic training had done for me as a soldier. Neither profession is for the faint-hearted; both seek out the shrinking violets and crush them brutally. And to be able to function it is also necessary to show steadiness under fire. The old fieldcraft training was not entirely wasted.

All the same, it was a great relief on my return to the Commons to discover the Pugin Room, a comfortable corner of the Palace of Westminster where I had not set foot before. Since I needed fuelling up for an adjournment debate, I approached its stern-faced custodian and asked for a cup of coffee.

'Excuse me, sir,' he asked, 'but are you an MP?'

7. Falling Cows and Other Cases

From Sarajevo to Tatton was about as far as it was possible to travel, in terms of the ways in which life could be lived, without falling off the edge of the planet.

The constituency's three main centres of population were Wilmslow, Alderley Edge and Knutsford. It had a reputation for attracting Manchester's money, as well as its revellers, and some of its most celebrated people. My constituents included a distinguished diaspora of vice-chancellors, surgeons and scientists from Manchester as well as Alex. Ferguson, David Beckham and Victoria Adams. Through no ambition of my own, I had become the Member of Parliament for Manchester United and its friends and partners. Pop stars and footballers lived in Wilmslow, as well as others who earned their wealth in less conspicuous ways. Useful shops were threatened with extinction, to be replaced by wine bars and drinking palaces – taverns measureless to man. Alderley Edge, a former copper-mining settlement, was regularly described in the regional press as 'millionaires' village'; it was the sort of place where an aromatherapy shop sold 'herbal Viagra'; and it boasted the highest per capita consumption of champagne in the country. This made it difficult for the parish council to win the wider support they required for the much needed bypass, or for the MP to get a hearing for the many cases of hardship that came his way. These were actually communities with a split personality. They were the headquarters of the Cheshire Set; yet, out of sight of the golf clubs and watering holes, they included two scandalously neglected Manchester overspill estates, in Knutsford and Wilmslow, and as great a discrepancy between the rich and the poor as anywhere in the kingdom.

Knutsford, the political heart of it all, was no ordinary market town. Although a Tory fiefdom within living memory, it was also blessed with a tradition of independence. In Victorian times its elections were vigorously and sometimes fraudulently contested between the great houses: Tatton for the Conservatives, and Tabley or Arley for the Liberals. It was said that the dead voted first. And the Conservative agent in 1882, having drawn £400 in silver and £100 in gold on the day before the election, reckoned each vote to have cost six shillings and eight pence. The corruption of more than a century later would hardly have raised an eyebrow.

Knutsford was also Cranford. Elizabeth Gaskell's gentle and affectionate portrait of the place, first written for Charles Dickens's periodical *Household Words*, featured a town that was run entirely by its women. 'Cranford is in possession of the Amazons,' she began; 'all the holders of houses, above a certain rent, are women.' The men were away in commerce in Manchester, in shipping in Liverpool, or serving the Crown in a distant regiment or outpost of Empire. They were not among those present in that other universe bounded by Princess Street at the top and King Street at the bottom.

A century and a half later, it seemed that nothing much had changed. Elizabeth Gaskell would have felt entirely at home. There were a few token men about the town, such as the MP, the mayor and the street cleaner, but the women ran it now just as much as then. I welcomed this, because I do not believe in the equality of the sexes. I have benefited greatly from the kindness of women and have always believed that they are the superior species – kinder, gentler and more civilized than men. So what better place for a newcomer to practise politics than a town where, as Mrs Gaskell put it, 'somehow the gentleman disappears'? When I turned down an invitation to 10 Downing Street (my one and only) for a previous engagement to address the seventy-five ladies of the Knutsford Tangent Club, it occurred to me to wonder where exactly the gentlemen had disappeared to, but I was too outnumbered and diffident to ask.

The Tatton constituency contained all sorts and conditions of people, but Cranford Woman was alive and well and prominent among them. The better I knew her, the fonder I became of her. She did not so much walk into my little office on Princess Street as sail into it, majestic in motion, stately as a galleon and as well trimmed. There was nothing casual about her. She came prepared, with matching hat, scarf and gloves, and a list of half a dozen issues requiring the MP's attention by yesterday at the latest. These ranged from the uneven pavement outside her house, to the state of Knutsford's public toilets (a notorious rendezvous for homosexuals, later damaged by a vengeful vigilante with a fork-lift truck), to the situation in Southern Sudan. She even sought to enlist my help in a dispute with her dry cleaner.

She never lost her capacity to surprise. One day a special Cranford Woman came to see me. She shook me cordially by her gloved hand, and then took it off – not just the glove, but the hand. It turned out to be her reserve artificial hand. Its predecessor, the first choice artificial hand, had been lost in a ladies' toilet at Heathrow, where she had left it in a rush to catch a flight. The hand was an expensive item, and her insurance company had been unsympathetic and reluctant to pay for its replacement, believing that its loss was the result of negligence on her part. I wrote to them as eloquently as I could, pointing out that this was not so. One could as easily lose a hand as a handbag – indeed, my constituent just had. I believe that her claim was accepted.

No less striking was the case brought to me by an elderly couple on behalf of their son. This too was an insurance problem. It was about his damaged car.

'What happened to the car?'

'It was hit by a falling cow.'

'It was hit by *what*?'

'A falling cow. At two o'clock in the morning.'

The young man had been driving home along a sunken road between two high embankments. What appeared to have happened was that a cow on one side, seeing an animal of the same species but the opposite sex on the other, chose that moment to go for it

– with the most damaging consequences both to itself and to the car. Neither survived. The insurance company refused to settle – perhaps because the story, although true, seemed unlikely; and there was also the issue of the farmer's liability. I tried, but could not persuade them. I then gave the story to the local papers, whose headline writers had a field day with it, on the many variants of the cow jumping over the moon. The company relented, scenting a public relations dividend, and offered an *ex gratia* payment of half the car's value. I advised the young man to accept, and put him in touch with an insurance consultancy which specialized in animal casualties.

At the time of my swearing-in, I had thought that the main attraction of the job would be to sit on the green leather benches of the House of Commons, the showpiece of democracy and model of parliaments, to absorb its history, to listen to its great debates and just occasionally to participate in them. The details of constituency casework, I supposed, would be less compelling. In fact, the opposite happened. There were very few great debates to be listened to in a House where the government's majority was so large, its supporters so submissive and its principal opposition so demoralized for so long. Only on the free votes – fox hunting, gun control or hanging – or when it felt its liberties threatened, did the place really come to life. At other times, as in many theatres, the reviews bore little relation to the reality. It was marginalized by the power of Downing Street, and the victim also of its own verbosity. I never heard a speech of sixty minutes that could not have been delivered more cogently in six.

By contrast, the constituency business belonged to the real world. Sometimes I won and sometimes I lost; and I soon discovered that it was easier to win when dealing with private enterprise than with the Macclesfield or Vale Royal Borough Councils. All MPs have to do business with their local authority, and I envied an MP I met from Botswana, whose local authority was the tribal headman, the Paramount Chief. I wished there were a Paramount Chief in Macclesfield. Instead there was only the Chief Planning Officer.

On the occasions when I lost, my reputation as a miracle worker was bound to suffer. I had already worked one miracle – or rather, others had worked it for me – in the General Election. I was unlikely to produce another, even for the very young who had so touching a faith in my powers. How was I then to reply to ten-year-old Abigail Percival of Wilmslow? She was one of my liveliest constituents, and wrote to me as follows: 'We are bored of the shops in Wilmslow, in Grove Street. The clothes what we buy are too big or too small. We are asking you if you would build a mall.' She went on to name the dozen stores, from Marks and Spencer to Toys 'R' Us, that she wished me to include in this great enterprise.

The mall was never built, but Abigail received a shoal of letters from the chief executives of the companies on her list, and even some gift tokens with them. It was her interest, and others', that made me see the inadequacy of my former style of life. For far too long I had lived as a news nomad, with no real home except where I dumped my suitcase. After years of racketing around the world, and in some of its least salubrious corners, I was finally putting down roots in a real community. I was getting a life, finding a home which was rather more than a resting place for a suitcase.

It was a tiny cottage in Great Budworth, two rooms up and two down, with beams so low it might have been built for gnomes, and with a manicured garden at the back. I was very lucky to find it. It was the property of a distinguished local artist, Isobel Barber, who at a certain age had found it difficult to cope with the near perpendicular stairs. Great Budworth itself, built by the lords of Arley Hall, drew visitors from all over the country, and indeed all over the world. Chocolate boxes and pub guides promoted it. There was nowhere else quite like it, even in my beloved Suffolk. It was Hollywood Central Casting's idea of the perfect English village.

The only drawback from my point of view was the vicar, the Reverend Derek Mills. On my first Sunday in Great Budworth, when I attended one of his services, I thought I detected a certain coolness, which puzzled me. I didn't regard the vicar and the MP as natural adversaries. On the second Sunday, in case I hadn't got the hint, he directed a hell-fire sermon straight at me, with my younger daughter Catherine sitting beside me. I do not anger easily, but he should have had more care for Catherine. A churchwarden murmured an apology as I left, and urged me to ignore the vicar's notes in the parish newsletter that he handed me. It was a strange and coded text, but it appeared to reveal the vicar as one of Neil Hamilton's most devoted supporters. I had no problem with that. He could have backed the Yogic Flying candidate if he wished. But I did wonder whether he needed to share his political opinions so widely with his parishioners, and to liken the result of Tatton's election to the braying of asses. 'Do you think that when all the asses bray, you get wisdom?' he asked. 'On the whole I do not think that wisdom has been increased in our constituency.' What he failed to notice, and should have done, is that, in biblical terms, the ass is a favoured animal.

One day when I was unlocking my door in Church Street a super-charged E-Type Jaguar screeched to a halt outside, with Jill Dando at the wheel. She had come to Great Budworth to promote the attractions of Cheshire for her *Holiday* programme. While we were chatting about old times and the BBC's iniquities (this was still in the John Birt era), her producer was being informed by the vicar that pictures of the church, then being filmed from the public road, were 'God's copyright'. He was no doubt theologically correct, but he might for once in his life have tried to be gracious. He even had an unexpected effect on the Great Budworth property market; but that is best left as a village secret, because no one outside would believe it. The vicar and I never did find common ground, before he left the parish in July 2000.

It was my good fortune that not all of Tatton's clergy were of his opinion. Disregarding the advice of supporters who wanted an elaborate network of committees and focus groups, I had been looking for a single figure outside politics – especially party politics – to help me with the constituency business. Small teams are better than large ones, and less fractious. I found the perfect choice in the Reverend Pauline Pullan of Wilmslow, who had been ordained just three years earlier and had reached retirement age at the time of the election. She could continue with what she did best, which was pastoral care, but in a rather more secular dimension. And she remained patient to the last on issues, like the fox hunting vote, where she felt that I had taken leave of my senses.

The team was completed by the redoubtable Frances Bowyer, who volunteered as our part-time secretary in Knutsford. With Pauline and Frances in Knutsford, the indispensable Mary Price in Westminster, and the MP and figure-head shuttling up and down the M6 between them, we were hardly a mighty political force – not a machine, but a contraption. But, which was more to the point, we shared the same objectives and liked each other.

The contraption had to be mobilized immediately. Six hundred and fifty-nine constituencies are represented in the House of Commons, and fate decreed that, since I was born unto trouble as the sparks fly upward, mine was the one with the second runway of Manchester airport in it: not only a change of career, but a change of war zone. The runway had been approved earlier in the year, following an inquiry in which its friends (the Manchester Airport Company) had outspent its opponents (my constituents) by a margin of ten to one. By the time I became an MP, the deal was done. All that remained, before the construction began, was an inevitable confrontation between the bailiffs and the eco-warriors. These veterans of the battle of the Newbury bypass were to make their next stand in the Bollin Valley, at the end of the existing runway. They were friends of the trees who had built platforms in the trees and elaborate rope walkways between them. They were friends of the earth who had dug tunnels in the earth. They were friends of the great tunneller Mr Swampy himself, although he was not among them at the showdown because of a disagreement about the degree of violence they were willing to use. And they were about to be evicted, during my second week as an MP, in an operation deliberately delayed until after the General Election.

The bailiffs moved in before dawn – violently, according to the protesters; with minimum force, according to Randal Hibbert, the deputy sheriff. I was certainly no stranger to conflicting accounts of controversial events, or to the pressure to believe only one of them. Jon Snow, having interviewed me at Westminster for his *Channel Four News*, urged me to get up there at once and stop the bloodshed. I was an MP, wasn't I? It was my constituency, wasn't it? What was I waiting for? I pointed out that I had a maiden speech to deliver that very evening. There were no excuses or alibis. Once Madam Speaker had been notified, the would-be speechmaker really had to show up.

Jon, who was once believed to have had political ambitions of his own, was deeply unimpressed. I had worked with him – or more accurately against him – in El Salvador fifteen years earlier, he for ITN and I for the BBC. It was a tense and competitive relationship, because neither of us liked to lose, especially to the other. His was a world without shades of grey. It was divided between good guys and bad guys. He had been a member of various solidarities. His sympathies were then with the rebels in El Salvador and now with the eco-warriors in the Bollin Valley. I knew him well enough to be confident that the deputy sheriff would not be one of his good guys.

As the least party political MP in the House, and learning the job by doing it (there was no other way), I was hardly in a position, at least at this point, to take off on crusades of my own. In fact, I was in a bit of a bind – the sort of dilemma for which regular politicians are elaborately rehearsed in hypothetical sessions at candidates' schools. I could not openly support the protesters, who were breaking the law by trespassing and resisting eviction, but neither could I condone the use of excessive force against them.

I delivered the maiden speech and headed north immediately, with some trepidation, for my second political battlefield, which like the first on Knutsford Heath, was not of my own choosing. In Tatton I picked up Pauline Pullan and the wellington boots which she thoughtfully provided, and headed for the mud of the disputed territory beyond the end of the first runway, where the ground sloped away into the trees of the doomed valley. Outside the wire, eco-sympathizers saw that I was being received as an official guest and shouted their anger at me. Inside the wire, Randal Hibbert took me to Zion Tree Camp, where the resisters had hoisted barrels of cement for 'lock-ins' in their tree-houses. Both they and the bailiffs – mostly ex-soldiers – had improved their techniques since Newbury.

The first evictions had been carried out virtually in secret, without independent witnesses. The stories of them lost nothing in the telling. Now reporters and photographers were on the site, but penned into a compound with a very limited view, and with most of the action taking place beyond their line of sight. I claimed – with some justice, I thought – to be a connoisseur of hazardous situations, and the battle of the second runway certainly qualified as one. I urged Mr Hibbert to change his way of working.

'It's in your own interest,' I explained. 'Whatever you do has to be done in the open, where the press can see it.'

'There are too many of them – more than we can handle.'

'They still have to see it. Make them form a pool. It's been done before, indeed I've done it myself. And if it's that or nothing, they'll accept it.'

'Actually, it's a plan that I've had for a while in my back pocket.'

'Then now is the time to bring it out and make it happen.'

I suspected that the deputy sheriff did not have a notably high regard for the press – and after my own recent experiences, I didn't altogether disagree with him. But at a news conference in the mud, which was my first experience since the election of being on the other side of a press line, I tried to persuade the journalists themselves to co-operate. I put the case for neutral observers. I urged a 'model eviction'. And then, having done what little I could, I went off to the installation of the new mayor of Macclesfield. Politicians do that kind of thing. I was already noting a little forlornly that, just a couple of weeks into my parliamentary episode, I was dancing away from trouble, trying not to offend people and balancing conflicting interests like an MP whose principal idea of politics was a never-ending campaign. What Neil Hamilton would have done I had no idea: probably stayed at Westminster, if he had any sense.

In the month that followed, a model eviction was more or less what happened. The serious casualties that could so easily have occurred were avoided. My guess is that the two sides not only understood each other better, but even respected each other more. They did this by themselves and because of the dangers they shared. The independent observers were never admitted, perhaps because the most prominent of them, Terry Waite, was not seen by the deputy sheriff to be neutral.

There are few people whom I admire unreservedly, and Terry Waite is one of them. I knew, and I think that he knew, that he and not I should have been the Independent MP for Tatton. Instead, he had moved from Cheshire to Suffolk, as I had from Suffolk to Cheshire. I was his substitute. Even when the eviction was complete, we continued to campaign together against the second runway. We refused to believe that the cause was lost as long as local people believed that it wasn't, and the new government was committed to an integrated transport policy, of which the over-reaching by the Manchester Airport Company was clearly not a part. With placards over our shoulders, Terry and I led a protest march of many hundreds along a footpath beside the airport's new perimeter, a wall of wire as offensive and hideous as the one which had divided the two Germanies. We started and finished at Hill House, a timbered seventeenth-century farmhouse with gentle gardens and exquisite lawns, which lay in the path of Manchester's ambitions.

I realized that over more than thirty years I had reported protest marches all over the world, from Lisbon to Luanda to Little Rock, but had never before taken part in one. And again I asked myself, since these days of apprenticeship were a time for self-criticism, whether I was merely playing the political game, making capital out of an opportunity, and backing my constituents, right or wrong in their own back yard. I cleared myself of the charge without much difficulty. They were right to oppose the runway, and I was right to support them. It threatened the entire communities of Mobberley and Knutsford. It engulfed a great swathe of the Cheshire countryside, and for no sufficient reason. A British Airways pilot wrote to me, 'My daily experience of airport operations makes it abundantly clear that the airport's existing runway is under-utilized. For extended periods, there are few, if any aircraft movements.' We had our future to safeguard, and our past to respect: and what would Mrs Gaskell have made of the Islamabad-bound Boeing 747 creating mayhem in the skies above her Cranford?

Still not accepting defeat, I carried the campaign to the House of Commons in my first adjournment debate. I would have been a lone voice anyway, but I probably made a tactical mistake in allowing other Members, from Manchester's powerful Labour caucus, a chance to contribute. My idea of a debate was that different voices should be heard in it; but Robert Sheldon, the veteran MP for Ashton-under-Lyne, gently and kindly corrected me. 'You were too gracious,' he said.

What was really dismaying was the response of the government minister, Glenda Jackson. In her other career, as an actress with an impressive range from high drama to light comedy, I had admired every performance that I had seen. I did not admire this one, in which she spoke in leaden tones to almost empty benches. I could not help seeing her, not only in her temporary eminence as Minister of State for Transport, but in some sense still in her former glory as Elizabeth R. I expected at least some passion and commitment in defence of the government's position, if it had one. Instead, she hardly lifted her eyes from the text prepared by civil servants, with no sign that she cared about a word of it. Gloriana she wasn't. I wondered why good people let politics do that to them. At what point and through what mechanism was the passion filtered out? If it happened to me, one term in the House would be half a term too much.

The adjournment debate was followed by a petition to Downing Street by my constituents, the victims of the second runway, led by the mothers of Mobberley. (True to the spirit of Cranford, the men were elsewhere.) Neither event moved the stony heart of officialdom. Within weeks the earth-movers were on the site. By winter the valley and its pastures were an ocean of rutted mud. Flying over it out of Manchester, I felt that I might as well have been the MP for the battlefield of the Somme. I was struck by the irony of it, that quite by chance I had stumbled into yet another war zone.

The war was a territorial one. Its cause was its terrain, the Cheshire countryside. The might of Manchester had annexed a thousand acres. A new motorway link between the M6 and M56, if approved, would swallow up more than half as much again. The big developers coveted it as building land. It had its warlords too – a small minority of ruthless landowners who did not so much farm the land as terrorize it. They invited the profitable dumping of waste; they defaced the landscape with advertisements for their enterprises; they intimidated their neighbours; they built Berlin walls; they encircled their victims' gardens with old farm rubbish; they seemed to need enemies as much as most of us need friends. I suggested to Kate Adie that she should pay us a visit. She would surely have felt at home.

And did you ever hear of *intimidation by trees*? I certainly hadn't, until I became an MP. The principal culprit was the leylandii, a hybrid of the Alaskan and Californian cypress, which could reach a height of twenty feet in five years, and keep on growing. This was the hedge from hell, a nuisance even to those who planted it, and a frequent weapon in our pastoral hostilities. It would be used to screen an illegal development, or to threaten a neighbour by turning his garden into a permanent twilight zone.

And the MP's role in all this? It had to be more than to urge a return to the English virtues of the privet and the hawthorn, or to add his signature to an early day motion deploring the tyranny of leylandii – although I will confess to having done just that, a sad and sorry example of gesture politics. Neil Hamilton, to his credit, was said not to have bothered much with early day motions; and since I was inheriting some of the problems that he had dealt with, I should like to have been able – just occasionally – to seek his advice, but it somehow didn't seem appropriate, and he never left me a single record of any of his casework. There was too much past between us.

My own solution was to spend more time than many MPs in the constituency, on suitable occasions, and less in the House itself. Whether the government's majority was 171 or 172 on Clause 65 Amendment 14 of the Finance Bill seemed to me to be a matter of no great consequence, and as my own chief whip I could take a liberal view of my voting record, even when it stood at less than 35 per cent. The *Sunday Express* affected surprise, but my constituents never bothered, and Alex Salmond assured me nor did anyone else. They deserved my attention and received it – all except the minority of intimidators. To be close to such people is the surest sign of a suspect and dodgy MP.

I also took it upon myself to question the role of the local authorities, and especially the Planning Department of Macclesfield Borough Council, the designated defender of the green belt. In its defence it must be said that its officers had suffered intimidation, and even violence, from frustrated developers. Even so, it seemed to me that too often they gave ground, quite literally, to those who came to the negotiation armed with lawyers and a detailed knowledge of the loopholes of the law. Planning law is rich man's law. It leaves the little people at a disadvantage.

These included an elderly couple, Eric and Veronica Shaw of Pickmere, who had extended their garden by buying a strip of a farmer's field next to it, so that their grandchildren would have enough space to play football, and they themselves could add a little rock garden. When the council heard of this, it ordered them to restore the fence, to flatten the rock garden and to keep the new bit of grass at meadow height. Then one December it proceeded to deny them the use of their entire back garden, on the grounds that it too belonged to the green belt. The spirit of Scrooge was flourishing in Macclesfield. The Shaws, who had done nothing wrong, were left living in fear and dreading the arrival of every morning's post. 'Don't mow that lawn!' was the planners' stern instruction – and this in a corner of Cheshire where others were turning farmyards into building sites and fields into an airport runway.

Council officials, who ran the planning department with proprietary zeal, objected that I did not have a sufficient understanding of planning law. In fact I had been at some pains and expense to educate myself about it. I understood it all too well. The rich got richer and the poor got shafted. William Cobbett would have recognized it: it was like that in his time too. Like Cobbett, although less eminently, I had a platform rather than a party; and I counter-attacked through the power of the printed word. Macclesfield's planners didn't like it up them. They accused me of being undemocratic in using my columns to express my personal views. But that is what columnists do. And with 29,354 votes behind me, I could surely claim to be more democratic than most.

Coming to the war zone of Cheshire from the war zones of the world, I was inclined to encourage my constituents to count their blessings. There was nothing fundamentally wrong with a country where the great disputes were about the green belt, and whether its grass should be cut to a farmer's length or a gardener's. But there was a great deal wrong with a country where there was, in effect, one set of rules for those with lawyers and consultants and another for those without, where the big developers could bend the law to their purposes, and the little people were not allowed so much as to mow their own lawns.

After more than a year of these experiences, I tried to work out if they were steering me into party politics, or placing me anywhere on the known political spectrum from left to right. The answer that came back was no, and nowhere in particular, and of no fixed abode. An ally of the late Screaming Lord Sutch described me as 'mainstream fringe', which seemed fair enough. My political heroes, few in number, ranged from William Cobbett and George Orwell of England to Václav Havel of the Czech Republic, each of whom in his time and in his way had opposed the prevailing orthodoxies, the party machines and the big battalions. Bill Cash, the Tory MP who was no mean rebel himself, assured me that I was an Independent Whig. In my own view I was a sort of radical liberal conservative – as much a hybrid as the leylandii of Cheshire, although more benign, I hoped. Once, after an appearance in David Dimbleby's TV studio, the veteran Conservative MP Tom King looked at me in some dismay. 'You're a bit of a populist, you know.'

'Am I? I had never given it a moment's thought.'

'You are, and it rather surprised me.'

I think he meant it as a reproach, but I took it as a compliment. Lacking a party or doctrine, I was free to chart a course of my own according to certain principles. I would do what seemed right, and what I could for the little people. I would never make the headlines of political history; but I wished to be remembered, somewhere in its footnotes, as one who had made a difference.

8. Minefields

The beginning of wisdom is to know how much you don't know – and not to be afraid to admit it. From the outset, I resolved to adopt a self-denying ordinance, and to avoid some obvious pitfalls, by speaking in Parliament only about what I knew about. (A revolutionary and heretical practice that stood little chance of being widely adopted.) That was why my speeches were so few and so short. If you blinked you missed them, and it may well be that there wasn't that much to miss, but at least I spoke from the heart, from personal experience and without a moment's thought of re-election. As the time went by I tried to extend the range, but I refused to accept a connection between length and quality. Indeed, the dreariest Commons performances were generally the longest, while it was difficult although not impossible to be both brief and boring: better a mediocre minute than an excruciating hour.

There were 658 MPs, I reasoned, who knew more about parliamentary procedure than I did – and more about the bread and butter issues which were the stuff of domestic politics. They tabled questions to ministers of such a technical detail and complexity as I had not dreamt of in my philosophy. Norman Baker, the new Liberal Democrat Member for Lewes, asked questions of ministers on an industrial scale: more than 600 in a single session. He was one of the marvels of the new Parliament. I, on the other hand, was not. I must have been in the House of Commons for a whole year before the helpful clerks in the Table Office, through whom these things are submitted, would accept one of my questions without amending it. I was learning fast, but would still take a while to catch up. But there were a very few issues about which I knew more than they did. These included not only the second runway of Manchester airport, but the nature of modern warfare, the weapons with which it was waged, the state and morale of the British army and the threats to peace represented by the collapsing states of Africa and the Balkans.

That was why my maiden speech was about land mines. It would have been impertinent to talk about pay or pensions; but about land mines I hoped that I might receive a hearing, as the Member of Parliament most often nearly blown up by them. I had been close to these engines of death – how close, I could not always be sure – from Vietnam to Bosnia. They were the devil's handwork and carried his signature; they were cheap to make and expensive to clear, easy to lay and hard to detect; and besides, they knew no cease-fire. The mines I had met had ranged from anti-personnel devices the size of cigarette packets, to sophisticated anti-tank mines with anti-lift and anti-tilt devices, to old television sets packed with explosives and left abandoned in hedgerows in central Bosnia. They had the effect of freezing the front lines. They substituted for infantry. They taught me fieldcraft and vigilance – to look for trip-wires and to tread carefully, never on the grass verges but always on hard surfaces or in the footsteps of others. They carried the ever-present menace of being the last mistake of your life – the lurking terror and the killer that lived in the long grass.

I was bemused, when I stumbled into politics, to come across the issue of countryside access. It was code-named the right to roam. I was besieged by causes seeking endorsement, and this would not be one of them, although I saw the merit of it. To me the right to roam, to ramble at will across open land, was a luxury confined to our peaceful societies, which undervalued it and too often took it for granted. I took nothing for granted, and ever since an accident in Sarajevo five years earlier, I regarded myself as living in extra time. There was surely no right to roam in Bosnia – but only, for its two million refugees, a desperate and driven *need* to roam.

I had looked for a pattern in the wars of my life, especially the civil wars on the Bosnian or Nigerian or Angolan model, in which government collapsed, and a territory was fought for by the peoples who used to share it. A common feature of these conflicts was that they mocked and defied the Geneva Conventions, the so-called laws of armed conflict. These were framed to protect civilians. But in the wars of the new world disorder civilians were not only not spared, they were targeted with special and singular ferocity. Two groups of people suffered disproportionately: the very old and the very young. One had too little mobility and the other too much. Because of the energy and curiosity of children, who would poke around in the ruins almost as soon as the guns fell silent, the anti-personnel mine was unique among the weapons of war, in that it had the effect of seeking out the innocent. That was the peculiar horror of it. And there were children yet unborn who would continue to be its victims, maimed and killed, in the next generation and beyond.

The soldiers, by contrast, were schooled in survival and more or less untouched by it. It was a weapon of trench warfare whose time had passed, except in civil wars like Bosnia's, which reinvented the defensive systems of the First World War, the trenches and bunkers, and the charge to certain death across no man's land. To a main force unit in manoeuvre warfare, armed with the technology of high intensity assault, a belt of land mines had about as much deterrent effect as a field full of garden gnomes. The First British Armoured Division went to war in the Gulf in 1991 with a mechanical mine scatterer called the Minotaur, but never used it except in demonstration. Rather, they swept past the Iraqi minefields, laid in accordance with Soviet doctrine, as if they didn't exist. I was with them at the time, and – speaking as one who knows fear when he feels it – did not experience so much as a tremor of unease. The campaign against land mines was subsequently joined, on military as well as moral grounds, by General Norman Schwarzkopf, the American commander of Operation Desert Storm. A former Commandant of the US Marine Corps, General Al Gray, was of the same opinion. They had both been colonels in Vietnam, where a high proportion of the Americans' casualties were caused by their own land mines.

But the politics of de-mining was itself something of a minefield. A long-standing tension existed between those who worked to ban land mines (the political and rhetorical side of the movement) and those who worked to clear them (the practical and soldierly). A number of organizations were in the field, of which the Mines Advisory Group and the HALO Trust, both initially staffed by ex-servicemen, were the most prominent and effective, and doing heroic work in manual mine clearance from Angola to Cambodia. Yet they were losing ground, quite literally: more mines were being laid every day world wide than were being cleared. According to the gloomiest estimates, even without any more being laid it would take a thousand years to lift those already in the ground. These estimates were later revised downward. Mechanical and electronic mine clearance systems were being proposed, and developed, to close the gap. These too competed with each other, and were viewed with some scepticism by the manual de-miners, since they could work only on accessible terrain and cost more money than was likely to be available. The British government was devoting one twenty-fifth of 1 per cent of its aid budget to mine clearance, and yet claiming a position of leadership in the campaign.

This was the same government which, in March 1999, committed the Royal Air Force to dropping more than 500 cluster bombs on Kosovo, as part of the NATO action against the Serbs. Each bomb had 208 bomblets in its casing. A high proportion of them failed to explode, and fell in a wider pattern or footprint, because of the height from which they were dropped. The bomblets, which looked like pineapples with spidery fins, had all the characteristics of land mines – except that they were sown from the air. When the military intervention was over, they claimed more lives and limbs than the Serb-laid land mines. Yet still we were invited to applaud a famous victory.

And then there was the seminar circuit – the UN's 'Mines Action Conference Calendar' listed twenty-seven international conferences between April and October in a single year. If the land mines could have been talked out of the ground, the problem

would have been solved. Guy Willoughby, director of the HALO
Trust, made the point most tellingly:

'These global conferences extend from Washington to Shanghai, Nova
Scotia to Johannesburg, Ougadougou to Albuquerque. If each conference
attracted 100 people who spent $1,000 on air tickets and hotels, then
the summer conference circuit will have cost $3 million . . . HALO's
de-miners would clear very, very many mines for $3 million.'[1]

It seemed to me then, as it seems to me still, that there was scope
for the establishment of a British *disarmament* industry – committing
to the clearance of land mines and cluster bombs something of the
ingenuity that had gone into their manufacture. Or to put it another
way, why should the devil have all the best scientists?

The cause had one priceless asset: the blowtorch charm and
personality of its principal champion, Diana, Princess of Wales.
After her separation from the Prince, she had reduced the hundreds
of causes with which she was associated to just five. Of these, the
campaign against anti-personnel mines was the most visible, and
the one in which she had the greatest impact. Her visit to Angola
in January 1997, when she walked in a cleared minefield and held
in her arms children who were victims of land mines, had a greater
effect in mobilizing world opinion than any speech or conference
in the gilded chanceries of Europe. It was charismatic diplomacy,
projected by the global force of television. Its images changed the
climate of the times. It challenged the reflexive indifference of
politicians. It caused them to take initiatives – notably, the signing
of the Ottawa land mines treaty later that year – which without her
they might not have taken. And of course, because the Princess
troubled the mean-spirited, it put her within range of her detractors.

These were mostly politicians of the Tory right. In an unguarded
moment she once described them as 'those dreadful Conservatives',
and one of their own senior colleagues dismissed them as 'head-
bangers'. There were only three or four of them, which was three
or four too many. They were hungry for headlines and of no great

consequence, but a standing reproach to those whom they had persuaded to vote for them. They accused the Princess of trespassing into politics. One of them, who had served in four Parliaments without creating so much as a ripple on the waters of politics, had the nerve to ask her to observe 'a period of silence'. His wish was granted all too soon, and he surely lived to regret it.

In my first month in Parliament, I was invited by the excellent veteran Labour MP Frank Cook to be a supporting speaker at a meeting of his All Party Group for the Eradication of Land Mines. The Princess of Wales had expressed a wish to attend. There was no constitutional obstacle. The event was to be held not in the legislative precincts but in the Grand Committee Room. The Duke of Edinburgh had set a useful precedent. Diana was not even a Royal Highness at the time, having been stripped of the title by an arbitrary decision of the Palace. The news of her visit leaked out to the tabloids. They in turn called the usual suspects on the Tory right, whose reactions duly made the following day's headlines. At that point, the Princess cancelled.

I had a question about land mines to the Defence Secretary on the Order Paper that afternoon. I took the opportunity to regret the cancellation, and to make the point that the Princess's involvement in the issue was not political at all, but humanitarian. It turned out that from the discreet distance of her palace she took a personal interest in these exchanges, and was grateful to have someone speaking up for her in the House. I knew that, because I then received an invitation to go and see her. Whether or not she was a Royal Highness, it had the force of a royal command.

We met in Kensington Palace on the morning after her thirty-sixth birthday. I felt that I must have taken a wrong turning. Overflowing with orchids and exotic blooms, it looked and smelt like a transplanted rain forest and the grandest floral emporium in the world. Through the thickets of flowers and vegetation her butler flitted in with the morning coffee. It was the strangest of places to be discussing the scourge of land mines.

Journalists – and I was only just an ex-journalist – are no great respecters of reputations, especially royal ones. My previous life had tended to leave me unimpressed by the famous – celebrities are of little consequence to anyone but themselves. But Diana was different. I had met her before, on her honeymoon tour of Canada with the Prince in 1982. It was an event of such exquisite tedium from coast to coast, with not a ceremonial tree unplanted or visitors' book unsigned, that I wrote my final report on it from Prince Edward Island in iambic pentameters and rhyming couplets, and no one even noticed. But fifteen years later, and after all that had happened, she was no longer a supporting player in the royal road show – or if she was, she ran her own, an alternative court with quite distinctive values. In her altered state she possessed a surpassing charm, an underestimated instinctive intelligence and a passion to make things happen. She touched with her magic an entire constituency of all kinds of people otherwise indifferent to royalty. She was also defiant, and not one to shrink from challenging the established order of things. She had a plan to visit the minefields of Bosnia, and found herself obstructed. 'They are trying to stop me going,' she said.

'Who are they?'

'Oh, the usual people,' she answered.

I was left to infer their identity – an alliance of her enemies in the Palace and those elements in the Foreign Office who still believed, against all the recent evidence, that diplomacy was best left to the diplomats.

We also talked of our children. Each of us admired the other's. She described Melissa as my 'drop dead gorgeous' daughter – a considerable compliment from such a source. (Afterwards I was reluctant to pass it on lest it swell the girl's head. But I did – and it didn't.) As for the young Princes, one of her principal anxieties was about their press coverage, as well as hers, from which they were already beginning to suffer. 'How am I going to bring them up,' she asked, 'without a contempt for the press, and a feeling that all journalists are their enemies?'

She walked me to my car, which was the last I ever saw of her.

In the following weeks she managed to dodge the praetorian guard of protocol and make her trip to Bosnia. It was a private visit, and thus beyond the scope of official obstruction. In another month she was dead: officially the victim of a traffic accident in a Parisian underpass, but in my view hunted to death.

I have seen revolutions in other countries, but never before in my own. It was quiet and unspoken and profoundly British, but none the less a sort of insurrection. We, a notoriously unemotional people, were expressing our feelings publicly on a scale never seen before. And it wasn't even a state funeral. The outpouring of grief that swept over the capital in that first week of September 1997 was not orchestrated by anyone – least of all the press. We surprised the press. We surprised each other. We surprised ourselves. We shed our trivial and selfish cares. We felt as one people and mourned as one people, as if for a loved one in our own closest family – which in a sense she was. Much later, the tribunes of the chattering classes sought to dismiss and diminish what had happened as some kind of hysterical reaction. They were wrong, and it was nothing of the kind. Their best rebuttal came from the Reverend Donald Reeves, Rector of St James's Piccadilly, who was moving day and night among the crowds to which his was the closest church: 'What I experienced over that long week was a surprise, and a heartening one at that – a glimpse of the solidarity of what it means to belong to one another. The death of Diana brought out our best selves. There was no mass hysteria. Eyes were full, and occasionally there were silent tears as couples held each other. But it was the restraint that I noticed.'[2]

It was not in any sense a republican movement, but rather obstinately royalist, wishing to reclaim the monarchy, and to remind it that it was ours and no one else's – certainly not theirs. Without the people to sustain them the royal family were just rich people living in big houses, and the institution would wither and so die. Without commanding the love that she did, they none the less needed the loyalty. The empty flagpole on top of Buckingham Palace during that critical week was a standing reproach to the

Queen and her satellites of courtiers. Their antennae were some-how left untuned. They, who lived by symbols, had not understood the importance of the symbolism of the unflown flag at half mast. They were in every way too distant from their people. Had the Queen not returned from Balmoral when she did, and made the unprecedented live broadcast that she did against the backdrop of the massed and silent crowds outside the palace, she might well have been booed during the funeral procession. I heard that saving speech described as 'a diving catch at third slip'. It was probably the worst week of the Queen's long reign. She would not wish to be seen, ever again, so out of touch with her people.

I attended the funeral. A line of Shakespeare insisted on a hearing: 'If you have tears prepare to shed them now.' I certainly did and so did those around me. I cannot remember glimpsing anything in my life through such a mist of mourning. The wonder of it was that Elton John, who was two seats in front of me and as grief-stricken as anyone, summoned up the composure to sing his reworked version of 'Candle in the Wind'. And when he had finished that anthem of love and loss, broadcast on loudspeakers to the vast crowd outside, their applause drifted back into the Abbey like the sound of breaking waves on a pebbled beach.

Then Earl Spencer spoke, the Princess's younger brother and now head of the family. His eulogy was more than a tribute. It was a challenge – that the young Princes be brought up with the love and care that their mother had bestowed on them, and that the baser sections of the media be held to account for their malicious attempt to bring the Princess down. 'My one and only explanation is that genuine goodness is threatening to those at the opposite end of the moral spectrum.'

The effect was electrifying. The applause surged into the Abbey for a second time, enfolding us into it on a tide of devotion that seemed to carry all the way to the standard-draped coffin, and on to the Spencer family, only to stop short at the House of Windsor. There were medieval echoes here of the rival houses of York and Lancaster – except that, in the modern version, the two young

Princes belonged to both; and they were in the Abbey rather than the Tower.

When the service was over I drove north to Knutsford, for much of the way along the route of Diana's last journey, and about an hour later. What a trail of tears it had been, and of flowers too. The bouquets thrown carpeted the road all the way past Lord's Cricket Ground to the Finchley Road and beyond. More floral tributes adorned every bridge over the M1. And banners on bed sheets delivered messages of farewell: 'God bless you Diana', 'Diana for ever' and 'Goodnight, England's Rose'. I felt her presence all the way to Northamptonshire. It was a lonely road beyond.

In the months that followed there were many attempts to revise the history of what had happened – none of them convincing – and many schemes proposed for a fitting memorial: statues and gardens, stamps and coins, and new names and wards for hospitals. The best tribute of all, it seemed to me, would be in some way to take up the torch, and to continue to work in the causes to which her last years were devoted. This turned out, in the case of the land mines crusade, to be difficult and deeply frustrating. It led me to wonder, not for the first time, whether there was any point at all in my new career.

I travelled to Sheffield, where in the stygian gloom of a foundry which had armed the British military for a hundred years (and was the only factory ever visited by Queen Victoria), the welders' sparks were dancing around the prototype of the Minelifta, a flail machine for the mechanical clearance of mines. It was the invention of Nick Kirk, an ingenious manufacturer of customized lifts, who had been inspired by the Princess's example to design and build a practical de-mining machine. It was a refinement of military technology and an attempt to turn the dream of a disarmament industry into a reality. But two years later, he still had no funding for it and no encouragement either. I tried to open some government doors for him, but found them firmly closed.

The mine clearing agencies were similarly disappointed. For the two years following her death they received no money at all from the £85 million contributed to the Diana Memorial Fund; indeed they found themselves even poorer than they had been before the Princess's involvement in their cause. The Mines Advisory Group had to suspend its projects in Bosnia, and was close to laying off locally trained staff in Laos and Cambodia. Lou McGrath, MAG's director, commented bitterly, 'I think it's incredible that they're calling it the Diana Memorial Fund when it does nothing to support the causes she was committed to.'

So quickly did the cause lose momentum, that even the formality of the ratification of the land mines treaty came perilously close to failure. The treaty was signed in Ottawa in December 1997, with China and the United States among the notable absentees. It would not come into effect, even theoretically, until forty states had ratified it. It was imperative that the United Kingdom, claiming a leadership role, should be among the forty. Yet Parliament's legislative programme was a log-jam. The business of the Commons was mainly to do with devolution for Scotland and Wales, and then – quite rightly – the Northern Ireland agreement. The months slid by, and the government's managers insisted that not even a single day, which was all that was needed in the Commons, could be set aside for the Ottawa Treaty. It was the saddest of commentaries on our priorities – of what mattered to us and what did not.

By then I was beginning to get the hang of things. The way to make things happen in the House of Commons is to get the government's attention outside it. A parliamentary speech will be ignored, a contribution to Radio 4's *Today* programme may not be – it is the jungle drum of the political classes. I was invited to discuss the ratification issue with George Robertson, the Defence Secretary – he in the studio in London and I in an ancient BBC radio car parked beside the bowling green in Great Budworth. Old radio cars go to the north of England to die. George recited the usual reasons why, with the best will in the world, nothing could be done. I countered that it could be done – indeed it had to be done. MPs could forfeit a day of their long recess, and come back to ratify the treaty on 31 August, the anniversary of the Princess's death. What better way to honour her memory?

This simple idea was taken up the following day by the *Express*, which turned it into a front-page campaign. That afternoon the government capitulated, and mysteriously managed to find the time that had previously been declared unavailable. The *Express*, of course, proclaimed a great victory, which it had every right to. It didn't matter to me who claimed the credit. The important thing was that the cause had won a small but significant victory. So indeed had Princess Diana. Nearly a year after her death, she still had the politicians running for cover. We do not need perfect people to be our examples, and to ignite an idealism in us that we may not have known that we had. We need special people. Flawed and fallible as she was, she was also a special person. No wonder that the politicians felt challenged, and responded by trying either to cut her down, or else to co-opt her. It is not in the nature of politicians to leave good people unobstructed to do good things.

She had the ability, in death as in life, to create a sense of community transcending the usual social barriers, to revive our sense of belonging to each other, and to make us feel more at home in a society of strangers. No political party could achieve that, and probably none should aspire to it. (Beware especially of the politicians, like the soldiers, who believe themselves to be charismatic.) But I do believe that there was a general principle at work here, of which politicians at least would do well to be aware. It had to do with the example she set, and the difference she made, in the last few years of her life. Call it the Diana Principle: *Good things happen because people make them happen, and bad things happen because people let them happen*. It was best expressed in a verse she quoted at a grand charity function in Washington. She apologized for it in advance, fearing that some might find it naive. I don't think it is naive at all. It speaks to the heart of the matter, and serves to remind us of a life unlike any other.

Life is mostly froth and bubble;
Two things stand like stone,
Kindness in another's trouble,
Courage in your own.

9. Loose Cannons

On the field of battle there are two sorts of incoming fire. One explodes far enough away for you to dare to defy it. This is known in the trade as the 'F★★★ you!' The other explodes so close that it scares you witless. This is known as the 'F★★★ me!' The odd thing about Gulf War II, which lasted for seventy hours from 16 to 20 December 1998, was that the fire was entirely outgoing, at least from the British and American points of view and in terms of allied casualties. For the first time in military history the 'F word' was probably redundant among British forces. It was also unusual in that the attack was signalled clearly and well in advance. Since becoming an MP I had developed an alertness to new sorts of dangers, but the antennae from the former life were well attuned to picking up the old ones.

If you have been long enough in dodgy places you don't need the sound of the 'incoming' to alert you. The sign that hostilities in the Gulf were imminent was a last-minute change to the programme of the parliamentary carol service at St Margaret's, Westminster. The Prime Minister's advertised place as reader of the sixth lesson was taken by the Home Secretary, Jack Straw. In the season of peace and goodwill, and instead of delivering tidings of joy between a carol and an anthem, Mr Blair was busy in Downing Street planning a small war. He was consulting with President Clinton about the Anglo-American blitz of Iraq, using air- and sea-launched bombs and missiles. It started four hours later.

Anglo-American was probably the wrong word for it. It was American with a token British ingredient. It was the Prime Minister's military baptism of fire, and the first major foreign policy crisis of his government. All MPs would have to take a stand on it. They duly did so, despite their doubts and divisions, and the personal reservations of many of them. The armed forces were on active service and in the line of fire. For the politicians it was like a muster parade, which is the army's way of finding out who is present and correct. The established parties dutifully rallied to the government side and carried their rank and file with them, with the exception of such habitual mutineers and free spirits as Tony Benn, Dennis Canavan and Tam Dalyell. I had never for a moment expected to find myself in agreement with them, and yet like them I was both present and incorrect. The Independent Member for Tatton had serious personal misgivings and no party to hide behind.

The timing of the attacks was deeply troubling. Intermittently throughout 1998 the UN weapons inspectors of UNSCOM (the United Nations Special Commission) had been seeking to discover and destroy Iraq's weapons of mass destruction, under the terms of the cease-fire agreement of March 1991. Sometimes the Iraqis complied and sometimes they didn't. Armed conflict was narrowly averted in February by the personal intervention of the UN Secretary-General, Kofi Annan, and in November by an unambiguous Iraqi assurance delivered to the United Nations even as the American bombers were in the air. But UNSCOM was turned away again; its Head of Mission, the undiplomatic Richard Butler, presented a negative report to the Security Council; and armed conflict was imminent.

So was impeachment. The American and British offensive was launched on the day before a vote was scheduled in the House of Representatives on whether President Clinton should be impeached, and stand trial in the United States Senate, for perjury and the obstruction of justice in the Monica Lewinsky affair. It wasn't only the conspiracy theorists on both sides of the Atlantic, but senior British army officers in a position to know, who suspected a connection between the two events: that these were 'Monica's missiles'.

The decibel level of Mr Clinton's rhetoric against Saddam Hussein rose perceptibly during 1998 as the scandal drew him deeper into the mire. It had happened in February, and was happening again in December. The domestic and international crises meshed together. If it had been a screenplay for the movies any self-respecting script editor would have rejected it as altogether too far-fetched; but from the recollection of my time in Washington over twelve years and three presidencies, I reflected how much the Americans needed someone to demonize and think ill of. The Iraqi ruler was the latest in a long line of them. Assorted ayatollahs, colonels, sheikhs and banana republic dictators had gone before him. Some had fallen, like Noriega of Panama and Ortega of Nicaragua. Others had survived, like Gaddafi of Libya and Saddam Hussein himself. All of them were ill-matched adversaries of the last superpower left standing, which constructed its scenarios on the lines of a Hollywood film.

Operation Desert Fox lasted for four days, and ended predictably with both sides announcing victory. The Americans claimed that their 650 aircraft missions and 425 cruise missiles had destroyed 100 targets in Iraq. The Iraqis admitted to the loss of sixty-four 'martyrs' among their military. The allied pilots sustained not so much as a scratch. The lives of Britons in Islamic countries were put at risk – and in the Yemen four innocent tourists were killed. Saddam Hussein remained in power, and probably stronger at home and abroad even as his barracks and bunkers crumbled under the bombardment. As General Sir Peter de la Billière correctly observed, who was the British Gulf War Commander the last time around, you do not and cannot bomb people into submission. 'It tends to make them despair, and there's a considerable risk that this will happen, not just in Iraq, but across the Islamic world.' Bombing does not tear countries apart but bind them together, and it hands their governments an alibi for tyranny and mismanagement. I wished for the first time – and not the last – that just once in his career a Prime Minister innocent of these things could have known what it was like to tremble under such a bombardment.

How rapidly do the politicians forget, if they ever learned. General Colin Powell had made a similar point six years earlier when he was Chairman of the United States Joint Chiefs of Staff:

'We should always be sceptical when so-called experts suggest that all a particular crisis calls for is a little surgical bombing or a limited attack. History has not been kind to such an approach to war-making.'

The limited attack on Iraq was not so much a war as a punitive air raid with deeply damaging consequences, diplomatically as well as materially. As it unfolded, I kept myself under observation for symptoms of wishing to return to the war zones in my former rather obsessive occupation. Like an old war horse I might have been hearing the trumpets from afar and pawing the ground, but to my great relief I found that the curse was lifted and that I was cured. I sat the thing out from the safety of Westminster and without a twinge of nostalgia. Others could cover the arcade game warfare of the twenty-first century, which would be conducted in something known to the military as 'digitized battlespace'. These were wars of the post-heroic age.

The laser-guided bombing of the allied offensive was a prelude to it. The cost-free remoteness of it troubled me greatly. I did not wish to report it, partly because it was a reporter's nightmare. It was accompanied by a propaganda war in which lies were accorded the same status as truths, access was fragmentary and very little was verifiable. The BBC qualified its coverage with the 'health warning' that its reporters were not allowed to move freely about Baghdad; that was true. But neither were they allowed to move freely about Kuwait, or just about anywhere else amid the shadings and manipulations on either side.

Even the metaphors were confusing. Who were the 'loose cannons' in this adventure – the dissident MPs or the two front benches? And who were the 'rogue states' – the Iraqis or ourselves?

I carried these misgivings over into the Commons debate on the crisis. It happened on the second day of the bombing, which was the eve of the Christmas recess. Not only the usual suspects on the Labour left but some of the Tories were seething with indignation. One called the bombing campaign 'outrageous' because of its timing and the life-line it threw so conveniently to a beleaguered

American President. Yet the Conservative outrage and indignation never broke surface; the Liberal Democrats followed the all-party consensus, although many of them had doubts; and most of the Labour back-benchers fell into line. Only a few MPs dissented — all on the Labour side except myself.

The debate was one of those rare Commons occasions when the moments of drama were worth the hours of tedium. The Prime Minister, on his first outing in khaki as de facto commander-in-chief, seemed unusually ill at ease, especially on the issue of the Clinton coincidence. 'I want to deal with one thing straight on,' he said. 'There are suggestions that the timing of military action is somehow linked to the internal affairs of the United States. I refute this entirely. I have no doubt at all that action is fully justified now. That is my strong, personal view.'[1] He had somehow absorbed the Ministry of Defence's Pentagon-inspired vocabulary, and spoke of 'degrading the enemy's capability'. It sent a slight shiver through me, because I had been there before and knew what it meant. It meant a lot of things. One of the things it meant was killing people. I wondered if Tony Blair had ever seen a dead person — or, more to the point, a killed person. They are not quite the same.

The dissenters, myself included, were unconvinced by the Prime Minister's explanation. George Galloway, a lone ranger of the Labour left and friend of the Iraqi regime, declared: 'We are diminished and degraded by being reduced to the tail on this verminous and mangy Desert Fox.' And then when he was interrupted he rounded on the hecklers, all of them Labour MPs on the benches beside him: 'This is a free Parliament, and I will have my say in it.'[2]

Tony Benn, whom I was coming to admire more than I ever expected, was compelling. The sweetest music an MP hears is the sound of his own voice. Mr Benn was one of the very few who could draw others into the House, and whom they genuinely wanted to hear besides themselves. (I was greatly complimented one day, in the rebels' division lobby, when he described himself as a 'Bellite'.) It was the sixth war that he had seen debated in

Parliament: on the day he was first elected, he claimed, President Truman had threatened to use atomic weapons in Korea.[3] The Member for Chesterfield extemporized passionately, waving his notes like a baton in front of him and hardly referring to them for a moment. He dismissed the argument that, once British armed forces were sent into action, it was unpatriotic to question the decision to commit them.

The truth is that chair-borne troops, who sit here planning strategy with their marvellous knowledge of military matters, are the ones who can betray the troops. The most scandalous thing that can be done is to commit troops to a war that is wrong and then shield behind them, saying that because they are on the front line we must never criticize.[4]

The iron arithmetic of the House of Commons prevailed. Observing the usual ratio of waiting time to speaking time, I waited for three hours to speak for three minutes. MPs were surprised, but there really is no merit in length, and three minutes were all that was needed. Much longer than that, and the message loses impact. I drew on my experience in the Gulf War of eight years previously (I was in camouflage then, but not now) to point out that the international support that had been mustered for that campaign had failed to materialize for this one. It was a mirage of the desert. Britain and America stood totally alone.

Study the silences. I urge all honourable and right honourable members to study the speeches that have not been made and the actions that have not been taken. Where is the support in the Arab world, the United Nations and the world community at large of the kind that we enjoyed seven and eight years ago? Now we face a really difficult situation, in which we are in danger of being perceived as acting as the deputy sheriff of the world, with the United States as sheriff . . . I sit in this House as the only elected Independent. I vote with the Government more often than against them. On the whole, they are a good Government. On most issues, they serve the people well. I cannot support this enterprise.[5]

The speech drew much comment – most of it adverse from Conservatives dismayed at the company I was keeping, and accusing me of inconsistency. I had supported air strikes against the Serbs in Bosnia; so why was I opposing them against the Iraqis in Baghdad? The answer of course was that the United Nations did not exist to be used when it suited us and bypassed when it didn't. The NATO actions in support of UNPROFOR (the UN Protection Force) in Bosnia were properly authorized by the UN Security Council, while the raids on Iraq were so far from authorized that two of the Council's permanent members were defying the other three. One was an action which had widespread support and an achievable objective; the other was a bastard and orphaned project with neither.

In hearing the debate out, I found myself not only handicapped, but declared to be a literal nonentity, by the archaic traditions of the House. I had moved from my speaking position beyond the Liberal Democrats, to my viewing position on the cross bench beneath it. With a commanding view of both front benches, it is the best vantage point in the House except the Speaker's, although technically not a part of it. The Conservative MP for Canterbury, Julian Brazier, wished to take issue with me on the merits of the bombing. 'I am particularly aware,' he said, 'of the presence of the honourable Member for Tatton.' The Deputy Speaker, Sir Alan Haselhurst, rose majestically to interrupt him: 'Order! The honourable Member for Tatton is not in the Chamber, so the honourable Gentleman should not refer to him.' 'I stand entirely rebuked, Mr Deputy Speaker,' replied a chastened Mr Brazier. 'Although we can see him, I accept that he is outside the Chamber.'[6]

There were times when I felt that the Deputy Speaker must be right, and I didn't exist. It was all some kind of a dream. I was not in the House of Commons at all, but had somehow strayed into a parliamentary pantomime or an unpublished chapter of *Alice in Wonderland* – a sort of Mad Hatter's debate. (Top hats had indeed played a part in the crazy rituals of the place until the previous session.) I was especially alarmed by this turn of events, since it had followed exactly Neil Hamilton's prediction during the election campaign. He had warned that, in the unlikely event of my becoming an MP, I would be lost without trace. I belonged to no party and would therefore be marginalized. I would serve on no committees and have no clout. It was a perfectly reasonable argument, although he was wrong about the committees. But even he never foresaw that I would be officially declared invisible. I wrote to the Modernisation Committee asking them to change the rules of the House in such a way as to recognize the cross bench and restore my visibility. It was a matter of confidence. This kind of thing could affect morale: I saw no future in being the only Member of Parliament to doubt his own existence. There was actually an old movie about an invisible man: it starred Alec Guinness and was called *The Man in the White Suit*.

Yet in the case of this crucial debate I was not alone. The entire opposition to the bombing of Iraq was declared non-existent by a parliamentary manoeuvre. The motion actually being debated was one for the adjournment of the House. As the clock ticked towards 10 p.m., when it would run out of time and hit the procedural buffers, Tony Benn rose from his seat to demand that 'the question be now put'. The front benches wanted a show of unanimity, or the next best thing which was an absence of any recorded opposition. The government reached deep into the rule book and found it could achieve this by refusing to provide any tellers for a division. The rebels laid siege to the Speaker's chair, and the recriminations filled two full pages of Hansard. Twenty MPs might have voted against – all on the Labour side except myself; and mutiny was also stirring among the Liberal Democrats. We were denied our democratic right to register our opposition. Like the bombing itself, it was an exercise in futility. Not for the first time, I had a sense of what it must have been like to serve as a deputy in one of the rubber stamp assemblies of a socialist 'people's democracy'. In this respect would we not have felt thoroughly at home in the old East German *Volkskammer* in Berlin? The *Volkskammer* was no more democratic than the royal palace on whose ruins it was built.

The ambush on Knutsford Heath became one of the defining
images of the campaign (© *Knutsford Guardian*)

Learning to field questions after years of asking them
(© *Knutsford Guardian*)

One of the most used pictures from the campaign. Overhead lighting
by courtesy of the Longview Hotel (© *Knutsford Guardian*)

With Melissa at Knutsford Royal May Day.
Christine and Neil Hamilton in attendance (© *Knutsford Guardian*)

Campaigning with Terry Waite. The second runway of Manchester airport was an immediate and continuing issue for the constituency

Being an MP has revealed talents I never knew I had

UNICEF official mission to Burundi, July 1998.
(UNICEF/UK/Victoria Scott)

Kosovo, March 1999.
(*Below*) With Milos Stankovic,
central Bosnia, January 1993.

With some of my most important constituents (J.Codes)

Was our 'people's chamber' at Westminster any better? It was a melancholy reflection. We are a free people, and the doctrine of unity at any price should have no place in our Parliament.

On the morning the bombing of Iraq was over, the Sunday before Christmas, I was awakened by the bells of the Church of St Mary and All Saints in Great Budworth, and by my younger daughter Catherine using her mother's mobile phone to call me from the Great Wall of China. It set me thinking, what extraordinary technical advances we have made when we can chat to each other across the planet, yet human nature remains obstinately the same. That is not a reflection on Catherine's nature – a matchless blend of intelligence, sweetness and charm. It is a reflection on what I have come to see as the increasingly perilous nature of the new world disorder.

Not only communications but weapons systems have advanced spectacularly, even in the interval between Operation Desert Storm in 1991 and its poor relation Desert Fox in 1998. The technology of star wars is not science fiction but already within our grasp. An attacking force delivers most of its destructive capacity by remote control and from a long way over the horizon. A single cruise missile is itself a weapon of mass destruction. I have actually witnessed the *baptism* of such a missile, at the factory in Florida where the very first Tomahawk Cruise missile was made. In a religious ceremony of sublime and surpassing incongruity, it was blessed by a US Air Force padre as an instrument of world peace. Yet no bomb or missile is so smart that it can distinguish between a soldier and a civilian. And the politicians who take the decisions to launch them are not only much as politicians always were – driven by domestic and international pressures and sometimes flawed perceptions of the national interest – but they are themselves increasingly remote from the effects of their decisions. They are also under pressures not known to their predecessors – to satisfy the demands of the media, to wage a parallel war on television and to deliver an instant and inexpensive victory.

Tony Blair's government had no lack of message merchants and spin doctors, but it was the first this century to have no one in it with any real military experience. The same was true of all but a handful of MPs. None of the defence ministers, or any of the other ministers, had ever worn the Queen's uniform or followed the colours. That is not a criticism of them: it is an inevitable percentage of the peace dividend, that we have lived more or less at peace for fifty years, and war is now a part of our islands' history rather than their politics. We field the smallest standing army since the 1820s, and the soldiers are uneasily aware of living in the margins, where their lives can so easily be set at risk by an ill-considered gamble. I know that this is how they feel because the regimental sergeant-majors, the beating heart of the army, have told me so. I know it also from the House of Commons door keepers, the lieutenants of the Serjeant-at-Arms. They are all ex-soldiers or ex-marines, and any one of them could deliver a better speech on defence than most of those they routinely have to listen to. We would discuss this mournfully, as old soldiers together, in the entrance at the back of the Speaker's chair.

Britain is a civilian society, with only the remotest notion of the realities of warfare. Those that it has are dangerously distorted through the filtered images of the large screen and the small one. From *Apocalypse Now* to *Salvador* to *Welcome to Sarajevo* I have never viewed any of the movies of wars that I knew about, directly or indirectly, without wishing to walk out. I refused to be trapped by fictions, and could not abide the myth-making falsehoods and revisionist nonsense applied to them. Oliver Stone was the worst offender, and Steven Spielberg the only one of them who caught the true reality. As for television, I had personal experience from Saigon to Sarajevo of a sustained editorial campaign, in the interests of good taste and easy viewing, to remove the scenes of horror and bloodshed from the coverage of real world violence. The BBC was not solely responsible for this campaign, but was its most persistent and influential promoter. I was more than a witness of this. I was an accomplice. *Mea culpa.*

This is where it gets dangerous. We are living in a culture in which warfare is seen as a relatively cost-free option and an accept-able means of settling differences. Our politicians, when issues of life and death are set before them, cannot fail to be affected by this serendipitous vision. It makes the difficult decisions so much easier. In the Falklands War, the casualties were sustained a long way away and not known about in detail until after it was over, when the euphoria of victory dulled the pain of loss for all but the families of the fallen. In the Gulf War of 1991 the casualties were statistically negligible in terms of the ground forces committed, and inflicted more by 'friendly' than by enemy fire. In the bombing of Iraq in 1998 they were zero. The same applied to the bombing of Kosovo in 1999. I cannot think of a more dangerous or misleading lesson for the consideration of future wars. In these and subsequent crises I used my position as an MP to stand up and say so on all possible occasions, whether in the House of Commons itself, to university audiences, to the armed services' academies, to church groups in Wilmslow or even to the North West Chrysanthemum Growers in Allostock. I tried, but I frankly doubt if I had any effect. It is in the nature and tradition of prophets of doom that their warnings are unheeded.

On the bombing of Iraq, I had expected to find a storm breaking over my head. Anticipating it, I had even offered to resign my position as patron of the Association of RAF Wives. This admirable organization of air force families, sprung from the grass roots and indifferent to rank, was under threat of being closed down by the high command. I reasoned that its chances of survival would not have been strengthened by the patronage of someone who had opposed the bombing, even while RAF pilots were at risk and flying their missions over Baghdad. The Association declined my offer; but I retained an alertness to incoming fire, and knew that there must be an air marshal out there somewhere fuming apoplec-tically.

I did not hear from any air marshals, although I did receive a call from a serving wing commander. He was facing disciplinary action on some other issue, and wished to move to Knutsford in order to be my constituent. (And he wasn't the first: it was hardly a pattern of migration to be encouraged.) But my mail on the bombing of Iraq was totally supportive of the position I had taken. The expected letters of outrage never arrived – not a single one. A correspondent from Devon called the military action 'a political miscalculation of ridiculous proportions'. An expatriate wrote from France – her first-ever letter to an MP: 'I feel ashamed to be British. I feel sick as I sit here watching the news, and when I saw you on the news it was a ray of hope for me, that not everyone accepts the rubbish that we are being told.' And one of my constituents added: 'When "national emergency" strikes, a craven and dangerous closing of ranks takes place by the men in grey suits.' My mailbag was the only barometer of public opinion that I had, and all that a party of one could actually afford. It suggested to me that the government had miscalculated its support, and was acting against the grain of the national mood. It was also profoundly mistaken.

Astonishingly, the only dissent came from within the ranks, or perhaps I should say the rank, of my own party. That may seem difficult to achieve in so small an outfit, but it was accomplished against all odds by my issues adviser and nephew, Oliver Kamm. Oliver, who played a leading part in the election campaign, has a day job as the chief strategist of an investment bank in the City. He is very good at it. And since he is a human computer and ideas factory, his more important occupation is to advise me sagely on the issues of the day, and to keep me on a reasonable and consistent political path; but since his expertise is in economics I had not actually sought his thoughts on the bombing of Iraq.

I received them anyway in faxes and e-mails, and a letter to the *Guardian* answering an article I had written while the bombing was in progress setting out my reasons for opposing it. He wrote, 'Martin Bell's rhetorical question as to who appointed us and the United States to act as the world's sheriff and deputy sheriff is inapt. The bombing of Iraq was a grim necessity precisely because no sheriffs exist.'

I reflected on this act of open rebellion during my half-hour drive to Westminster the following morning. And then as a matter of grim necessity – what a dreadful cliché, Oliver – I composed a press release signed by myself as Party Leader and my secretary, Mary Price, as General Secretary. It was not actually sent to the press, but e-mailed directly to the dissident faction:

The Executive Committee of the Independent Party has been meeting in emergency session, following allegations of disloyalty and perfidy made against its issues adviser, Mr Oliver Kamm. The allegations came from two loyal party cadres, Ms Fiona Goddard (the leader's wife) and Ms Melissa Bell (his daughter). After a lengthy discussion it was concluded that Mr Kamm's ignorance of the issues on which he wrote his letter to the *Guardian* was a substantial mitigating circumstance. It was further concluded that the risibility of his arguments drew attention to the strength of the leader's own *Guardian* article, and thus had done the party no damage. Mr Kamm is therefore invited to remain in the party and to continue to sound off whenever he pleases.

Oliver was unconvinced. But, in keeping with the family's long tradition of non-belligerence, he wrote back, 'You'll have to sack me and expel me before I resign – especially on matters where you know a lot more than I. I am the Neil Hamilton of the Independent Party – you'll never be shot of me.' That he hadn't been dismissed, he added, was a weight off his mind.

And there the matter rested. In the looser and more consensual politics which I favour, I recommend it as a model of how to deal with a rebellion within a party.

10. Soldier's Story

'What do they know of England who only England know?' Rudyard Kipling might as well have added: 'What do they know of Cheshire who only Cheshire know?' The soldiers' poet would surely have understood that the first I knew of Cheshire, whose heartland and Shangri-La I was later to represent in Parliament, was the compacted snow and deep-rutted mud which were the home of the First Battalion of the Cheshire Regiment at Vitez in Central Bosnia. I had not a political thought in my head at the time, but I did believe that I knew something about the Balkans. Having survived the war's first summer in Sarajevo almost intact, I had addressed the Cheshires at Fallingbostel in Germany before their departure. I am not always proved right, but this time I was. I predicted that the operation on which they were embarked would be an entirely new dimension of soldiering, and one that would change their lives. I was with them during their six months of ordeal and achievement. I rejoiced with them when half-way through their tour of duty they celebrated in more than orange juice their liberation from a deeply unhappy amalgamation with the Staffordshire Regiment (the Staffordshires reciprocated). And in May 1993 I was alongside them up to a certain point on their way home. The certain point was Mostar, which was then exploding. They kept going with their Union Jacks flying and I stayed behind. Their commanding officer, the admirable Lieutenant Colonel Bob Stewart, remained a steadfast friend. Long before I became an MP they graciously accepted me as an honorary member of their regiment, the 22nd of Foot. I even acquired a tasteless bow tie, cerise with buff spots, to prove it.

Any regiment is a family, and in Bosnia theirs was an extended one. The Cheshires had almost as many men under their command who were not of their cap badge but belonged to other units – attached infantry, cavalry, medics, engineers, logisticians and others. They dealt well with such auxiliaries, as one of their more fashionable successor regiments did not. As far as one individual soldier was concerned, who was with them but not of them, those days had consequences which reached to the Army Board, to the House of Commons and to Downing Street. They began for me with an encounter in a cookhouse.

In January 1993, in the Cheshires' camp in Vitez, I met a British officer who was introduced to me as Captain Mike Stanley of the Parachute Regiment. We greeted each other over one of the army's high cholesterol breakfasts. He probably thought no more of it, since the Paras took a regimentally dim view of the press, for all sorts of reasons: they knew from experience the untold damage that could be done by a single adverse headline. But I thought a great deal more of it. There was something about him that intrigued me because it set him apart from the others. It wasn't just that he was the only sky-diver among all the foot-slogging infantry. He would have been one of a kind in any company. Appearances mattered little to him: he wore a flak jacket but seldom a helmet – a style that was later adopted by the secret soldiers who guarded the British commanders. The SAS men, who became known to us as 'Her Majesty's Hooligans', also wore no helmets, in the clear belief that they were immortal and the bullets would bounce off their heads. Mike Stanley was not one of Hereford's typical products (indeed he was not SAS). He was not one of Sandhurst's, either. He had eyes and depths which smouldered. He was quieter, more intense and reflective than the officers around him. Nor, unlike so many of them, had his vowel sounds been strangled at birth.

He was not a secret soldier, but he was a special one. He was assigned to Bosnia for a particular reason. He was one of only two British soldiers serving there who spoke the language with fluency. The other was a captain in the Light Infantry known to us as Nick Costello. Both names were fictions – aliases bestowed on them by an army which thought it prudent to disguise their families' origins, and had even considered baptizing an Abbott as well as a Costello. The two men worried about entrusting their lives to people who could entertain such daft ideas. Both were the sons of refugees who had made a new life in England.

Mike Stanley's real name was Milos Stankovic. His father was a Serb. His mother was partly Serb and partly Scottish. His father had served with the Royalist forces against the Germans in Yugoslavia, and his mother with Montgomery's 8th Army, as an ambulance driver, at the Battle of El Alamein. After the war they came to England and started afresh. Their son was born in 1962 – a British citizen, of course. He was educated at private schools, and decided on a military career. At Sandhurst he was selected to serve in the Parachute Regiment – itself no slight distinction.

When he first signed on, a sergeant took him through the usual questionnaire. 'Do you have any languages?'

'Yes sergeant, actually I do. I speak Serbo-Croat.'

'Fat lot of use that'll be,' said the sergeant.

If he had only kept quiet, he later reflected, his life would have turned out differently.

Stankovic worked for senior British officers: Colonel Bob Stewart in Vitez, Brigadiers Andrew Cumming and Robin Searby in Split, and Generals Michael Rose and Rupert Smith in Sarajevo.

The generals were the British commanders of the UN force in Bosnia. Their role was at least as much political as military. They needed a path-finder through the murk of the Balkans where the only truth was a lie. He was their eyes and ears and sense of history. His mission was to translate the people as well as the language. It was especially to win the trust of the Bosnian Serbs. He served as the UN's liaison officer with them, and spent more and more time in their territory. He called it 'travelling to the dark side'. He described the whole imbroglio as 'Yugo-Disney' and the Balkan obsession with death as 'necrowar', because the dead meant more to these people than the living, and a corpse was worth two cans of petrol. He had a way with words and a courage which I envied. He relayed messages, unblocked convoys and arranged cease-fires.

The Serbs discovered where he came from, but also understood where he belonged. He knew them but was not one of them. 'Captain Stanley is a nice enough guy,' said their Vice-President Nikola Koljevic to a visiting Anglo-Serb, 'but we must never forget that his loyalty is to his Queen and his Regiment.'

The quiet captain from the Parachute Regiment served longer in Bosnia than any other British soldier; and he saved lives. In Vitez in May 1993, he ran out under fire and rescued a Muslim woman who was wounded and lying in the road. In 1994 and 1995 he and Costello were the essential link-men of a covert and deniable UN operation to smuggle civilians – Muslims, Croats and Serbs – out of Sarajevo and through Serb-held territory to be reunited with their relatives abroad. Close on 200 were brought to safety in this way. The operation had the tacit consent of the two British generals. It was known to the UN inner circle as 'Schindler's'. One of the rescued Sarajevans, a Muslim, wrote to her saviour from the safety of Canada: 'We really must consider you our friend since what you have done for us is a huge thing. Such people who are prepared to help others risking their own lives are people who really must be considered friends. Therefore, one more huge thank you for what you have done – you and that great humanitarian, General Rose.'

Milos Stankovic was promoted to major and awarded the MBE, which he received at Buckingham Palace from the hand of the Queen. He left Bosnia for the last time in April 1995. The cease-fire was melting with the snows, as it did at that season every year, and the armies of Bosnia's three peoples were preparing to do battle in the last and fiercest summer of the war. It was a period that included a costly attempt by government forces to break the siege of Sarajevo, the first significant advances by Croatian troops against the Serbs on the western front, and the infamous massacre of Muslims by Serbs at Srebrenica. The Bosnian Serb commander, General Ratko Mladic, was a key figure in all these events. There was only one UN soldier who knew him really well, and to whom he would speak when he refused to deal with all others. Yet on his posting home, Major Stankovic was not even debriefed. That was a failure of intelligence in both senses. He thought it strange, but cheerfully returned to regimental duty.

He tried to set this chapter of his life behind him. It was hard to do so. His work for the UN at a time when it was calling in air strikes on the Serbs had strained his relations with his father, then living in retirement in Cornwall, where he died; indeed Milos Stankovic believed that the stress of it killed his father, who like many Serbian exiles was appalled by the disintegration of Yugoslavia and by the part played in it by the governments in Belgrade and Zagreb.

I kept in touch, as I try to do with good and interesting people. Major Stankovic was by then a company commander with the First Battalion of the Parachute Regiment. He was a natural for the Paras, who do not take to the airs and graces of the old army's officer class. He was good at the job and loved it. I was still a TV reporter then, and at the request of his commanding officer, Lieutenant-Colonel Julian James, I visited them at Aldershot and gave a talk about army press relations. For more than a generation, since 'Bloody Sunday' in 1972, the Parachute Regiment had taken a battering from the Sinn Fein publicity machine, and had developed a bunker mentality towards the press. I don't know if I helped them break it, but I do know that I left the garrison with the feeling that, after all that had happened to my friend, the clouds that hovered over his head had lifted, and he was settling back with relief into regular soldiering. He and the army belonged together: he was as good for it as it was good for him. He was accepted into the Joint Services Staff College at Bracknell, a necessary step towards further promotion.

In the meantime I had embarked on a new career – indeed, according to Neil Hamilton, I had been parachuted into it. The phrase reminded me of the intrepid Major Stankovic, and I wished that on hitting the ground I could find my feet as easily as he found his. The Tatton campaign was not my idea of a soft landing.

The next thing I heard of him was at the end of October 1997. I received a call from Kate Adie. 'Have you seen the *Sunday Times*?'

'No chance. I'm on a personal boycott of Mr Murdoch's papers. I only read other people's. Tell me what's in it.'

'It's the Ministry of Defence Police. They've arrested Mike Stanley, under the Official Secrets Act.' Observing protocol, she used his alias.

'They can't have done.'

'Believe me,' she said, 'they have.'

They came for him at the Staff College at 8.24 in the morning. He was not charged then, or at any time later. He was driven to Guildford police station and formally arrested there under Section 2 of the Official Secrets Act 1989, a Thatcherite extension of state power, on suspicion of having disclosed information to the Bosnian Serbs which would have compromised the integrity of the United Kingdom and jeopardized the safety of British soldiers in Bosnia. A man who had saved lives was suspected of having endangered them. This was a strange notion indeed. The UN ran a transparent operation; in Bosnia as elsewhere its documents and signals were never encoded, although the Royal Welch Fusiliers did use the Welsh language on the radio net between Sarajevo and Gorazde. It was difficult to see how Major Stankovic, as a serving UN officer, could have passed on the secrets of an organization that didn't have any. An SAS major who had served with him in Bosnia was arrested at the same time and questioned separately. The police even had a code-name for it: Operation Bretton. The suggestion was that there was not just a single spy at work, but perhaps an entire ring of spies in a setting of Balkan intrigue. The connection with reality was already broken. Fantasy policing took over.

The prospect was an enticing one to the Ministry of Defence Police, generally and unflatteringly known as 'MoD Plod'. They were not well regarded by the armed services, or even by other police forces. They guarded gates at camps and barracks. Their standard inquiries were into the embezzlement of funds and the thefts of wallets at military establishments. In the Stankovic case they were adrift and out of their depth. From start to finish they could never get their heads round it. They knew little of espionage and nothing at all of the Balkans. Nor did they possess even the fragments of knowledge that might have illuminated for them, like a parachute flare, the landscape of their ignorance. So they blundered on, ineptly and inequitably. The result should serve the police academies for years to come as a text book study of how not to conduct an investigation.

A British officer of good character and unblemished record was thrown into a cell and held for eight hours. Lit cigarettes were passed in to him through a spy hole in the door as if he were an apprehended felon. He was not allowed to telephone even his family. (The Guildford police countermanded this order after two hours, as an infringement of his rights.) He was suspended from the Staff College – an action that would ruin his army career, however the investigation ended. The Ministry of Defence detectives ransacked his house and stripped it of just about everything but the furniture – some 30,000 documents in all, including Christmas cards, an old copy of *Playboy* magazine and even a sheet of sandpaper. It was not a search but a trawl: they took so much because they had no settled notion of what they were looking for. Nor did they know what they were looking *at*. They dismantled and confiscated a collection of old photographs and medals that he kept as a shrine to his father. They also went through his room at the Staff College. From his desk they seized his course work, and from his mess uniform they took his miniature medals. There were four of these, all earned the hard way on active service: the General Service Medal for Northern Ireland, the UN Kuwait Medal, the UNPROFOR Medal and the MBE. His entitlement to them was never in doubt, yet the later summary of witness statements showed that it had been questioned, so ingrained and entrenched was the hostility against him. Heroism was an alien and suspect notion to the MoD Police. They would not have recognized it if it had stood up out of the file and saluted them.

He was assured that the investigation would probably be over in two months. It took fourteen. The first time that his bail was extended he received the news in a letter sent to 'Mr Stankovic'.

To a soldier facing the Kafkaesque procedures of the secretive constabulary, the inference was clear: as far as Major Stankovic was concerned he had already been found guilty, and stripped of the rank and medals that his soldiering had earned him. He had every right to believe that all that was now required was to find a charge to hang on him, or to hang him on. In his state of mind it seemed very much the same. 'I've had enough of this isolation,' he wrote. 'It gets worse with each passing day.'

He was too proud a man to ask for help, so I called him up and received a melancholy account of the story so far. Even then I judged him to be close to breaking point.

'Milos, I'm not a reporter any more and I know that if I were you wouldn't be allowed to talk to me. But things have changed. Rather improbably I happen to be an MP. I'm on your side, and I can't believe what I'm hearing. Who else is helping you?'

'My police-appointed lawyer from Guildford, and that's about all.'

'What about the army?'

'My commanding officer told me that all I'm permitted to do is prepare my defence. Apart from that, if I contact any of my mates, or they contact me, it's a disciplinary offence.'

'No soldier's friend?'

'Not even a soldier's friend.'

This was extraordinary. The humblest private soldier in serious trouble is provided with a soldier's friend, an officer outside the case who will be someone for him to talk to and to advise him. For more than two months Major Stankovic had no such officer, and when he was finally allowed to nominate one, Brigadier Andrew Cumming of the 17th/21st Lancers, the Ministry of Defence Police tried to block that too.

It made me wonder about the Parachute Regiment. They had rallied behind one of their own, Private Lee Clegg, who had been convicted of murder in Northern Ireland. Many brave souls stood by Major Milos Stankovic, who was so far not accused or convicted of anything. Some broke the rules and talked to him directly.

Others sent messages of support through their wives. Two of the regiment's serving generals, Rupert Smith and Michael Jackson, were steadfast in their belief in his innocence. But there were some who ignored the case, or spoke of it in whispers, and left its central figure to his loneliness. Was this because he was an officer, and therefore supposedly able to look after himself? Or was it because he was not entirely of British origin? Did it have anything to do with an army personnel file that described him as being 'Brit Nat / Foreign' by birth? The more I considered his ordeal – the isolation, the murmured suspicions, the institutional betrayals, the unspoken and insidious presumption of guilt – the more he seemed a victim of racism as well as injustice. He was the British Dreyfus.

Alfred Dreyfus, the French staff officer falsely charged with selling military secrets to a foreign power, was court-martialled in 1893, primarily because he was Jewish. He was the victim of an anti-Semitic conspiracy, his sword was broken on the square and he was exiled to the penal colony of Devil's Island. A century later a similar suspicion hung over Stankovic – and the same reproach, that he had betrayed secrets to an enemy and that he was not 'one of us'. Events were driving towards the same conclusion. This case was as shameful as that.

It was time to rattle the cage. I asked for and was granted an adjournment debate – a parliamentary manoeuvre which requires the government to put up a minister to answer a backbencher's argument on the floor of the House. The only difficulty was that the conscripted minister, Dr John Reid of the MoD, was among those absent, having been misinformed by his staff about the timing of the debate. He duly apologized. But the upshot was that for all but the closing peroration, I regaled the inattentive green leather of the government front bench, occupied by no one but a deputy whip, with my account of the grave and continuing injustices suffered by a serving British soldier. 'What kind of a people are we,' I demanded, 'and what kind of a signal does it send, if we reward our heroes by arresting them? Heroes are ordinary people who do extraordinary things. Major Milos Stankovic is such a man.'[1]

John Reid is a good and decent politician, whose only enemies were inside his own party – itself a melancholy reflection on party politics. His subsequent promotions were a loss to the armed forces, and not of his seeking: in the Labour government's first reshuffle, he was the one minister who sat by his telephone hoping it wouldn't ring – and so, of course, it did. Before leaving to be Transport Minister and then Scottish Secretary, he arranged a visit for me to enemy territory, the headquarters and nerve centre of the Ministry of Defence Police. It was a remote and isolated garrison on the disused airfield at Wethersfield in Essex – a parcel of paramilitary England marooned in the countryside, and frozen in time around the 1950s. That was the ethos and atmosphere of the place, although the force itself was of more recent creation.

The Chief Constable, Walter Boreham, was a bluff and four-square veteran of the service with a sense of grievance to match my own. He had in front of him, highlighted in yellow, a list of the allegations that I had made against the force under his command. He was proud of it, and angry with me. We faced each other over coffee and biscuits, seething with indignation.

'You say here, Mr Bell, that we are politically motivated. I wish to assure you that we are an impartial service and proud of it.'

'Chief Constable, that is the one charge that I haven't made against you. It was the decision to refer the case to you that was politically motivated. I think I know who made it. A very senior soldier, responding to an allegation by another country's intelligence service. He should have told it then and there to get lost. My complaints against your force are about the injustice of its procedures.'

We went over these at length and without result. I found him obstructive, and have no doubt that he found me difficult and adversarial. He sought to mollify me with the remark that if he himself were ever in trouble he would wish to have me on his side. I thanked him for that, but to every point that I raised he pleaded the constraints and confidentiality of an operational police investigation.

'Including the seizure of the medals?'

'The medals may be needed as evidence.'

'Evidence of what?'

'You will understand that I can't tell you that.'

'And the shrine to his father?'

'We didn't know that it was a shrine,' he said.

I made two requests. One was that the investigating officers, who had taken evidence from so many marginal witnesses who had not even met the suspect, should travel to Bosnia and interview Jovan Zametica, his principal contact with the Bosnian Serbs. The other was that he should have access to his confiscated documents. Both requests were denied. And the access to the papers continued to be refused right up to the brink of an expensive judicial review.

By this time Major Stankovic had a new lawyer, Steven Barker, who became a steadfast friend as well as an adviser. He was outraged by the case: he had never known anything like it in eighteen years of legal practice. The injustices multiplied. When he sought evidence from a number of serving soldiers on the major's behalf, they were sent a memorandum by the Ministry of Defence advising them in effect, not of their right to testify, but of their right to remain silent. Many felt intimidated. Two were ordered not to co-operate. And a distinguished ex-officer, giving evidence to the investigators, found them using the major's diaries as a means of trying to turn a friendly witness into a hostile one.

'To the best of my knowledge,' he informed them, 'Major Stankovic served at all times with propriety and honour.'

'Very well,' said the inquisitor, 'then you might be interested to hear what he wrote about you.' There followed a candid and personal character assessment of the sort that any man might write of another in his diary. That is what diaries are for.

'You should be ashamed of yourselves,' said the old soldier, and stormed out.

The greatest of the investigation's many injustices was the sheer length of it. Major Stankovic was thirty-four when it started and thirty-six when it ended. The whispering intensified and the rumour spread that because it had gone on so long 'they must have something on him'. I heard this even from a general who should have known better. The reverse was true: the major's ordeal went on for so long precisely because they didn't have anything on him. The admitted cost of the investigation was £266,000. The real cost, including the investigators' salaries and the sacrificed alternatives (what they would have been better employed doing), was more than £1 million. British citizens had paid their taxes for that £1 million. And the penalty paid by the major himself was ruinous. He spent all the money he had – and some that he didn't have – on his defence; and because he was never actually charged he received not a penny from the Army Legal Fund.

He was summoned for questioning by the MoD Police at Guildford police station on 28 October 1998, more than a year after his arrest there. They were ready for a two- or three-day session. Before it began Steven Barker manoeuvred them into admitting that after all that time they did not possess the evidence to charge Major Stankovic. Nor would his client submit to their interrogation. Major Stankovic explained his reasons for refusal in a quietly incandescent four-minute statement that read like the climactic speech in a courtroom drama – except that no playwright could have imagined it, because no playwright could have lived it. Stankovic had, and survived with his confidence shattered and his career in ruins but his integrity intact. He had travelled twice to the dark side – once abroad among the Bosnian Serbs and once at home among his shadowy and nameless accusers.

'It's a cheap and dirty trick you've played on me,' he told his inquisitors,

if you think I'm going to answer your questions when you've given me no indication that this is a fair investigation. I can tell you two days are not enough to discuss Bosnia. I could sit here for two weeks, two months even, and in so doing I would have to talk to you about things that would make your hair stand on end. I'll tell you another thing. The British

Army was my life. And not only was it my life, it was my soul. I committed myself wholly to it and you have destroyed that, you and your Chief Constable have taken that away from me.

The MoD Police submitted the papers to the Crown Prosecution Service on 30 November 1998. Still Major Stankovic was under a poison cloud of suspicion. I saw him regularly at La Gaffe, my habitual restaurant and alternative political headquarters in Hampstead. He was beyond the end of his tether. I wrote to both the Attorney General and the Director of Public Prosecutions expressing my fears for his health unless there were a quick decision. They both prevaricated, and pleaded as a reason for the delay the complexity of the case. This was nonsense. After twenty months of investigation there was no complexity, and not a shred of credible evidence out there.

The Crown Prosecution Service came to the same conclusion. On 23 April 1999 it announced that there would be no prosecution. The *Sunday Times* headlined: 'Spy Smears Wreck Major's Career'. The army, which had a duty of care in the matter, could have cleared Major Stankovic's name there and then at the stroke of a pen. An MoD 'mole' reported that a general had wished to do so, but his hand was stayed by a senior civil servant; and the case disappeared for six more months into the mists of the military bureaucracy. I even had time for a second adjournment debate in the House of Commons, nineteen months after the first one, to express a rising sense of outrage that was now widely shared in the army and in Parliament. I quoted a serving soldier who had written to me from inside the fortress of the Ministry of Defence, 'I hope – fervently – that some of those responsible will be held to account for the appalling way he has been treated. Only then will I be convinced that there remains some hope that the rest of us will be fairly treated in future.'[2]

Sadly, none of my military connections provided the leverage that Major Stankovic needed. He was by now a full two years into his nightmare. In the course of that time I had spoken extensively and passionately about the case to staff college seminars, regimental study days and dinners, and the annual convention of regimental sergeant majors at Sandhurst. I had included an uncoded message about the army's duty of care in an address to the top brass, and others, at the annual Guards' carol service at Wellington Barracks. I had cornered the Chief of the General Staff at a parliamentary reception. None of it made any difference. It was like arguing with a cloud of cotton wool. The buck stopped on no one's desk, but was permanently shuttling between the Army Legal Service, the Adjutant General and a mysterious brigadier in Bulford. To put it bluntly, I failed. I vowed to take on no more military commitments until the Ministry of Defence had cleared the major's name: not so much as a regimental carol service. That would bring them to their knees. Like hell it would.

Despite the best efforts of certain senior soldiers, the Ministry of Defence refused to take the honourable course that was open to it. Major Stankovic had served the army much better than he was served by it: and with his good name and security vetting still not restored, he took the only course open to him, which was to ask for a discharge and to return to civilian life. Two years and two weeks after his arrest he wrote to his commanding officer, 'It is with a sense of deep regret and profound sadness that I have decided to leave the Army while issues of honour and trust remain unresolved.' His own man to the end and not 'one of them', he signed his name in Cyrillic.

He left the army in July 2000, professionally exonerated but financially ruined. He never received a word of apology or a penny of compensation from the Ministry of Defence, which had traded on his courage and then abandoned him. But he had the last word – 200,000 of them, actually – in his book *Trusted Mole*, which was published during his last weeks as a soldier. A searing account of his journey to the dark side both at home and abroad, it was acclaimed by the critics for its literary merit and by the soldiers for its homage to the truth.

It meant a great deal to him, and to all of us, that the book's launch was attended by two serving generals of the Parachute Regiment, Mike Jackson and Hew Pike. Also present were many others who had stood by him through the ordeal, including Andrew Cumming, Steven Barker, Desmond de Silva, Lord Coleridge, Kate Adie and Olga Maitland; his own MP Virginia Bottomley, his mother's MP Colin Breed and my old parliamentary nemesis Gerald Howarth. It was a cause in which we were proud to have served. And it led me to reflect how much more important than a political party is a league of decent people.

11. KOSOVO

Towards the end of 1998 I received a message from Victoria Scott, parliamentary liaison officer of UNICEF, asking if I would travel to Kosovo on their behalf. I was wary of returning to the Balkans: they were haunted by too many ghosts of my past, I was the MP for Tatton and not Yugoslavia, and I had always been critical in my former life of joy-riding MPs more concerned (so it seemed to me) with headline-gathering than with fact-finding.

But Kosovo was no one's idea of a palm-fringed sun-trap, and Victoria was a hard person to say no to. The daughter of Sir Nicholas Scott, the long-serving Tory MP for Kensington and Chelsea who had been deselected in colourful circumstances, she had not hesitated to clash with her father when he was the minister responsible for the handicapped and she was a lobbyist on their behalf. She had recruited a parliamentary supporters' club for the UN Children's Fund, including Oona King and Hilton Dawson, who were among the more independent-minded of the new Labour intake – and I trust that I shall not blight their careers by saying so. Under Victoria's direction and to the constant beat of jungle drums, we had travelled through Burundi earlier in the year, in the week immediately following my marriage. It was a dangerous place. Our host, Luis Zuniga of UNICEF, was assassinated in a refugee camp a year later. The timing of our own trip was not terrific, but Fiona forgave me – even when Oona used her *Daily Mirror* column to tell the world that Martin Bell had spent his honeymoon with her. It was at that point that Fiona and Oona's husband Tiberio became good friends, and founded an informal league of non-political spouses.

In March 1999 Victoria and I flew to Belgrade, a city that I had visited often before in tense and difficult times. Nothing much had changed. The capital of the Serbs, which had been flattened seventeen times in its history, had the imminence of another catastrophe hanging over it. Up to that point Belgrade had escaped the damage that its leaders had inflicted on the rest of their collapsing Federation. This seemed unlikely to last. I knew that as soon as I saw the empty picture hook on the wall of the British ambassador's residence. My sense of war zone timing had not deserted me. The British knew full well what was coming, and had packed away the art work. The ambassador, Brian Donnelly, provided a gloomy overview of the rapidly deepening crisis, and dutifully repeated the Foreign Office travel advice to British subjects not to visit Kosovo.

'Ambassador,' I said, 'I made a career out of ignoring the British government's health warnings. Don't expect me to start paying too much attention now. But I promise this time to be careful, not least for the sake of Victoria's four-year-old son.'

The following day we drove to Pristina, Kosovo's capital. It is a grey and dismal place at the best of times, which this was not. Bitter weather was on the way, and there were more than snow clouds gathering. The peace agreement brokered by the American negotiator Richard Holbrooke the previous October was unravelling by the hour. The Verification Mission put in place to police it was ignored and defied by both sides, but more flagrantly by the Serbs. The thousand international monitors in their orange-painted vehicles were unarmed and powerless to intervene as Kosovo's Albanians were driven from villages which the Serbs then looted and burned. Fifteen thousand were made homeless in that week. The Kosovo Liberation Army had also proved themselves to be ruthless killers. As in Bosnia, there was no monopoly of wrongdoing, or of suffering.

I toured the UNICEF horizon and admired its provisional achievements – clinics, schools and even a project called 'smile-keepers' in which Albanian refugee children depicted the traumas of their recent past. They drew their hopes and fears in crayon. The images were vividly consistent. Their hopes were expressed as a house with flowers and flower pots around it, their fears as a house in flames. They were working not from imagination but from personal experience. And we feared that it was about to happen again. I think they knew it too.

In a three-quarters ruined village near Glogovac I visited a class of primary school children studying in shifts in what had been the local shop. The desks and chairs, paper and pencils were all provided by UNICEF. I saw the fear and hope in the eyes of the children as they followed me round the room. More refugees had arrived in the village only the night before: that was a sign that the Serbs would attack it again. Since I felt that I had to say something, I delivered a short speech which was full of the sort of empty phrases that politicians use. I said,

I am a member of the British Parliament, a member without a party, and I bring you the good wishes of the British people. I am here because I care about what happens to you, and I wish you to know that the rest of the world cares about what happens to you. You are not forgotten. I know about wars, because I have been in them. This war will end one day, as all wars end. And when it does, you will be able to live in peace and freedom like other people.

Knowing now what I did not know then, it is a speech that I am ashamed to have made. God alone knows how many of those children survived.

I had made a similar speech once before, in January 1993, to refugees sheltering from Serbian shell fire in a cave in Sarajevo. I had come to seek their views for a TV programme, but the session turned into a sort of town meeting in which they supposed that I represented the international community. I did nothing of the sort, of course, but I was all they had. I assured them of what I believed, that the West would come to their rescue within two months. In fact it took three and a half years. When would I ever learn?

During a break in the UNICEF schedule, in a moment of nostalgia and for old times' sake, I visited my friends in the international press corps in Pristina. It was the first time in two years I had felt the pull of my former occupation – not the dangers and the fear and the roadblock hassle, but the support and friendship of such a community of unlikely people. Sarajevo's veterans were at battle stations again: Kurt Schork, Elly Biles and Mark Chisholm of Reuters, Anthony Loyd of *The Times*, Emma Daly of the *Independent* and many others. They included some serious war zone addicts, especially Anthony, a former captain in the Royal Green Jackets who sought out the experience of living under fire and at life's edge. The title of his Bosnian memoir said it all: *My War Gone By, I Miss It So*. 'I cannot apologize for loving it so,' he wrote. 'It was like falling in love again.'[1] He painted so dark a picture of himself, that if anyone else had done it he should have sued for libel.

My wife Fiona, who was beginning to know these people, once described them as 'an interesting bunch of nutters', and who was to say that she was wrong? The press gang were living on borrowed time, and expecting to be targeted by the Serbs. Within a week they would all be expelled. Kurt and Anthony, who had attempted to flee into the mountains, were arrested by the Serbian Interior Police and had guns held to their heads. They were both on the black list and lucky to escape with their lives. In the end, Kurt's luck ran out. He was killed by rebels in Sierra Leone in May 2000. He was the best and bravest reporter I ever knew.

I left Kosovo two days ahead of the international monitors, and six days before the bombs fell. When NATO began its campaign to bombard the Serbs into accepting autonomy for the province under the Rambouillet peace plan, I was on the other side of the world, in Australia.

That was because of another conflict. In 1973 I had been diverted from a planned assignment in Sydney to report the Arab–Israeli war: and under heavy Syrian shell fire on the Golan Heights, I had vowed to the stone wall which protected me that if I survived I would one day make that trip to Australia. So it was that twenty-six years later I was speaking at the awards ceremony of the Melbourne Press Club, when I should have been in the House of Commons for a thinly attended debate on the Kosovo crisis. It is easy enough for a journalist to be in the wrong place at the wrong time. It can happen to an MP too: not that it makes much difference, you can reasonably argue.

The start of the bombing campaign, a month before NATO's fiftieth birthday, was the worst week in its history. An American Stealth bomber crashed near Belgrade. Three US soldiers were captured by Serbs on the Macedonian border. Serbs of all persuasions rallied behind their President. And worst of all, an action that was intended to protect the Albanians of Kosovo had the effect of victimizing them, with bitter and lethal results. Driven out by the Serbs' accelerated campaign of murder and ethnic cleansing, 300,000 fled across the borders in the first week; a million more were struggling to escape. It had some of the features of Srebrenica – a sequel to the massacre in Bosnia in 1995 from which the United Nations so disgracefully walked away. The greatest humanitarian catastrophe in Europe in fifty years was matched by brutal war crimes. The response of the Western democracies was to wring their hands, to bomb from a safe altitude, and to pitch their tents in refugee camps beyond the war zones. The British Army left its Parachute Regiment in Aldershot and Dover and mobilized its cooks to Macedonia.

Panic was infectious. A section of the press duly abdicated. The *Sun*, which claimed to stand alone as the only national newspaper totally backing the British forces, took the view that this was none of our business. 'DON'T SEND OUR TROOPS OFF TO DIE', it shrieked. Its idea of patriotism and principle was to support British troops so long as they didn't actually do anything. It is a sound rule of politics that, when the *Sun* leads off on one of its high-decibel campaigns, sensible people take the opposite course. The newspaper's readers certainly did, and voted in a telephone poll by two to one in favour of sending ground troops. Their verdict was buried in the small print.

In speeches and interviews and newspaper columns I argued for a full military intervention, or at least the forced creation of a safe haven inside Kosovo. Air power alone would never achieve the shifting objectives claimed for it. As a serving British general had written to me, 'you cannot change circumstances on the ground without boots on the ground'. I did not wish to damage his career by naming him, but I set out the argument as strongly as I could.

When did unsupported air strikes ever break a people's will or topple its leadership? Not in London or Coventry in the Second World War. Not in Dresden or Hamburg. Not in North Vietnam under American bombardment. And not to this day in Baghdad . . . I have seen the effects of genocide. I know one thing for certain about it. It is a crime that requires accomplices – not only the brutality and hatred that make it happen, but the indifference that lets it happen. The brutality and hatred are being practised by the Serbs. Will the indifference be ours?[2]

I would have cause in time to review that judgement, but not to revise it.

For all I know the words were completely in vain; for in the age of satellite television, it isn't arguments that persuade people, but images: 'no pictures, no news', as Alastair Campbell accused. Those TV pictures cascading into the nation's living rooms – pictures as if from the 1940s, of the mute columns of the dispossessed and the sealed trainloads of misery – brought a clamour for more effective action, including the use of ground troops to turn back the Serbian onslaught. People started to ask: if we would not make a stand to defend the unprotected Albanians of Kosovo, then in what cause would we make it? If not now, when? And if for fear of casualties we were reluctant to use our army, the best in Europe, then what was the point of having it at all? Or if it was an instrument too precious to be used, should we scale it down, like the Irish army, to the status of a moderately armed gendarmerie?

In the House of Commons, I asked the Prime Minister,

How, by the dispatch of more Harriers, can we stop the Albanians of Kosovo being murdered in barns and teachers being lined up on school playing fields and shot in front of their pupils? Surely we shall have to commit ground troops at some time; or, if the political will is not there, let us admit that and hang our heads and walk away in shame.

Mr Blair looked reproachfully at me, as he often did, as if to wonder why I didn't join the oleaginous ranks of MPs behind him in the queue for office also known as the government back benches. He insisted that air power alone would do it. 'I have no doubt that we shall succeed in our objective. We should have total resolve to see it through all the way.'[3]

The crisis cut across party lines completely. The Labour left joined the Tory right in arguing for non-intervention. Even the Labour 'awkward squad' divided – Tam Dalyell and Tony Benn against the bombing, and Ken Livingstone in favour. Harder to understand was the indifference of some back-benchers to the whole debate. I was sitting one evening in my speaking position, on the left flank of the Liberal Democrats, indignant about the way things were going and waiting to suggest to George Robertson the creation of safe havens inside Kosovo. One of the New Labour ladies strode across the floor to reproach me. I knew many of these people, such so-called 'Blair Babes' as Barbara Follett and Helen Southworth, and liked them. But this one was new to me and a real harpy. She accused me of inconsistency, not on the Albanian crisis, but on a couple of votes I had cast the night before on the Employment Relations Bill.

'Maybe I was inconsistent,' I answered pacifically. 'Maybe I was even mistaken. But it's only human to be mistaken sometimes. And if you don't mind, I am obliged to defend my voting record only to my constituents.'

'You must be exposed,' she hissed. 'I shall make it my business to expose you.'

And then she stormed off. I never heard from her again; but the incident summed up for me all that I most dislike about party politics – so much rancour and acrimony in it, and all to so little purpose. Nor did I trouble to find out who the harpy was, since I do not like to think ill of anyone – not even of my self-appointed adversaries. And besides, there was a war going on.

It intensified, with rising civilian casualties inflicted by NATO. In its third week, ten Serbs were killed in a train on a bombed bridge, and seventy-four Albanians died in an attack on a refugee column in Kosovo: their tractors were mistaken for tanks. The British sent a further reinforcement – the Prime Minister's press secretary Alastair Campbell – to shore up the operation of the beleaguered NATO spokesman, Jamie Shea, in Brussels. The campaign of murder and repression continued in Kosovo. And the Western democracies watched from afar, and bombed. In the fifth week, they hit the main TV station in Belgrade, which despite all the lies and distortions that it broadcast, was in no way a military target. Another sixteen Serbs, all civilians, died in the ruins. The raid was the first of the war which could not have been conducted without civilian casualties. It violated not only the Geneva Conventions, but common sense as well: lies are silenced not by missiles but by truths.

The capability of the Yugoslav armed forces was not much, in the NATO parlance, 'degraded'; but the will of the people was. It was the bombing of civilian targets – bridges and power stations – that mattered to them more. So NATO too, by violating the Geneva Conventions, would achieve objectives which it could not have achieved by respecting them.

I protested in the Commons to no avail. NATO seemed to be driven by some mysterious symmetry to match the Serbs' brutality with its own. No one benefited but the military academies at Sandhurst, Bracknell and Shrivenham: they were provided with a text book example of how not to conduct a campaign. (I would review that judgement too, but not revise it.) General Philippe Morillon of France, the former UN commander in Sarajevo and Srebrenica, wondered about the Kosovo enterprise with a veteran's melancholy eloquence: 'What kind of soldiers are these,' he asked, 'who are prepared to kill but not to die?'

An entirely novel doctrine was advanced, that British troops should be used, not to do battle against an opposing force, but only in a permissive or semi-permissive environment. Whatever jargon this was, it ran entirely against our military identity and tradition. Was Agincourt a permissive environment? Was Waterloo? Or more recently Goose Green and Port Stanley? The notion seemed dishonourable, whichever way you looked at it.

Every time that you thought it couldn't get worse, it did – and usually on a Friday, when with metronomic regularity NATO would hand the Serbs a gift-wrapped propaganda advantage. The location of the Chinese Embassy in Belgrade was no secret. It resembled no other building in the city, and every street map showed it. But on Friday 7 May NATO blitzed it, killing three Chinese citizens. This was an error and an outrage. It broke the domestic political consensus that had prevailed till then. It united the Conservative right, the Labour left and even such extreme moderates as the Independent MP for Tatton. In the heat of the crisis the genial Defence Secretary, George Robertson, had taken to calling me 'corporal'.

That was fair enough and undeniable, for I had been a corporal once (which in moments of self-doubt I told myself was more than he had been: we were paying the price for a stratospheric level of military inexperience). But even ex-corporals have a right to ask awkward questions, and I did so: 'Is the Secretary of State aware of the dismay being felt in the country that the world's greatest military alliance now resembles, in certain important respects, the gang that can't shoot straight?'[4] On the very next Friday ninety Albanian refugees were killed in the Kosovan village of Korisa, targeted by NATO as a Serbian military base. The errors were not just embarrassing; they were shameful. I suggested a Friday bombing pause, until the gang could learn to shoot straight. And I added that the likeliest outcome of half a war would not be half a victory, but three quarters of a defeat.

It is always the sign of an enterprise in trouble when those who are conducting it turn their fire on those who are reporting it. So it was with the bombardment of Yugoslavia. The BBC's John

Simpson, the most prominent of the British correspondents filing from Belgrade, was attacked by Downing Street sources, also known as Alastair Campbell, for allegedly giving too much credence to the Serbs' account of events. This was nonsense, of course. Mr Simpson was restricted by the Yugoslav authorities in what he could file and where he could travel; that's a common enough experience for war reporters, and hardly worth the breathless 'health warnings' with which the BBC prefaced all his dispatches. But it was important to have a believable witness in place to report the Serbs' reaction to the bombing, especially when it differed so markedly from the government's expectations. Mr Simpson anyway was an unlikely dissident: on a platform that we once shared at a literary festival he had described himself as an 'establishment creep'. I always felt he had missed his vocation, and would rather have been an ambassador. I trust that Kosovo didn't spoil his chances of a knighthood.

So intense did the war of words become that I felt obliged to fire a salvo on his behalf. John and I had been rivals rather than friends at the BBC, although I had been complicit in his secular canonization on *This Is Your Life*, and my relationship with him was easier than Kate Adie's, which had been a running skirmish across the world from Beijing to Bucharest. I seemed somehow to have offended him by plunging into politics. As soon as I did it he attacked my theories of journalism as nonsense, and reproached me for leaving 'his' world affairs unit at the BBC without so much as a word of good-bye. (What did he expect, I wondered – a farewell party on Knutsford Heath with Neil and Christine Hamilton as guests of honour?) I retaliated, as a free spirit should, by taking to the barricades in his defence. I wrote 800 words of unqualified tribute in *The Times*, under the headline 'Why We Need John Simpson'. And I was sincere about it. Journalism like politics can use a touch of human kindness: it is overrun by the shrill and the ill-intentioned.

After seventy-seven days of bombing and against most predictions, including my own, the Serbs capitulated. They accepted a peace plan, which was also a *démarche*, presented to them in Belgrade by the Russian envoy Viktor Chernomyrdin and the EU representative Martti Ahtisaari. It provided for the withdrawal of all Serb forces from Kosovo, and their replacement by an international force, under UN auspices, including NATO and Russian troops. The chain of command had to be left vague, because it wasn't agreed. The Serbs could have got a better deal at Rambouillet, but had refused to accept it. That is their genius, to pluck defeat from the jaws of victory, or in this case from the jaws of an acceptable settlement. On the same day NATO issued its estimate of Serbian casualties: 5,000 dead and 10,000 wounded among the army and police alone. This was a wild overestimate. The real figures were closer to 600 soldiers and police dead and more than 2,000 civilians. And NATO's battle casualties? Absolutely zero. Not so much as an airman with a broken ankle.

Nothing like this had ever happened before. It was an outcome that contradicted every lesson that soldiers had ever learned, and sought to pass on, about the nature of modern warfare. The warnings had been well founded. Up until the Kosovo techno-blitz and arcade-game war of 1999, a decisive result had never been achieved by the use of air power alone. John Keegan, the foremost military historian of our time, believed that we had been wrong and that the alliance had turned an entirely new page in the conduct of warfare:

After this war – caveats about Milosevic's compliance excepted – there will be no grounds for debate or dispute. Aircraft and pilotless weapons have been the only weapons employed. The outcome is therefore a victory for air power and air power alone. Usually one does not like to confess to error. In this case, I am delighted to recognize that I was, almost until the last moment, wrong and I reproach myself for not having seen the light sooner.[5]

In my view his recantation was premature and unnecessary, since the miracle had not been worked by air power alone. Indeed he should have recanted it. When the Yugoslav army's armoured columns came pouring out of Kosovo they seemed remarkably unscathed and gleaming with menace – more like an army on parade than an army in retreat. In eleven weeks of bombardment and tens of thousands of aircraft sorties, the world's most powerful military alliance had disabled only thirteen tanks. Air power had not crippled its principal target or achieved what its champions claimed for it. The Serbs capitulated when Moscow told them to, when KLA guerrillas were inflicting serious casualties on them, and when the NATO troops assembling on their borders presented a realistic prospect of an invader's boots on the ground. That force would have been led by 50,000 British troops – the entire British army available. There was no cause to rewrite the rule book of warfare. It remained as it always had been. It had only acquired an additional annexe, entitled *the thirteen tanks*.

The liberation of Kosovo, in June 1999, was a triumph of unopposed arms. It turned a province of Yugoslavia into an international protectorate. In a force which included Americans, Germans, French, Italians and finally Russians, the British were pre-eminent in quantity and quality. The men of the Parachute Regiment, finally mobilized, distinguished themselves in Pristina – an environment described by one of them as 'West Belfast in outer space'. The force was led by one of their own, Lieutenant-General Sir Michael Jackson, an unconventional soldier who was regarded with affection as well as respect by those who served under him (not always the case with generals). They called him, although never to his face, the Prince of Darkness. I knew him better than was good for my health, having argued with him into the small hours of the morning in the BBC house at Gornji Vakuf in Bosnia. My friend Major Stankovic wrote of him: 'We adored him but he was dangerous – if you drink with Jackson you die!'[6]

As for Tony Blair, whom I had still never met, but sometimes admired from afar and sometimes criticized, the outcome in Kosovo was to me the finest hour of his term of office so far. This was not so much because of the victory, which was in so many respects tarnished and tainted. It was because he understood that. He did not exult in it. Neither did he stand in the doorway of Number 10 and proclaim 'Rejoice, rejoice!' His non-triumphalist tone was entirely justified. There was a great deal not to rejoice about.

First, this was an operation launched with the stated objective of preventing a humanitarian catastrophe in Kosovo. It did not do that, but either precipitated a catastrophe, or accelerated one already in progress. The unmarked graves in a hundred villages testified to the consequences.

Second, there was an issue of truth and believability. The NATO and British publicity machines were micro-managing the media campaign, as if only the appearance mattered and not the reality. They were responsible for an accounting of the casualties and damage inflicted by the alliance. That accounting was inexact – or, to be accurate about it, downright misleading. It may not have been a deliberate distortion, but rather an effect of the safe and over-the-horizon range from which allied aircraft and warships were operating. This was the Vietnam body count where I began my career, extended into the world of high-tech warfare where I ended it. How could the allies know so surely what they were hitting? And if they didn't know it so surely, why did they report it in their communiqués? Even when the conflict was over the manipulations continued. In the early days of the intervention, when two Gurkhas were blown up by unexploded ordnance, 10 Downing Street tried to convince the BBC's *Nine O'Clock News*, at five minutes to nine, that they were the victims of Serbian land mines rather than NATO cluster bombs. That was an untruth.

And why, as soon as the troops went in, did the Number 10 press office have its own representative in Pristina? There is perhaps a place for spin doctors. A war zone is surely not one of them. Alastair Campbell himself showed up there, but only when it was safe for him to do so, and for what he later described as a 'magical moment'. I could reasonably claim to know the war zones better than he did, and to have found few magical moments in them. So how dare he, in his pugnacious defence of NATO's media strategy, accuse the journalists of cowardice? 'It was also striking how few journalists got into Kosovo itself, and how few even tried . . . The day of the daredevil reporter seems to have died.'[7] The day of the daredevil airman seemed to have died also; and how could a veteran of the wars of Whitehall have any idea of the real thing, and of the courage it takes to cross a border into a landscape of unmarked minefields?

Then there was the moral inequivalence of it. Although the alliance suffered not a single battle casualty, its immunity was bought at a high price. The price was paid by civilians, both in Serbia and Albania, killed and injured on bridges and in refugee columns and wherever the cluster bombs might fall. The number of civilian casualties exceeded the military casualties by a factor of about five to one. The death toll was the greater because the campaign was conducted by NATO bomb and missile crews without much in the way of line of sight, from the relative safety of warships over the horizon or aircraft three miles high. What we were saying in effect was this: British and American lives matter so much more than Serbian and Albanian lives, and are measured on so separate a scale of values, that we don't care how much your people suffer so long as ours remain unscathed. In this respect nothing had changed since 1995. The rationale of the Dutch retreat at Srebrenica had been just the same, and no more honourable: Dutch lives mattered and Bosnian lives did not. It was the doctrine of the permissive environment, and a discreditable way to wage any war, let alone a humanitarian one. It was also against our history, and our sense of the kind of people that we are. If we had always waited for a permissive environment, we should at one time or another have been Napoleon's off-shore dominion, or Hitler's.

Finally, there was the role of the Americans. The Rambouillet proposals were an American ultimatum, and the war that followed was in all important respects an American war. It was planned by General Wesley Clark and his American staff, with two British soldiers in token attendance and no other NATO country allowed a seat at the table. The United States provided 80 per cent of the air power, 100 per cent of the cruise missiles and most of the reluctance to commit to the use of ground troops. It dispatched its Apache helicopters to Albania, but was unwilling to use them, for fear of casualties from shoulder-launched missiles and anti-aircraft fire. ('We look after our own,' declared its President and Commander-in-Chief, rather ominously.) The other eighteen members of the alliance made much of their unity and cohesion during the greatest crisis in its history – but it was the unity and cohesion of subordinates, not of partners. And the British, who had an echo rather than a voice in the enterprise, were the principal lieutenants.

I am not anti-American. I lived and worked in Washington for twelve years, and loved every one of them, from 1978 to 1989. I was the BBC correspondent at Ronald Reagan's White House for both his terms of office. Reagan built his second career, like his first, on being underestimated. Rather unfashionably for a servant of the BBC, I admired not only his communication skills but also his diplomacy (or that of the staff around him, especially James Baker). Against all the received opinions, it won the cold war.

But from my own perspective, I would rate the United States as the most foreign country of the eighty-one in which I have worked. Since the cold war ended, and especially from the mid-1990s onward, the Americans have seemed to me to be less a guarantee of our security than a potential threat to it. Their interests are not our interests – and neither are their principles our principles. If there is a lesson to be drawn from the Kosovo crisis, it is the need for a considered and concerted European defence policy as a counterweight to the Americans' tendency to blunder around the planet as if they own it. I call it the SSS – the Single Superpower Syndrome. It is not an evil empire or ill-intentioned, but reflects a mismatch between strength and understanding.

Quite by chance, and at exactly this time, a constituent sent me a perfect parable about the SSS. It comes from the sea, and may be apocryphal, although it resounds with a ring of truth. It is the transcript of an exchange of radio messages between the Americans and Canadians in the North Atlantic in October 1995.

AMERICANS: Please divert your course 15 degrees to the North to avoid a collision.

CANADIANS: Recommend you divert *your* course 15 degrees to the South to avoid a collision.

AMERICANS: This is the captain of a US Navy ship. I say again divert your course.

CANADIANS: No. I say again, you divert *your* course.

AMERICANS: *This is the aircraft carrier USS* Lincoln, *the second largest ship in the United States' Atlantic Fleet. We are accompanied by three destroyers, three cruisers and numerous support vessels. I demand that you change your course 15 degrees North, that's one five degrees North, or counter-measures will be undertaken to ensure the safety of this ship.*

CANADIANS: This is a lighthouse. Your call.

12. Happenings

Every morning, Mary Price assembled the incoming mountain of mail and divided it into four foothills: letters from constituents, invitations, letters from non-constituents who knew me (she called this the 'chatty' pile), and a larger stack of letters from other correspondents around the country and sometimes abroad (she called this the 'save the world' pile). These last were the hardest to deal with. They tended to be written in green ink liberally under-lined, or on manual typewriters with faded ribbons, and to say things like, 'I am the victim of a conspiracy, my own MP is part of the conspiracy, and you alone can help me.' I couldn't, unfortu-nately; and even if I could or had the time for it, the House of Commons rules were very strict about not trespassing into another MP's domain. But the letters made melancholy reading. Not all were from fantasists, and I did not doubt that there were genuine cases of injustice out there awaiting redress. With rare exceptions, the rules of the House allowed me to take up only those of my own constituents; and those who thought themselves the victims of conspiracies tended to live outside the plain of Cheshire. Except for Neil Hamilton, perhaps.

The green ink mail was not consistent: it ebbed and flowed. The new Parliament was well into its second year before we realized that there was a pattern to its irregularity. It rose inexorably like the tide once a month, not at random but *at the time of the full moon*. So it was definitely under a full moon that I was handed a letter by the parish clerk in my home village. The letter was postmarked somewhere in the home counties and addressed to 'All villagers, c/o the Village Hall, Great Budworth'. It urged them to disown and overthrow me. 'I've proved beyond all doubt whatsoever,' wrote this anonymous correspondent, 'that the BBC operated a secret overseas extermination policy in Bosnia, and that Martin Bell was a ringleader in its implementation . . . the camel incident did take place.' I was intrigued. What extermination policy, I wondered, and what camel incident? The last camel I met was on manoeuvres with the Queen's Royal Irish Hussars in the Saudi Arabian desert just before the Gulf War, and so far as I could remember I had treated the animal with the respect that was its due. So had the regiment's commander, Lieutenant-Colonel Arthur Denaro. The letter had the outline of a camel crudely drawn on it. That is the charm of green ink mail: it opens windows on new and unimagined horizons, and has a logic all of its own.

It was also at the time of a full moon, in April 1999, that I was taking the train to Macclesfield for a day of constituency events. Just short of Stoke-on-Trent, the mobile phone rang. It wasn't any of the usual callers: constituents, colleagues or radio stations. It was the Cheshire police, with news of a death threat.

'Who's it against?' I wondered nonchalantly.

'I'm sorry to have to tell you,' said the inspector, 'it's against you.'

Someone with a northern accent, and who knew my schedule that day, had telephoned a London news agency to announce that if I went ahead with my planned visit to a show home in Wilmslow, I would be shot. Since Jill Dando had been assassinated on her doorstep only ten days earlier, and she was someone with no known enemies, the police were taking it more seriously than they would otherwise have done. My own opinion was that professional killers didn't call news agencies to announce their intentions in advance. But the police were the experts: if they took a serious view of it, so would I.

I looked down and noticed my hands were shaking, and reproached myself for cowardice. Bosnia hadn't prepared me for this, or maybe I had run out of the courage to deal with it; and I know from experience that courage is a limited resource. One moment you have enough and to spare, and the next you are running on empty. There is also a world of difference between standing in someone else's line of fire, and being personally targeted. A soldier's bullet is somehow less threatening than an assassin's. Colonel Denaro had taught me a lesson about fear, that it helps to keep you alive, while panic can be what kills you.

I was met at Macclesfield station by a detective sergeant, who checked my car for explosives, and shadowed me on an errand to buy a bottle of milk at the village shop in Great Budworth. I didn't know if he was armed, and it seemed discourteous to ask. The only protection that I saw was his two-way radio, which no doubt he could have thrown at an attacker in an emergency. But the entire armed response unit of the Cheshire Police, an extremely professional looking outfit, were waiting in the yard of Wilmslow police station. So was the Divisional Superintendent, Derek Barnett. The conversation repeated itself. 'This is very impressive, Derek, but what on earth's it all about?'

'It's about you.'

The police were in plain clothes. Some of them were checking and aligning their automatic weapons; others were doing a recce of the housing estate. They reported back that the show home I was to open was in the line of fire of more than sixty potential sniper positions. I was advised to cancel, which I did reluctantly and rather indignantly. Outside Ireland and the Irish connection, we have no settled tradition of political assassination in these islands. But it occurred to me to wonder whether, under the media pressures of the age, every threat of violence spawns imitations, and we are becoming a nutters' and hoaxers' paradise. I went into hiding for the rest of the day, but emerged in the morning, with the undaunted Fiona, for Knutsford's Royal May Day: marching bands, costumed children, horses and hornpipes – everything in its place as it had been for more than a hundred years. There are things that an MP can get away with, but being a fugitive in his own constituency is not one of them. Nothing untoward happened, except that people asked after my health with special vigilance, as if to check for bullet holes. They didn't say 'How are you?', they said 'Glad to see you alive.' They made it clear that they didn't want a by-election. I was with them there. I didn't want a by-election either. I would have found it extremely inconvenient and tiresome to have been extinguished just then. The Parliament was at its half-way point, and there was plenty left to do.

One of the most compelling causes was the campaign for a government gratuity to former Far East prisoners of war. More than 7,000 of these old soldiers are still alive, out of the 50,000 taken prisoner at the fall of Singapore. A quarter of those captured suffered every ordeal from neglect to execution, and did not survive their brutal treatment at the hands of the Japanese. I had a military interest in the matter, since the 4th and 5th battalions of my old regiment, the Suffolk Regiment, were lost there as part of the 18th East Anglian Division, the last East Anglian Division that went to war. The 4th, 5th and 6th battalions of the Royal Norfolk Regiment, and the 1st and 2nd battalions of the Cambridgeshire Regiment had also been taken prisoner. The churchyards of East Anglia record their sacrifices. I was by no means a distinguished soldier in my later term of service, but I was the only MP in this Parliament who had worn the uniform of any of those regiments. And I had a family interest, since my father's first book *Corduroy*, a lyrical story of his apprenticeship on a Suffolk farm, was packed in many soldiers' kitbags and was a source of solace to them. One of them wrote to me that he had learned it almost by heart in Changi jail: 'Nightly, his writings transported me in memory from a bug-ridden prison cell to the cool English countryside.' And a military psychiatrist added, 'My abiding memory of these men is the quiet dignity shown by all of them and their reluctance to make any demands on the country they had served so well.'

We could make the demands for them that they would not make for themselves. I initiated a Commons debate that attracted wide all-party support. Within a month the government changed its position. The Prime Minister himself became involved. It was on his initiative that in November 2000 the government announced the award of £10,000 to each of the former POWs, the youngest of whom were then in their late seventies. British heroes every one of them. We owed them more than we knew or could repay. Their widows and the civilian internees were also compensated.

The recognition mattered more than the money. One of the old soldiers, whose earlier letters had been bitter and angry, remarked, 'Now I can meet my Maker with a great big smile on my face.' Another wrote, 'We have waited 50 years for this. You made it happen.' There were other letters to the same effect. They made me feel that my excursion into politics, however bizarre, at least had something to show for it.

Other campaigns offered slimmer prospects. One offered none at all. That was the campaign for shorter speeches in Parliament. I was not alone. I was joined by John M. Taylor, the quietly spoken former minister and Conservative MP for Solihull. He was the only man I ever heard who stood at the dispatch box and summed up a debate in one minute – and it wasn't a minor debate either, but the concluding argument on the settlement in Northern Ireland. For that achievement alone he deserved a knighthood. One day in July 1999 we sat and suffered through four hours of wind-driven rhetoric in a debate on manpower in the army – an important issue at an important time, because of the recent deployment in Kosovo. Then, just as despair set in, we caught the Deputy Speaker's eye, one after the other. John weighed in for four minutes on behalf of the Army Cadet Force. I followed with a three-minute attack on the Ministry of Defence Police. I had promised the shortest speech of the evening, and he had doubted if I could do it. 'We must persist,' I said. 'Indeed we must,' he encouraged me. 'We have to believe that success lies just over the horizon.'

It didn't, of course, and I doubt if it ever will. I blame Gladstone, whose two-and-a-half-hour orations are part of the history of the House in which we sit. Something of them must be ingrained in the stonework: even today's MPs are too often blind to the sight of each other's eyes glazing over. Some of the worst offenders, as it happens, are from the descendants of Gladstone's party, the Liberal Democrats – Mike Hancock on defence and Robert Maclennan on the constitution. Both are good people and accomplished parliamentarians, and I shall yield to no one in my admiration of them. But Hancock's half hours seem longer than that. And when at night I cannot sleep, instead of counting sheep I try to remember a Maclennan speech on Scottish devolution. The eyelids drift together immediately.

There is hope for our politics if we listen to the young; for the children will not just keep us awake but keep us humble. I learned this lesson when I was asked to present an award to Alderley Edge County Primary School, one of the best in Cheshire. The head teacher introduced me to her 200 pupils. 'Do you know who he is?' she asked. 'He's Tony Blair,' replied Abigail, aged about six, with great conviction. With this misunderstanding cleared up, the head teacher asked another question, 'And do you know what he does?' The hand of Molly, Abigail's classmate, shot up. 'I think he does a magic show,' she said. Oh, if only I did! There is so much more magic in our primary schools than there is in the Houses of Parliament.

That goes for the pre-schools equally. One day in Knutsford I sat down with paintbrush in hand, at the request of the Pre-School Alliance, to publicize the excellent work they do. I was in the company of some extremely gifted young artists, and trying to depict a scene from my father's Suffolk farm, so long ago that all of the loading and stacking were done by hand. I painted a passable wagon laden with sheaves, and an acceptably graphic stick figure of myself as a boy on top of it. The shafts weren't too bad either, as shafts go. But I failed with the horse. 'That's not a horse,' chanted the four-year-olds in unison, 'that's a dinosaur!' I had just turned sixty, and to the kids of Knutsford I was not only old – I was positively *Jurassic*.

Two MPs who published their diaries, Alan Clark and Gyles Brandreth, appeared to regard their constituencies and constituents in Plymouth and Chester with a conspicuous lack of affection. I found that strange, and was sure that Tatton would have struck them differently. I had an especially soft spot for Alan Clark, an original historian and gifted orator. His passing was not only a loss to the House. It deprived me of a rough guide to how to vote in an emergency: if in doubt, I could wait to see which lobby he entered, and go the other way. He found out about this, and gently reproached me for inconsistency when we voted together on a bill to ban fur farming. I pleaded guilty.

One of the things he was wrong about was constituency politics. An MP's best moments, except for a few great legislators, will almost always be outside the House of Commons rather than in it. So it was when I made my one and only flowery speech: three minutes in praise of roses. It was at the opening of the National Rose Show, part of a grand northern venture by the Royal Horticultural Society at Tatton Park – the Chelsea Flower Show transplanted to more pastoral and spacious surroundings. I was presented with a rose created for the occasion, a burnt orange floribunda named after the park; following the commotion of the not-so-distant past I liked the idea of a rose called Tatton, and the place being identified with the queen of flowers rather than with the corruption of politics.

The Rose Show opened on the day of the by-election in the neighbouring constituency of Eddisbury. It was a contentious and acrimonious campaign in which the Conservatives fought off a strong Labour challenge to hold the seat by 1,600 votes. Seventy Labour MPs were thrown into the front line on a single day – the political equivalent of the Battle of the Somme, except that they lived to fight another day. And so, I wondered, why not a rose called Eddisbury? Because gardening is about what unites us and politics is about what divides us. That surely is what's wrong with politics, especially in an age when there seem to be greater differences within the parties than between them. There has to be a better and less gladiatorial way of practising it.

I thought for a moment that I had found it in the week after the Eddisbury vote. I was walking into the House of Commons through the main St Stephen's entrance, when I espied a phalanx of forty Conservative MPs lined up on either side of it, like guards of honour at a wedding. All that they lacked was uniforms and ceremonial swords. 'How good of you to turn out for me like this,' I said, 'I really didn't know that you cared.' A great, if ironic cheer resounded, and they urged me to join their parade. It was only then, going into the building, that I met William Hague and the Tory winner at Eddisbury, Stephen O'Brien MP, coming out, and I realized why the troops were there, as the back-drop to a photo opportunity. A second and not much larger cheer went up. So I knew what it felt like to win a by-election, without the inconvenience of having to fight one.

One of Tony Blair's great strengths as Prime Minister was that, from time to time, he understood the futility of the parties' trench warfare, and dared to praise an opponent or even to co-opt one. To keep Lord Carrington's experience and wisdom available to the House of Lords, when the sitting rights of most hereditary peers were ended, he topped up the lifelong Tory's hereditary peerage with a life peerage. Carrington shook with laughter. 'I'm one of Tony's cronies now!' he chortled. And Mr Blair was exceptionally gracious to Paddy Ashdown, in the same week as the Rose Show and the Eddisbury by-election, on the Liberal Democrat leader's last appearance at Prime Minister's Question Time. 'Can I at least pay tribute to the tremendous contribution he has made to British politics? On Kosovo he was well ahead of us and right long before us.'[1] For the rest of the session Mr Blair returned to the ritual polemic of the party battle; but he had for a moment stepped out of it into untrodden territory; and there is surely a great future, even a rosy one, for such a politics of generosity. A politician who will say to another, 'You were right and I was wrong,' deserves to reap a harvest of votes for his honesty.

Constitutionally MPs have no business to be partisan. They represent those who didn't vote for them every bit as much as those who did – perhaps especially those who didn't, for these are the people needing extra reassurance that they still have an MP working for them. (The classic case is the Reverend Ian Paisley's assiduous service to the minority voters in his North Antrim constituency – and I couldn't help wondering whether the old teetotaller extended this to its distillery at Bushmills, the home of Protestant whiskey.) It was in the cause of bending over backwards that, when the election was over, I announced a willingness to speak to Tatton's Conservatives at any time. I dealt with them individually on a daily basis and I never answered Neil Hamilton's attacks on me. Indeed I even drew attention to them. A friend in Wilmslow surfing the internet came upon an obscure American interview with Mr Hamilton in which he described me as a complete irrelevance, a useful idiot and a political babe in arms. For some reason peculiar to the politics of Tatton I thought that this deserved a wider hearing. In more than two years in Parliament I had issued only one press release, to publicize a protest march for a bypass in Alderley Edge (it only half worked: we got the publicity, but not the bypass). But I fed this stuff to the local papers, as a sort of reverse press release, and the *Knutsford Express Advertiser* duly headlined 'Hamilton Attacks On Internet: MP Bell Branded As Idiot'. With an enemy like Neil, I hardly needed the many friends that I had. He could never get his head around the idea of politics without rancour.

One of his former supporters bore down on me one day in Princess Street in Knutsford. She was definitely of the blue rinse brigade and the Cheshire set, from whom many of Mr Hamilton's most devoted loyalists were drawn. She could not have been more charming. 'You know,' she said, 'I'm sorry to have to tell you that I voted for Neil, but I'm so glad you won!' And the odd thing was that because I value loyalty I knew just what she meant.

MPs don't represent parties, they represent people. From time to time and in special circumstances – a dreadful crime in the constituency, perhaps, a serious accident or the death of an admired public figure – they will be expected to have something appropriate and non-partisan to say, and to speak for the whole community. On such occasions a party label is actually a handicap, and I was lucky not to have one. The challenge in my case came from an unlikely quarter. The departing curate of Wilmslow, the Reverend David Leaver, who had been filling in during the long interregnum between one vicar and another, used his last parish newsletter to deliver a resounding jeremiad. He denounced the townspeople – especially those of his own generation, the thirty- and forty-somethings – for materialism verging on paganism. He wrote, 'I have never before met people who are quite so obsessed with money.'

It happened at a quiet time for news and touched off such a journalists' feeding frenzy as only ever occurs in the silly season. Reporters and camera crews descended in droves and roamed the streets in search of the pagans of Wilmslow. They stopped at the usual ports of call: St Bartholomew's Church, the *Wilmslow Express Advertiser*, the Ferrari showroom, the Porsche showroom, the Mercedes showroom and the shops and watering-holes of the Cheshire set. Wilmslow's misfortune was that it lent itself too easily to caricature. By the time the visitors had done their stuff, with purple prose and immoderate headlines about the town 'too posh to pray', I felt like the Member of Parliament for Sodom and Gomorrah.

So I went to work, and in interviews and articles I defended my constituents, many of whom were churchgoing people deeply offended by the fabrications about them. I thanked the curate for shaking us up and making us think, and pointed out that this was in part the historic role of the clergy: prophets prophesy regardless of focus groups and public opinion polls. Just as the people of Israel had Jeremiah, so the people of Wilmslow had the curate. But there was another side to it.

Just for the record, Wilmslow has many more poor people than rich people. It also has many generous people. I present their cheques to so many good causes – whether from the George and Dragon for the Kosovo appeal, from the Rotarians for Hope and Homes for Children, or from Ruby's Indian Takeaway for flood victims in Bangladesh. They are as kind a people as any I have met . . . Just because Wilmslow has a Ferrari showroom – and a very good one, if I may say so – that doesn't necessarily mean it's a vortex of godlessness. After all, in a strictly theological sense God creates Ferraris too – or at least the world in which Ferraris are possible.[2]

I wrote that last bit carefully, and hoped that I got it right. For there was nothing that touched off an avalanche of mail more quickly – not all of it green ink mail – than an ill-considered reference to religion. Of all the issues that came before this Parliament there were two that prompted more letters than any other, both in volume and in passionate commitment. One, to no one's surprise, was fox hunting. The other, by no means so obvious, was the right of churchwardens not to be suspended by a bishop. It generated hundreds of letters from all over the country, especially from Norfolk.

I was asked by Madam Speaker, whose request for me had the force of a command, to serve with fourteen other MPs on the Ecclesiastical Committee, together with an equal number of peers. This committee, which is as close to the establishment as I shall ever penetrate, inspects measures submitted to it by the General Synod of the Church of England, and is expected reflexively to approve them – or, as tradition has it, to declare them 'expedient' – on their stately passage through Parliament. But the Churchwardens Measure, with which we tangled for more than two years, was as undemocratic as could possibly have been imagined. It was couched in the language of absolute power. It gave bishops the authority for any reason that seemed to them sufficient to suspend a church-warden for up to two years. We therefore thought it inexpedient, and twice threw it back at the Synod. It felt good to do so, for that is the historic function of MPs – to defend the liberties of the people, including churchwardens. If we fail in that, our minimal duty, we are truly a waste of space; but if we stand for freedom, especially in these days of robotic politics, we shall have achieved something in line with the best traditions of the House of Commons. Sometimes things don't go, after all, from bad to worse.

It was while the House of Commons was debating another of the measures laid before it by the Ecclesiastical Committee that I underwent one of the strangest moments of the entire parliamentary episode – not exactly a religious conversion, but an out-of-body experience. I was sitting in a quiet corner within range of the annunciator – the green television screen which shows at all times when the House is sitting what the business is, who is speaking, and for how long he or she has been going on (almost always too long, in John M. Taylor's view, and mine). A change of speaker was announced by a muffled chime. The chime sounded, and I glanced up to see whose name was up in lights. It was my own. There was no doubt about it. Mr M. Bell of Tatton had the floor. I wondered how I was doing, what eloquent points I might be making about the Cathedrals Measure and with what rapt attention other MPs might be listening – or more likely not. Two minutes later the chime sounded again, and the annunciator corrected its mistake. The speaker was Mr S. Bell of Middlesbrough. Until the people of Tatton spoiled it for him, he used to take pride in being the only Bell at Westminster besides Big Ben.

Thus in the space of six months I had been declared to be not present in the chamber when I had been present, in the debate on the bombing of Iraq. And I had been declared to be speaking when I had not been speaking, in the debate on the Cathedrals Measure.

In my former life as a war reporter, the first question I asked myself on waking up was always 'Where am I?' (If this is Tuesday it must be Fernando Po, and if it's Friday it must be Nicaragua.) In my new life, the question was '*Who am I?*' Or even, more metaphysically, '*Do I exist at all, or is this a dream?*' The House of Commons is so strange a place that if it wasn't there it could never have been invented. That is not to disparage it. It is venerable, yes. But deeply improbable too.

13. New Labour, New Sleaze?

I never liked the 'S' word and seldom used it, even in the heat of battle in the Tatton campaign. Sleaze was a powerful and emotive issue, which had swung more votes in the 1997 election than any other; but by the time the headline writers had played their word games with it, it was a portmanteau term covering everything from minor sexual peccadilloes to the use of public office for private gain. According to the opinion polls, people were rather more forgiving about the first than they used to be, and very much less forgiving about the second. This was the engine that had propelled me into Parliament, and was fuelled by a widespread and genuine public anger. It was best described by one of my most eminent constituents, the chrysanthemum grower Reg Lawrence of Over Peover, as the politics of the pig trough. The voters of Tatton had given me a mandate on it, and would not expect my sword to sleep in my hand. Those grand-sounding phrases on election night would return to haunt me if I let the issue lie, although I could and did argue that something substantial had already been achieved. The constituency's reputation had changed overnight, and the spirit of Tatton was entering the phrase book as a political force for good. There was even a boat named after it, and a flower.

It occurred to me that, from the point of view of reputation, plunging from journalism into politics was not the smartest of moves. I had exchanged a job that stood low in public esteem for another that stood even lower. Sir Gordon Downey, the Parliamentary Commissioner for Standards, quoted an opinion poll on professional trustworthiness conducted before the new rules came into force – the rules that had tripped up Neil Hamilton, among others. Doctors and teachers came top with 84 per cent. Politicians and government ministers came bottom with 14 per cent and 11 per cent respectively.

Journalists were the only others with a score of less than 30 per cent.

Perhaps we should have learned from the South African example. The most respected political leader of the age, Nelson Mandela, served his prison sentence before taking office. The tendency with British politicians, if ever the law caught up with them, was to do it the other way round.

Confidence was so far eroded that there were those who saw MPs not only as untrustworthy, but as hardly having a proper job at all. One day I was at a petrol station near Knutsford when a motor cyclist from outside the constituency accosted me.

'Don't I know you?' he asked. 'You're that TV reporter.'

'I used to be,' I replied. 'I'm an MP now.'

'Oh,' he said, rather disappointed. 'You're out of a job. I'm very sorry to hear that.'

He wasn't being ironic. He really believed it. And he had a point: from the end of July until the middle of October, Members of Parliament were absent with leave, and the government had no one to hold it to account as the House of Commons chamber gathered dust. The House didn't sit for more days than it did.

Clearly there was a mighty mountain to climb in changing the perception of MPs as pariahs and parasites. But how to begin to set about it as a politician with no party, no leverage, no knowledge of how the system worked and no right to a place on any of the House's committees? It was true that the Labour Party had stood down their candidate for me in the General Election; but now they were in government they owed me no favours, and seemed even to resent a lone Independent as a challenge and reproach to their controlling tendency. After an intervention that he disapproved of, John Prescott glared at me across the floor and muttered, 'You're only here because of us.' (I thought that a touch ungracious from the man who had swung the crucial meeting of the Tatton Labour Party in April 1997: would he really rather have had Neil Hamilton? Maybe he would, because the new government could have exploited such a living symbol of the old one's disrepute.) As far as Labour were concerned I had served my purpose; would I please now sit quietly for four years, toe the line obediently and then vanish? I had met that attitude once before, in my first and most ferocious sergeant-major.

Help came from an unexpected quarter. One morning in the second session of the new Parliament, I was minding my own business in the House of Commons Tea Room when I was approached by the gangling figure of the Conservatives' chief whip, James Arbuthnot: Ann Widdecombe had just resigned from her seat on the Standards and Privileges Committee, and would I be interested in taking her place? I went away to think about it, and the more I thought about it the more I liked it. The committee's function is to enforce the rules governing the conduct of MPs, to deal rigorously with conflicts of interest, and to restore public confidence in the House. The committee's consideration of the Hamilton case, in which I could not have participated, was over. The Conservatives' offer to give up one of their seats to an Independent, with the explicit assurance of no strings attached and no pressure applied, came from their leader William Hague. I welcomed it as a sign of their determination to keep the committee, unlike its predecessor, completely non-partisan and free from the suspicion of interference by the whips. So I accepted.

Except on rare occasions, such as Neil Hamilton's high voltage statement to the committee before I joined it, its proceedings are hidden from public view. They have to be. It could not function otherwise, for public hearings might encourage grandstanding, and would certainly make it harder for the eleven members to leave their party allegiances at the door. Nothing enters the public domain about the committee's deliberations except its reports and their annexes, the reports submitted to it by the Parliamentary Commissioner, and transcripts of the evidence of those who come before it – usually MPs accused of breaking the rules. I trust that I shall not be breaking the rule of confidentiality in stating that the committee's proceedings – in their dignity, fairness and diligence – left me with a far greater respect for the House of Commons than the sometimes dismaying scenes in the chamber itself. One was for most of the time what Parliament should be, serious and purposeful. The other – not always but too often – was a long way from my idea and ideal of democracy in action.

The committee's prestige derived from its non-partisan status, from the weight of its judgements and from the authority of its chairman in the 1997 Parliament, Robert Sheldon. Mr Sheldon, the MP for Ashton-under-Lyne, was a wise owl, a former Treasury Minister who first entered Parliament in 1964. He enjoyed an early reputation as a free spirit and firebrand and had not been afraid to challenge a Labour Chancellor (but that was in 1967, before the rise of the obsequious back-bencher). He also presided – and I hope he won't mind me saying this – over the parliamentary equivalent of the last-chance saloon. If the present system failed, Parliament would have finally and decisively been proven incapable of policing itself. Public trust would be eroded even further. That laid a heavy burden on us. New rules had been drawn up, and a new office had been created – that of Parliamentary Commissioner for Standards – because of the failure of previous Parliaments to discipline erring MPs. The House in those days was seen as a gentleman's club, in which a Member's word was his bond. Maybe there once was such a place, a legislative Nirvana and parliamentary equivalent of Blandings Castle, although I rather tend to doubt it. I prefer the wisdom of my Chesterton, that 'the class of English gentleman has in its time been as corrupt as any upon earth'.

Nothing was more dismaying to Mr Sheldon – and again there was no secret about this, for he expressed it on the floor of the House – than suggestions in the press that his committee was Labour dominated, which is code for Labour controlled. Its actual composition was seven Labour MPs, two Conservatives, one Liberal Democrat and one Independent. This left the Independents rather heavily over-represented at the expense of the Nationalists; but otherwise it reflected democratically, as do all the select committees, the relative strength of the parties in the House of Commons. And as Mr Sheldon correctly stated, 'It did not divide on party lines.'[1] This is not to say it worked in perfect harmony. All committees have their tensions and disagreements, and it would be surprising if this were not the case with Standards and Privileges.

Consensus requires compromise. I felt that I could do more good inside the committee's tent than outside it. But I also believe that its composition should be reformed. First, it should contain no new Members. (In this I am arguing against myself, for I was one of four new MPs on it.) Second, it should contain no Parliamentary Private Secretaries. A PPS is a diminutive cog in the machinery of government, but part of it none the less and should be excluded from the committee's deliberations.

The previous Parliament had passed into history, unlamented and having outlived its mandate and its welcome, under a cloud of public opprobrium. The minority of its Members who had brought it so low – a small minority, but not a negligible one – had all been Conservatives, and without exception had either resigned or been defeated in the General Election. Nineteen ninety-seven was not a good year for spivs. I sometimes wondered, had the voters of Tatton decided otherwise, how William Hague would have dealt with having Neil Hamilton MP among his back-benchers. The Conservative leader never thanked me for it, but I think that the people of Tatton did him a favour.

The new Parliament was to a significant extent composed of a different group of politicians. Nearly 40 per cent of its Members were newcomers to the House, and a few were 'retreads' returning after a democratically enforced leave of absence. Many had expected to lose, and some may even have preferred to. There were winners on that election night at least as shocked as the losers; and there were others, such as the unwhippable Bob Marshall-Andrews of Medway, whom Labour would not have selected for the seat in the first place if they had thought he had the outside edge of a sporting chance of winning it. They were the kind of people more likely to register their outside interests, and not to have any interests at all in the grey and perilous area of political consultancies. They were not the kind to go into politics for what they might get out of it. Sir Gordon Downey, the outgoing Commissioner for Standards, noted this change of the landscape in his final report: 'The number of commitments involving the provision of parliamentary services has fallen by some two thirds since the time when the new rules came into force.' He also commented on the committee's conclusion on the Hamilton case, which was rather less decisive than his own: 'My own view is that the Committee under-estimated their capacity to reach a judgement on the evidence provided . . . The seeds of doubt were, of course, sown by Mr Hamilton's unchallenged and very public statement which produced no new evidence and was grotesquely misleading.'[2]

Because the 'Tatton effect' was a new phenomenon and much debated, I was invited to attend one of those country house conferences of the great and the good which occur from time to time. Its theme was the decline of public trust in politics and possible ways of reversing it. Its participants were parliamentarians and academics from both sides of the Atlantic. Since I was the MP most newly elected, and cast as the political Alice in their Wonderland, I put forward the heretical view that the best way for politicians to be trusted more was to behave better. There was a sharp in-drawing of breath around the table. An American congressman recently in trouble with the state police and his local press looked at me in astonishment. 'I can tell you one thing for sure,' he said, 'they'll nickel and dime you to death.'

The preponderance of Labour MPs in the House, more than 60 per cent of the total, made it statistically inevitable that they would come under more scrutiny and criticism in this Parliament than the last. So indeed it happened, to a variety of Members on a variety of issues – whether Ernie Ross for leaking a select committee report to his friends in the Foreign Office, Bob Wareing for failing to register a Serbian business interest, or Ron Davies for taking a walk on the wild side of Clapham Common. And whenever it happened, I would receive calls from the press, or letters from indignant citizens, saying, 'There, you see, this lot is at least as bad as the last lot; since you campaigned against Tory sleaze, why are you not denouncing Labour sleaze with equal vigour?' My answer was threefold: first, that Mr Davies's recreations were none of my business; second, that I had continued to criticize so-called 'sleaze' even-handedly, and could quote the chapter and verse of where I had done so, usually in my monthly newspaper columns; and third, that there was in this Parliament, as far as I could see, no established pattern of politicians abusing public office to enrich themselves. There was no cash for questions. No used bank notes in brown envelopes. No parliamentary palm being greased for favours. That was an important and substantial difference. What there was instead on the Labour side from time to time was an extraordinary lack of common sense, an arrogance and a sublime indifference to the appearances of things, all the more remarkable in a party that had exalted the art of the spin doctor, and set such store by massaging the headlines.

Two cases stood out, which could not be 'spun' in any convincing way. One was that of Geoffrey Robinson, MP for Coventry North-West, Paymaster General and Labour millionaire who apparently held more directorships than he remembered. He was twice rebuked by the committee for failing to include them in the Register of Members' Interests. And on the second occasion his public apology was so brief, at fifty-four seconds, and so lacking in contrition as to amount in the opinion of many to a contempt of the House. His difficulties deepened when his company, TransTec, went into receivership amid allegations of fraud. These difficulties cast their shadows backward, on the judgement of leading Labour politicians – Tony Blair and Gordon Brown among them – who had benefited from his generosity. The Book of Exodus – 'thou shalt take no gift' – had something to say on the matter.

The other case was that of Peter Mandelson, MP for Hartlepool, Secretary for Trade and Industry and the government's in-house Machiavelli. Just before Christmas 1998 it emerged that he had financed the purchase of his house in Notting Hill with a £373,000 loan from his friend, Geoffrey Robinson. This he topped up with a £150,000 loan from the Britannia Building Society, without declaring to the Britannia his existing mortgage on his home in Hartlepool. There was a further complication: the department that he headed was investigating some of Mr Robinson's business affairs. There was no suggestion in any of this of corruption or the abuse of power –

but a lack of understanding, a remoteness from the lives of ordinary people, and a breathtaking carelessness in not seeing that an apparent conflict of interest can do almost as much damage as a real one. That wasn't sleaze but myopia. After twenty-four hours of trying to ride out the storm, Mr Mandelson resigned as Secretary of State, at least for a while. Mr Robinson also returned to the back benches.

Complaints about the case were inevitably referred to the Parliamentary Commissioner for Standards. By this time Sir Gordon Downey had retired and been succeeded by Elizabeth Filkin – a very different character, less sphinx-like in demeanour but in her own way just as formidable. She was formerly Adjudicator of the Inland Revenue and (quite by chance, in the Mandelson connection) a non-executive director of the Britannia Building Society. It was said that the first question asked about any proposal to come before the Britannia board was, 'Will this pass the Elizabeth Filkin test?'

Mr Mandelson did not pass the Elizabeth Filkin test. He failed it spectacularly, and there were even those who felt she could have been harsher than she was. She upheld some of the complaints against him and concluded that in his incomplete mortgage application he had breached the code of conduct for Members of Parliament which requires them to be as open as possible about their decisions and actions.[3] Mr Mandelson protested vigorously. 'I think with a new Commissioner coming in, as she is fully entitled to do . . . making an interpretation of the code which is tougher and harder than the previous interpretation . . . is not fair on me.'[4]

I asked him if he felt that his mortgage was the committee's legitimate business. He answered, 'You could make a technical case in terms of the Code, as the Commissioner has, that a Member of Parliament has to be as open as possible in the conduct of their affairs. I do think it is stretching it a bit in relation to the filling out of a mortgage application form.'[5] Until that day I had not encountered Peter Mandelson except in the corridor or voting lobby. I was struck by a commanding and brooding intelligence; and relieved that, as a one-term MP without a party, I would never be beholden to him for political advancement. His evidence to the committee, which ran to twenty-two pages and was entirely in the public domain, repaid the most careful study. It illuminated my new-found occupation better than anything else that I came across. And this was the lesson I drew from it: that politics as a profession was worth trying for a while – but as a way of life it was missing something, like sunlight without shadow or a coastline without a hinterland. Give me the war zones any time. The obsessions there were rooted in realities.

The committee was less censorious than the commissioner, and its report reflected its uncertainty. Did the new code of conduct, devised by Lord Nolan and including rules of honesty and openness, apply only to MPs' actions in their public life, or did it apply to *everything* they did, including taking loans from friends and filling in building society application forms? Did it matter that Mr Mandelson's Britannia form 'might not have been perfect in every last dot and comma – and whose is'?[6] Should MPs, because of the trust reposed in them, be held to a higher standard of behaviour than anyone else? I believed that they should be, although the case could honourably be argued either way, the libertarians on one side and the puritans on the other. And it was a testament to the change Lord Nolan had wrought, that MPs in this Parliament were wondering whether the rules had been drawn too strictly, whereas for most of the previous Parliament such rules as there were had not been drawn strictly enough to provide a defence against the politics of the pig trough.

Mr Mandelson's second fall from grace was as illustrative of the problem as his first. In 1998, while still the Prime Minister's right-hand man at 10 Downing Street, he had made a call to the Immigration Minister, Mike O'Brien, on behalf of a wealthy Indian businessman, Srichand Hinduja. Mr Hinduja was not a constituent: but he had offered to donate £1 million to the Faith Zone of the Millennium Dome. He sought a British passport and obtained it in six months – against the twenty months it would have taken an Indian without his special connections, and who even then could have been refused.

Here again, as in the Bernie Ecclestone affair, was a prima facie case of cash for access. The rich and well-connected had special privileges. The Prime Minister and his spokesman Alastair Campbell felt misled by Mr Mandelson's account of his actions. The MP for Hartlepool lost his ministerial job. It was his second downfall in a single parliamentary term. It did great damage to the government and to public life as a whole. As Clare Short put it with her usual bluntness, 'He has got problems with the truth.'

The other alarming development was a whispering campaign against the commissioner. It happened in the spring of 2000 and coincided with a number of cases involving high-profile MPs. Elizabeth Filkin's investigations were thorough and rigorous, and conducted without respect to rank. Junior back-benchers and former prime ministers were treated equally. MPs on both sides of the House, ever conscious of their dignities and privileges, began to realize the full implications of the code of conduct they had so blithely signed on to. At the time of writing the issue is unresolved; but if the commissioner resists the pressure, as I know she will, and the committee remains non-partisan, as I trust it will, then progress will be made in restoring public confidence.

Does this mean that our turn-of-the-century politics is free from the taint and suspicion of corruption? Unfortunately it means nothing of the kind. The slithering beast has moved out of range of the nets and harpoons of the parliamentary policing system. But it still lurks out there somewhere, offering favours and preferential treatment in return for cash donations to needy causes – not charitable causes, but the expensive campaigns of cash-strapped political parties. The areas in which the beast lives and thrives are the honours system and the funding of parties. These should be entirely separate, but despite the best efforts of Lords Nolan and Neill, a subtle and sinister connection remains between them. The ghost of Lloyd George, that notorious magician and trafficker in peerages, casts its shadow even today over our democratic process.

It is true that certain reforms have been set in motion. It is also true that they were embarked on only after the Bernie Ecclestone affair, in which the government appeared to adjust its policy to accommodate the business interests of a man who had given a million pounds to the Labour Party. The furore that followed had two consequences. One was that the Formula One tycoon was given his money back. The other was that Lord Neill's Committee on Standards in Public Life was asked to report on the funding of political parties. In its eleven months of deliberations, none of the evidence it heard was more remarkable than that of Lord Pym, the former Foreign Secretary, who was at that time chairman of the Political Honours Scrutiny Committee.

This body existed to check nominations for political services, including life peerages, and to provide an independent assurance that they could not be bought and sold. Appearing before Lord Neill's Committee, Lord Pym was asked whether there was any linkage between financial donations to a party and the subsequent award of knighthoods and peerages. Since he and his fellow scrutineers were supposed to stand guard at the gate and prevent such abuses, I expected him to say: 'No, and under no circumstances, and over my dead body.' But that was not what he said. What he said was:

On the whole, the principle we follow is that if somebody gives their money to a political party, that is a bonus point rather than a minus, because they are supporting what they believe in with their own money . . .Our responsibility is to look at the totality of contributions made by individuals and weigh them all together. Donations may be an aspect of their achievements; it may be a minor one, but it is an aspect.[7]

I found this astonishing, and said so in the debate on the Neill Report, in which I called for Lord Pym's resignation. Since when was signing a cheque considered an achievement? It was possible that the accumulation of wealth might be an achievement – depending of course on how it was accumulated – but certainly not the spending of it. What Lord Pym was saying was that, all other things being equal, money given to political parties *could* be the decisive factor in awarding someone an honour. Party benefactors were better placed than others. They had the inside track. In that case he might just as well have published the rate card. How much for a peerage? How much for a knighthood? How much for a humble MBE? What would £50,000 a year for five years actually buy you? The public surely had a right to know. People are hungry for these things: someone wrote and asked me, 'Where's my damehood?' The ghost of Lloyd George was up and about and haunting the Political Honours Scrutiny Committee.

The government at least went some of the way to laying that ghost to rest. In its proposals based on the Neill Report, it insisted that honours should be given on merit, regardless of party donations. But it went on to quote with approval one of the Scrutiny Committee's criteria: to consider 'Whether the achievements of the individual overall are meritorious to an extent that makes any donation of lesser significance.'[8] Here again in weasel words lurk hidden shades of meaning. People can have no confidence that honours are not for sale until the system is fully and transparently reformed, and political donations are ruled to be not just of *lesser* significance, but of *zero* or even *disqualifying* significance. Such a reform will restore public trust, and be better for the nominees as well. In how much more respect will Lord Moneybags be held, if it is known that he did not have to pay for his peerage?

The problem lies with the parties themselves, who spend more money than they can safely raise. They become unhealthily dependent on big contributors, the Bernie Ecclestones and Michael Ashcrofts. The case of Mr Ashcroft, a buccaneering businessman of dual British and Belizean nationality, was especially illuminating. His £3 million in donations kept the Conservative Party afloat during and after its electoral débâcle in 1997. He was also, and not entirely by chance, its treasurer. He was duly nominated for a life peerage, at first rejected, but awarded at the second attempt following pressure from William Hague. On top of that, he was given a knighthood for his services to Belize. A political party is in good health if it doesn't need such people, however blameless in character, but can finance itself from the small and moderate contributions of the rank and file. Whatever else could be said of Mr Ecclestone and Mr Ashcroft, they hardly qualified as rank and file.

Neither did Lord Archer. Here was a sharp operator and a

chancer who stood high in the esteem of his party, and whose wealth blinded eyes which should have been opened by it. In his case it was not only his own money, for he made and lost some fortunes in his time. It was the money that he was able to coax out of the pockets of fellow Conservatives. Why were they so gullible? In a party by then rather short of charisma, Jeffrey Archer was the magician of the rubber chicken circuit, the patron saint of the patrons' clubs, and could wipe out a constituency association's debts in a single evening. That bought him a kind of immunity.

I was a latecomer to politics and never well enough connected to attend his champagne and shepherd's pie parties, but I was a witness to his extraordinary powers as a charity auctioneer. And more than thirty years earlier, when I was an apprentice TV reporter and he was an upwardly mobile charity worker and the BBC news was still in monochrome, I had conducted what was probably his first television interview. Was I thus an accomplice in his rise to fame, as I had been in Ian Paisley's? I don't think so. He owed that to his skills as a self-publicist and to the patronage of successive party leaders: Margaret Thatcher who first promoted him, John Major who ennobled him and William Hague who endorsed him as the Conservative standard-bearer for mayor of London, 'a candidate of probity and integrity'.

Long before Lord Archer fell from grace, the party could have spared itself embarrassment by submitting him to the early scrutiny of its newly formed Ethics and Integrity Commission (itself a postscript to the Neil Hamilton affair). It declined to do so. Such was the power of money, which in the party system could corrupt the judgement of otherwise honourable people. And so it was that in the third year of the new government, Geoffrey Robinson and others notwithstanding, it was the Conservatives' A list of Aitken, Archer and Ashcroft who hijacked the headlines. The government's spin doctors didn't do that to them. They did it to themselves. Money and politics don't mix – or when they do, they damage both the givers and the takers.

In the General Election of 2001, after the government's proposed campaign limits came into force, the political parties were still allowed to spend up to a maximum of £19.77 million each. That was far too much. It exposed them to the ambitions of chancers and grafters. It turned our political parties into supplicants, and their annual conferences into trade fairs. For those who care about public trust, there is a compelling case to be made for a limit of £2 million, or at the very most £5 million. There is an extra twist. Much of the £19.77 million will be spent on billboard advertising, which has become increasingly negative and destructive. It is political trench warfare. Party A will use its posters to bring party B into disrepute, and party B will retaliate. Politics and politicians generally will suffer, and the door to the buying and selling of influence will have been opened in the process of discrediting them. What an extraordinarily daft way to carry on!

We have seen the corruption of money in America, where a Senator towards the end of his term will spend half his time raising money for re-election, and will inevitably be beholden to the people who contribute it. I remember in 1988 being told by Senator Lawton Childs of Florida, an honourable and trusted public servant, that he found this burden intolerable: he therefore quit. Such distortions of the electoral process must not happen here, and yet we have blindly written them into the statute book.

We have two options. One is to use taxpayers' money, rather than millionaires' money, to fund the parties. The other is to run shorter, cheaper and more honest campaigns (without those mendacious billboards, for instance, that upset even the advertising industry). The people would rise in wrath at the first option, but my guess is they would rather approve of the second. This is not an argument for a community of saints and angels, but only for a system in which the shady characters lose their rights of privileged access.

14. The Pledge

In journalism as in politics defeat comes in various shapes and shades, from minor setbacks to unredeemed disasters. The unredeemed disasters can happen to anyone at any time. It is sound advice, to those with ambitions in either career, never to lose sight of that.

The BBC News Division, when I left it rather abruptly in April 1997, was still scarred by the folk memory of its own Waterloo – a wipe-out by ITN during the Turkish invasion of Cyprus a generation earlier in 1974. As with most scoops, luck played a significant part in it. The TV news teams, expecting an amphibious landing by Turkish marines, headed out to the island's northern coast – all except Michael Nicholson and his ITN crew, whose car broke down half-way between Nicosia and Kyrenia. Suddenly out of a clear blue sky Turkish paratroopers were falling all around them. They had stalled in the middle of the drop zone. Whether Michael was wise, on camera, to welcome them to Cyprus was another matter: the point was that he and his team were there and no one else was. With his rivals cut off in Kyrenia and unable to file, he capitalized on his good fortune for the rest of the week, and for a long time later. Indeed he spent much of his distinguished career trying to replicate that triumph. The BBC's defeat became a tragedy. A brave young sound recordist, Ted Stoddard, was blown up and killed in a minefield; two reporters, Chris Morris and Simon Dring, were wounded. When things go wrong in news, they go terribly wrong. Successes will be forgotten by the day after tomorrow, and disasters remembered for years.

I reflected on this when I impulsively agreed to throw my hat into the parliamentary ring. It occurred to me, when I was already too far committed to back out, that the Tatton campaign might well prove to be my personal Cyprus, or Waterloo. I was riding for a spectacular and inglorious fall. I had no political qualifications, and very little idea what I was getting into. I was the novice and outsider. Neil Hamilton was a professional politician, a formidable adversary, well entrenched and with his battle-axe beside him. (I am not being ungallant – Christine took the term as a compliment and exploited it commercially.) As for the evidence against him, he had countless supporters happy to believe that it was no more than a media conspiracy led by a media candidate. The London *Guardian*, which had set out the case so comprehensively, was not widely read in the constituency. The *Knutsford Guardian*, which *was* widely read, was cautious to a fault. Its editorials thundered regularly about pedestrianization, pelican crossings and the state of the town's public toilets. But in all the three years of the Hamilton affair, it never offered an opinion about its own MP until after the publication of the Downey Report. Indeed, before the election it printed in colour 3,000 copies of Neil Hamilton's answers to its soft-edged questions, which the Conservatives then distributed as campaign literature.

Matthew Parris of *The Times*, whose judgement as a political analyst I greatly respected, predicted that the tabloids would destroy me, and recommended a modest bet on Hamilton to win. 'I'd give Martin Bell a week,' he wrote, 'until his character is torn to shreds.'

With the incumbent resting on a notional majority of 22,000, I calculated that to be in with a chance I had to woo and win 12,000 of his voters. Party loyalty runs deep with Conservatives; it is one of their strengths. Because I don't like losing I hit upon the idea – which I never discussed with anyone, but just announced – that I would offer myself as a candidate who, if elected, would serve the people of Tatton for one parliamentary term and one term only. If it were not too flippant an analogy, I wasn't asking these Tories for a lifetime commitment, but only for a one-night stand. They could then return to their former and natural allegiances. The promise was clear and unambiguous, and repeated on election night in front of great crowds of people.

In the first couple of months as an MP, still tired from the campaign and struggling to find my feet in the House of Commons, the one-term pledge was actually something of a comfort. I would never have to submit to such an ordeal again. But then to my surprise, after six months or so, I found that I was actually enjoying it. I was not alone. MPs do that, even – and perhaps especially – those who complain about the long hours, the drudgery and the tyranny of the whips. As a way of life it is addictive. It offers membership of the best club in town, a riverside terrace and a beguiling illusion of being at the centre of things. That is why people of power and standing in their own communities, councillors and leaders of councils, regularly seek election to a Parliament where they have no power and standing at all, and no prospect of them; and then after four years or so not just of obscurity but of servility, obsequiously doing the bidding of others, they will campaign as tirelessly for re-election. They will see themselves as servants of the public good, rather than as fragments of the rubber stamp which is the British House of Commons at its worst; and it is at its worst quite frequently.

I thought little more of the promise I had made. I would be obliged to keep it however much I regretted it. That wasn't the view of regular politicians. A veteran Labour MP, then in his tenth Parliament, stopped me in the corridor and asked me about it.

'You are like a breath of fresh air in this place,' he said. 'You must stand for a second term.'

'I can't. I promised not to.'

'There are promises, and there are promises,' he said. 'The passage of time has its way of sorting them out.'

The issue lay dormant until the beginning of 1999 when there were stirrings of revival in the Conservative Association. Tatton was one of three constituencies which the Tories knew they should never have lost and were especially determined to retrieve. In all three they authorized fast track procedures to select early candidates for the next election. The other two were Lewes in Sussex, a Conservative citadel stormed by Norman Baker for the Liberal Democrats, and Leominster where Peter Temple-Morris had crossed the floor and joined the Labour Party. Tatton probably hurt the most because it need never have happened. They threw it away in a fit of absence of mind.

The Tatton Tories would probably have welcomed a heavy hitter, a party grandee or one of the cabinet ministers unseated in the 1997 landslide. The names of Michael Portillo, Malcolm Rifkind and Ian Lang, the former Scottish Secretary, were wafted around more in hope than expectation. Mark Stocks, chairman of the association, invited applications: 'I hope that whoever we choose will be very worthy of the Tatton electors' support, and will have the potential to be a high flyer in the next Conservative government. I also hope that our new prospective candidate will be able to work closely with the present Independent MP, Martin Bell. Mr Bell doesn't represent any political party, and is not standing again at the next election.' I liked the co-operative tone of that, but was not so sure about the high flyer. The Tories' selection process was none of my business and I stayed scrupulously out of it. But I contributed a few paragraphs to one of my newspaper columns in praise of low flyers; because their political ambitions are more modest they are actually better placed to serve their constituents than those who fancy themselves as cabinet ministers in waiting.

The last truly local MP to represent Tatton was Lieutenant-Colonel Sir Walter Bromley-Davenport, who retired in 1970. A famously low flyer himself and the target of satirists, especially the young Bernard Levin in the *Spectator*, he is still remembered by older members of the community as the best constituency MP they ever had. His son Bill serves with distinction today as Lord Lieutenant of Cheshire.

At the opposite end of the scale was Jock Bruce-Gardyne, to whom indirectly I owed my political episode. Double barrels carried political clout in those days. In his time he was Conservative MP for a number of constituencies, including Knutsford and Wilmslow, as Tatton was then called. He took a notoriously relaxed view of his constituency duties, and wherever he sat he had a habit of falling out with the local party executive, who duly retaliated by removing him in the course of a redrawing of the constituency boundaries. A story is told about him in Tatton to this day, which was repeated by Julian Critchley in his gentle political memoir, *A Bag of Boiled Sweets*. A farmer from the south west of Scotland, a former constituent, travelled through Knutsford one day and inquired about Bruce-Gardyne's new majority. He was told it was 20,000. 'Ooch,' said the farmer, 'that will nay be enough for our Jock.'[1] And the farmer was right: it wasn't. Bruce-Gardyne was discarded in 1983 and replaced by a politician better known now than he was then – Neil Hamilton. Some of the selectors had doubts, finding Mr Hamilton's manner even in those days too sharp and vaudevillian. But he came with Margaret Thatcher's benediction, which was all that mattered, and duly became the Honourable Member for Tatton.

To their credit, Tatton's Conservatives are a tenacious lot and not easily discouraged by self-inflicted setbacks. Some of those who had first picked Jock Bruce-Gardyne in 1979, and then Neil Hamilton in 1983, were still on deck for the selection process in 1999. They had no high flyers or heavy hitters to choose from. This was the cause of much speculation. Lawrence Matheson, editor of the *Wilmslow Express Advertiser* and the local grandmaster of mixed metaphors, reported that the Hamilton affair had turned Tatton into a hot potato and poisoned chalice, and had lingered on like a hangover. 'And then there's that man in the white suit, goody-two-shoes, Saint Martin. Who would want to follow in his footsteps?'

There was a more substantial local difficulty. A minority of the Tatton Tories, ever loyal to Neil Hamilton, believed that the vacancy should be left open until he had a chance to clear his name in his forthcoming libel action against Mohamed Al Fayed, which he was absolutely confident of winning. He was convinced that the way would then be open for him to return in triumph to the House of Commons. I was part of his vindication strategy. I knew that, because he told me so. He saw no contradiction in attacking me in public and seeking my help in private: indeed, in his last-roll-of-the-dice predicament, why should he? I obliged with a letter which went through four painstaking drafts, supporting his right to a court hearing – a right disputed not only by Mr Al Fayed, but for constitutional reasons by the government and the authorities of the House of Commons itself.

With the big names staying out of the race, and the high flyers grounded, the Tatton Conservatives still had more than a hundred applicants to choose from. They narrowed the field down to a long list of twenty-three, and then to a short list of four. From the short list they picked George Osborne, who was speechwriter for the party leader, William Hague, and secretary of the shadow cabinet. At twenty-seven he was less than half my age, but had been in politics longer than I had, with an early experience of its slings and arrows. He had been special adviser to Douglas Hogg at the Ministry of Agriculture during the BSE crisis, and had worked in the political office of 10 Downing Street during the débâcle of the 1997 election campaign. I couldn't help wondering whether the challenge of Tatton, with Neil Hamilton loitering ominously in the wings, would prove any easier for him. At least, unlike Neil, he actually joined the Tatton Conservative Association. He was its second youngest member.

The newly adopted candidate held a press conference in which he declared that the previous three years had been difficult ones for the Tatton Conservatives, and indeed for the people of Tatton. I had no quarrel with the first of these propositions, but I really did take issue with the second. So did many of those who wrote to me. I didn't dispute it publicly, however, but put it down to beginner's nerves. I had no doubt said some daft things at my own first press conference too.

The week after his selection I invited Mr Osborne to lunch at the Churchill Room in the House of Commons (he wanted it elsewhere, lest we be seen by his fellow Tories, but I insisted that neither of us had anything to hide). He struck me as a nice enough man and totally suited to politics. The ground rules were easily established. He could do as he pleased in the constituency and attend whatever functions he wished. He could make whatever speeches he was inclined to, although I would of course be aware of what he had said. Thanks to the enlightened chairmanship of Mark Stocks, the Tatton Conservatives and I had a sort of unspoken non-aggression pact; this would continue.

'You do know, don't you,' the candidate said, 'that there's only one thing that you can do to upset me?'

Actually I did know. And I didn't need to ask him what it was.

In due course he wrote an article for the local papers about his first month as the Tories' standard-bearer. They did not publish it, but I read it anyway. He said that on my pledge not to stand again I had struck him as a man of my word. And he added: 'I think he's shown the way to a new kind of politics based on honesty and principle. It's a kind of politics that I hope to continue after the next election.' That was more like it. The spirit of Tatton was getting to him. He was settling in.

At that point the local papers let loose a considerable campaign. I suspected a commercial motive, since the Tatton saga had boosted their circulations, which might well suffer from a return to the regularity of three-party politics. I think it is unusual for a politician to find himself reproached for keeping a promise rather than for breaking one, but that was what happened to me. The *Knutsford Guardian*, so sparing in its editorial comment under the previous regime, attacked me for defeatism in a rare column penned by the editor herself, Sue Briggs. Because Sue and I got on well personally, she felt obliged to fire off an editorial howitzer shell at me once a year: 'We believe Mr Bell owes the 29,354 people of Tatton who voted for him the chance to choose. Let the voters decide, Mr Bell. If they don't want you, you'll simply have to look for another job, or slip away to spend more time with your family.' The *Wilmslow Express Advertiser* was no less forthright. 'Break that promise, Martin,' it said. 'We urge you, Mr Bell – leader of the one man "People's Party" – let the people decide.' The paper commissioned a telephone opinion poll which drew a substantial response: 264 callers urged me to keep the promise, and 1,205 to break it.

The mail divided in the same proportions. A constituent wrote,

'Don't desert us, Martin.' And another, 'You have proved your point but you have not proved ours.' And I heard from a former Conservative cabinet minister, a notable high flyer in his day, who wrote from retirement urging me 'to accept popular acclaim to stay on after the next election; as an Independent you must have the right to change your mind in the national interest'. Against that, and with equal weight, there was the sensible reflection of one of the Wilmslow Tories: 'The interlude has been refreshing, but the future requires Mr Bell to keep his pledge and retire at the end of this Parliament.'

I studied the dilemma for quite a length of time. I held it up to the light, like a flawed piece of amber from the coast of my native Suffolk, and examined it from all angles. The more I looked at it, the more I could see of the flaws and the less I could see of the amber. For a fleeting and precarious moment I even considered the possibility of a sort of minimal non-campaign – just letting my name go on to the ballot paper so that people could vote for me if they wished. But even that meant breaking a promise. And the more I considered it the more settled I became in my conviction that whatever else Tatton's pioneering politics might mean, it unquestionably meant that a promise made was a promise kept. That applied even to an unnecessary pledge offered rashly in the heat of the moment and later regretted. There would be no second thoughts.

I allowed only one exception. If, by some outside edge of a chance, Neil Hamilton were to be re-adopted as the Conservatives' candidate in Tatton, I might be persuaded to reconsider, on the grounds that there was unfinished business still to be done. It seemed improbable, with George Osborne in place, but not impossible. You never knew with the Tatton Tories. They were capable of anything.

There was always the option, in theory at least, of accepting the blandishments of the regular parties and standing for one of them at the next election. I received discreet inquiries to this effect from both Conservatives and Liberal Democrats, and William Hague even asked me to join a commission he was appointing under the chairmanship of Lord Newton to find ways of restoring the authority of Parliament. The cause was a good one, but the commission was a Conservative Party exercise, so I had to decline. Once an Independent always an Independent – there could be no compromise on that. The same principle applied when I received an indirect approach from someone on the Labour side about whether I would be interested in being a candidate for mayor of London. The *Sunday People* reported that 10 Downing Street was so desperate to stop Ken Livingstone that it had even considered trying to recruit me as the official Labour candidate. This far-fetched scenario had only three things wrong with it: Labour's candidate for mayor should be a Londoner, a person with substantial business experience, and a paid-up member of the party. I failed on all three counts; and besides, I was developing a certain respect for Ken Livingstone. He was one of the few on the Labour back benches who paid little heed to his pager. I would remain an obstinate and pager-less Independent; and I could not have been persuaded to join the Labour Party, or any other. I could see no future for myself as a party politician – and probably none, beyond this Parliament, as an Independent and irregular.

But one further possibility did remain, which was to plant the Independent flag elsewhere and see if anyone would rally to it. The pledge applied only to Tatton. In due course I received approaches from serious groups of people in a number of other English constituencies. I was sceptical but attentive, and did not make any more foreclosing promises. It would depend on a number of things: local circumstances and *anno domini* among them. I had undergone one hip operation and needed another. Retirement would be by far the easier option. I did not choose it but went for Brentwood and Ongar instead.

There is a distinction to be made here between changing a policy and breaking a promise. The politics I would hope to stand for is both an idea and a destination: I haven't got there yet, because I came to it rather late in life, but I think that I see its outline. It has trust and integrity as its highest priorities, with party loyalties and personal ambitions so far down its order of things as to be out of sight and out of mind. People respond to it for that reason. It is unprofessional in the best and most creditable sense. It is politics as a conversation rather than an argument. It is not an alternative to party politics but an occasional corrective to it. It has principles but it doesn't have shibboleths. It can admit the possibility of error. It is thus open to the liberated and independent politician, to whom all votes are free votes, to use phrases that are nowhere to be found in the regular political lexicon: 'I don't know', 'I have made a mistake', or 'I have changed my mind'.

In my own case, I readily confess that I still don't know about a lot of things – no MP can be an all-issues expert – but I am willing to try to find out where I can, and where I cannot, to vote with those whose judgement I trust. I have made mistakes, as in my slowness in catching on to the profoundly undemocratic nature of the Registration of Political Parties Act, and the proposed new vote-buying arrangements in the City of London's elections (a difficult system to defend, said the party spokesmen – but they defended it none the less). And I have changed my mind, for instance on the legalization of cannabis for medical purposes, because I heard Paul Flynn MP advocating it in the House, and found his arguments unanswerable. But a personal promise about an MP's career belongs in a different category.

If I were to break that, people would merely shrug and say, what else is new? There goes another snake-oil salesman, a politician breaking his word, saying one thing and doing another: they always have been the same and always will be. It would add in a small way to the disrepute of politics, and cast a retrospective shadow over whatever might have been achieved in the interim. And as it was an issue of trust that got me into the politics of Tatton in the first place, it seemed only reasonable for an issue of trust to get me out of it too. There was a measure of honour in that, and of symmetry. The good stuff belonged at the beginning and the end – and whatever remained in the middle, remained in the middle.

15. Unfinished Business

Neil Hamilton took the all-comers' prize for tenacity. He was a hanger on to the cliff-top by his finger tips, even when the rest of the cliff was collapsing around him. No chapter ever closed for him, and he was never so far down as to be out. There were many in the Tatton constituency, and especially its Conservative Association, who wished devoutly that he would accept the will of the people and fade from the scene, but that was not his nature. I knew the type from the letters I received on a daily basis from conspiracy theorists all over the country. He did not need to add to them, since as his constituency MP I was willing to meet him at any time and did so twice, once in my office and once at his home. (It was a bleak day in December, the door bell at the Old Rectory in Nether Alderley didn't work, a cardboard cut-out of Margaret Thatcher presided in the hall like the ghost of patrons past, and the house was almost as cheerless inside as out.) Like the green ink brigade, Neil Hamilton saw himself as the innocent victim of ill-intentioned people. And also like them he was quite convinced that his own MP was part of the plot. A 'fraud on the people of Tatton' was how he described it. His determination to battle on against the odds drew the applause of the Tory right, especially the *Spectator's* dyspeptic columnists, and the grudging admiration even of his critics – more Macbeth than Henry V they thought, but none the less impressive. After two and a half years of the Hamilton comeback campaign, reasonable people started to wonder, why should he put himself through all this, unless he really hadn't taken cash for questions? Or was it that he had taken cash for questions, was a man without honour with nothing to lose, and could only ricochet from one lie to another?

Tatton was deeply divided for and against. So was I. I just did not know the answer. Some of my constituents were as suspicious of Mr Hamilton as ever, but others were starting to waver. I knew this not by instinct, but because I had just found a new role in life as an auction prize. Dinner for two with Martin Bell at the House of Commons was not in the stellar category of a Manchester United shirt signed by the players (it was more on a par with a Manchester City shirt, actually), but it was on offer at various charity dinners. And the Mere Golf and Country Club, where these auctions took place, was the fishing pool for most of the north-west's good causes. The highest bid was £1,000, even more expensive than dinner for two at the Ritz in Paris, to take an example not entirely at random. (It should go without saying, but I had better say it anyway, that I paid the real cost of the dinner myself.) The kind of people who won were more likely to have been in Neil Hamilton's social circle, and I listened to them carefully, because listening carefully was what I had always done. The prizewinners admired his persistence, and were inclined to give him the benefit of the doubt, at least until he tested the matter in court. It was an expensive but instructive way of conducting audience research.

Like so much that Neil Hamilton did, his chosen means of restoring his fortunes was a spectacular and high-risk adventure. He sued his old adversary, the owner of Harrods, for libel. Hamilton versus Al Fayed, one grand conspiracy theorist against another: it was a libel lawyer's benefit match. Taking sides was like picking a winner in the Iran–Iraq war. The issue was the one on which Sir Gordon Downey had ruled against Mr Hamilton, and which by the time of the trial had entered the political folklore of the nation: whether or not he had taken £20,000 in cash in brown envelopes from the owner of Harrods, as payment for asking helpful questions in Parliament.

My own position in the case was rather complex. I was an interested party, in that I had challenged and defeated Neil Hamilton in the election and was now his MP. But I was a disinterested party, in that I had based my campaign on other issues of trust, and supported his right to bring the matter to court. Al Fayed's attempt to block it in the House of Lords had failed. On the day that the five Law Lords ruled unanimously in Hamilton's favour, I congratulated his lawyer Rupert Grey with genuine sincerity. Mr Grey was leaving the Palace of Westminster as I was entering it. Forty yards away through the St Stephen's entrance, on the steps beyond the security machines, I espied the unmistakable figures of Neil and Christine Hamilton approaching. Christine must have seen me too, because by the time I reached them she had vanished. She regarded me as thoroughly bad news. I certainly bore her no ill will, but I doubt if she reciprocated. More than two and a half years after the election, she was one of the last irreconcilables – the two people in Tatton with whom I knew I could never hold a civil conversation. The other was the vicar of Great Budworth. I had tried at the church fête without success.

Neil Hamilton's end game, the libel trial of the decade, started on 15 November 1999 in Court 13 of the Royal Courts of Justice in the Strand. For its five-and-a-half-week run, the West End theatres just down the road could offer no drama to rival it, and none that lived up to its billing quite so spectacularly. Or maybe the pantomime season started early. There were tears and tantrums, insults and innuendoes, and at one point the judge stormed out of the courtroom to silence an unruly witness. The case attracted wide public interest and blanket press coverage, from the tabloids to the broadsheets, because of the notoriety of the contest and of the two principal characters. Neither was universally admired. There were some who suggested that they deserved each other, and regretted that only one of them could lose. I preferred not to comment on that, or on very much else until the trial was over. Although Rupert Grey had kindly offered me a seat in court, I chose to observe discreetly and from afar. But I did note in a newspaper column that what gave this legal grudge match its extra edge was that corruption is notoriously a crime without witnesses; and on the issue of whether Hamilton took the money from Al Fayed, one of them was lying and the other was telling the truth, and only they (and perhaps Christine Hamilton, who used to go through her husband's pockets every night) knew for certain which was which.

The barristers were equally well matched. Both came to the fray with formidable reputations and the capacity to inflict grievous verbal harm. George Carman QC, opening for Al Fayed, described Hamilton as 'a greedy and unscrupulous politician who was on the make and on the take . . . Do you not think a man as greedy as Neil Hamilton is capable of lying again and again about whether he took cash for questions?' Desmond Browne QC, for Hamilton, called Al Fayed 'a phoney Pharaoh . . . a man to whom lying has become a sickness and whose whole commercial life is founded on a lie. He is deeply vindictive, ready to take revenge on those he sees as responsible for exposing his lies.'

Of Neil Hamilton's further strategy, should he win the case, there was no doubt. I was its target. It was aimed directly at me. 'Hamilton Plans To Gun For Bell After Libel Case', announced the *Wilmslow Express Advertiser* gleefully, having talked to his friends. He thirsted for revenge and would challenge me as a man of honour to resign my seat. I was not sure that I wished to be included on Mr Hamilton's personal list of men of honour. He would then seek a special general meeting of the Tatton Conservative Association to deselect George Osborne and reinstate himself as Conservative candidate and then MP. He would return in triumph to the House of Commons. 'If I win this libel case,' he said, 'it would be deeply satisfying to be re-elected and then confront my accusers face to face.'

All this was fantasy. It ignored the party's new rules, changed as a result of its Tatton fiasco, which tightened Central Office control over the selection of candidates and would have excluded Neil Hamilton under any conceivable circumstances. It ignored the fact that he was not even a party member. It also ignored his admitted breaches of the MPs' code of conduct, matters of 'conduct unbecoming', which were the real cause of his downfall in 1997. And it failed to take account of the Carman factor.

George Carman, the most fearsome advocate in the land (Neil Hamilton's own description of him), was famous for the introduction of new and unexpected evidence. He had done this to such devastating effect in the Jonathan Aitken case as to put the former minister behind bars. On the first substantive day of Hamilton versus Al Fayed, he sprang another of his trademark surprises. In 1989 Mr Hamilton had tabled an amendment to Clause 116 of the Finance Bill that would have saved the oil industry £70 million in additional taxation. He then submitted a bill to Mobil Oil for a consultancy fee of £10,000, which the company to its astonishment and regret was embarrassed into paying. 'He was actually trying to change the law,' said Mr Carman, 'and seeking payment for that work.' In those days hiring an MP was like hailing a taxi. Peter Preston, the former editor of the *Guardian*, testified that Al Fayed had recruited 'a repertory company of MPs to do parliamentary business on his behalf'. A friendly committee member commented, 'If only I'd known, I could have made £150,000 on this year's Finance Bill.'

Of all Neil Hamilton's ordeals, which ranged over the years of his self-destruction from being censured by a Commons committee to being lampooned on *Have I Got News For You*, his cross-examination by George Carman in Court 13 was probably the hardest. It was merciless. It forced him to abandon his line that the alleged 'pack of lies' against him had cost him a senior position in the Conservative Party. It drove him to express contrition, and even shame, over his extravagant consumption of vintage champagne at the Ritz Hotel in Paris (the most expensive was a bottle of Krug Rosé at £140 in 1987 prices). It exposed a half-truth told to Sir Gordon Downey, that he had asked no parliamentary questions for Mobil, when in fact he had tried to amend a bill on the company's behalf. Hamilton's defence was semantic: 'At times I have behaved with a lack of candour, but one thing that I am not is corrupt.'

The judge's summing up, at the end of the trial's fifth week, tilted initially and strongly in Hamilton's direction. Mr Justice Morland described Al Fayed's evidence as 'inconsistent, confused and unreliable'. As for Hamilton's conduct over the demand for payment from Mobil Oil, the judge advised the jury 'It is important, you may think, not to be over-sanctimonious and priggish when considering Mr Hamilton's lack of candour.' That line was included, I believe, to make the summing up appeal-proof. But it shocked me at the time, and my spirits sank a little when I heard it. It could have come straight from Hamilton's own supporters' club. Politics, it seems, is a universe bounded by 'S' words. Those who are in it for what they can get out of it are condemned as sleazy. Those who are not are condemned as sanctimonious. Hamilton's backers scented victory. Lord Harris of High Cross, his principal fund-raiser, wrote 'Friends called me after the judge's summing up and said we were home and dry.'[1]

Except that it wasn't over. After a tense weekend, Mr Justice Morland resumed in more critical vein. The Mobil testimony appeared in a different light. This was the smoking gun or silver bullet (lawyers and journalists are partial to such metaphors) never known to anyone except the oil company's executives until two days before the trial, but credible evidence of Hamilton's corruption. It had nothing to do with cash for questions, but cash for amendments was in its way just as serious.

The eleven jurors, six women and five men (the twelfth had fallen ill early in the case), deliberated for eight and a half hours over two days. They were under instruction to return a unanimous verdict. On the afternoon of Tuesday 21 December they did so. The judge asked whether the jury had found 'on the balance of probabilities' that Mr Al Fayed had established corruption by Mr Hamilton 'on highly convincing evidence'. The foreman whispered, almost inaudibly, 'Yes.' Neil Hamilton slumped forward with his head in his hands, Christine fixed the jury with the baleful glare in which she specialized, and the last great trial of the twentieth century was over.

Two hours later I called a press conference at the Longview Hotel in Knutsford, only my second since becoming an MP. The satellite dishes were mushrooming again. It seemed the best thing to do, to feed the reptiles (my former colleagues) and draw a line as gently as possible under the whole extraordinary episode. I invited the Conservatives' chairman, Councillor Mark Stocks, to attend the press conference. He was even more relieved by the outcome of the trial than I was; it mattered less to me than it did to his battered constituency association, under threat of an attempted Hamilton comeback, if the jury had found in Neil Hamilton's favour. Mr Stocks suggested a joint press conference. I did not think that was a great idea, since we were not of the same political persuasion, so we held consecutive press conferences, with mulled wine and mince pies provided by the Tatton Independent Party. It was, after all, the season of goodwill, and champagne did not seem appropriate.

Asked if I felt vindicated, I replied that it was no time for triumphalism. No MP should welcome such a disgrace for a constituent. But Sir Gordon Downey was certainly vindicated, and so was the judgement of the people of Tatton who had removed Neil Hamilton as their MP. That is how corruption is dealt with in a democracy – not ultimately by lords and lawyers, commissioners and committees, but by the power of the people, whether as voters or jurors. There can be no better way.

The new Conservative Association distanced itself as far as possible from the old one. George Osborne declared, 'There can be no place for corruption of any kind in British politics.' Mark Stocks described the Hamilton affair as an unsavoury episode. Not all his members agreed. Even after the unanimous verdict a hard core of true believers protested Neil Hamilton's innocence. One of them who lived beside the heath came charging across it to berate Mr Stocks outside the Longview. 'You're a disgrace,' she protested, 'you're an absolute disgrace.' And Alan Barnes, who had been Hamilton's constituency chairman, added, 'This must be the most outrageous miscarriage of justice this country has seen in the last 100 years.' These people were unpersuadable. So were his supporters in the press. The guilty verdict might have been just a casual expression of opinion for all the difference it made to them. There was nothing that Neil Hamilton could do, and be found to have done by an impartial judicial process, that would cause them to lose faith in him.

Not only were these loyalists disappointed by the verdict, so was my friend David Soul. He had constructed a scenario in his mind in which the decision went the other way, Neil sought reinstatement as the Conservative candidate, and I was then obliged to break my single-term promise on the grounds of unfinished business. David sought to reprise one of his greatest roles – not on the stage but in the theatre of life, as the wooer of voters on the streets of Knutsford and Wilmslow.

Within days of declaring himself a broken man Neil Hamilton was considering a comeback – not a new career, but an appeal against the court's decision. He was encouraged in this by sympathetic interviews, and by the right-wing columnists and commentators who, by massaging his hopes, had contributed to his downfall. 'We are looking for new ways to go on the attack,' he announced. The appeal failed spectacularly a year later, surprising no one but the appellant himself. He called it 'justice in wonderland'. An ordinary litigant would have given up years ago. Neil Hamilton wasn't an ordinary litigant. He was a politician and a man obsessed.

The truth is, there is something about politicians that sets them apart from those they are elected to serve. They represent the people, but are not representative of the people. In the House of Commons there are, of course, many men and women of humility, honesty, quiet achievement and good judgement. But I would hazard a guess that such people are to be found in much greater proportion in the population at large. Parliament, by contrast, has always been attractive to shady characters. It possesses more than its share of adventurers, chancers, and fiercely driven individuals with no significant interests or obvious talents outside its walls, and who will thrive there and nowhere else. Such people live on the edge. Neil Hamilton fitted that pattern. So did Jonathan Aitken, Tim Smith and all those brought low by the cash-for-questions scandals. Ron Davies, the former Welsh Secretary, was another risk-taker and liver-on-the-edge. So, for all his talents, was Peter Mandelson; and in the end it ruined him.

The parties have only themselves to blame for those whom they recruit and promote. In advancing their cause on the floor of the House, they are on the look-out for public performers rather than public servants. ('No place for Trappist monks', was how the ex-lobbyist Derek Draper described it rather sharply when he and I crossed swords in a radio talk show.) The spivs and sharp operators are precisely the ones to catch the eye of the whips and secure advancement through their antic interventions, especially in business questions. This is the hour every Thursday when the Leader of the House sets out the parliamentary schedule for the coming week and is questioned on it. That is as it should be, and part of the process of holding the executive to account. But when it is hijacked by the parties' hit-men and point-scorers, it becomes a mockery of the democratic process. At least two of the regulars, on the Conservative side, are in evident need of psychiatric care. The futility of these proceedings is widely accepted − by Neil Hamilton himself, among others. A year after the voters pensioned him off, he saw his former profession in a different light: 'The little games and pantomimes in which I once enthusiastically took part now appear completely irrelevant. I jumped up and down at business questions and Prime Minister's questions to make some fatuous partisan jibe. What seemed from within so significant seems pointless and infantile when observed from without.'[2]

Were it not for his record, and a jury's verdict of corruption against him, the new Neil Hamilton could occasionally sound like a credible Independent.

16. Standing Alone

I was lucky that my short parliamentary career did not coincide with Enoch Powell's long one. Mr Powell, although he was no lobby fodder and crossed party boundaries with agility, dismissed the very idea of an Independent MP as an 'irrelevant absurdity'. I am not sure why he bothered, since he entered the House in 1950 when the university seats were abolished and the Independents were banished. Maybe he feared their return. 'A single imaginary question settles the point,' he argued. 'Mr candidate, if you find you have the deciding vote in an evenly balanced new House of Commons, will you use it to turn the Government out or keep them in? The candidate cannot refuse to answer; and when he does so, he ceases to be an independent candidate.'[1]

The imaginary question is in fact quite easily answered. The Independent MP may be reasonably reluctant to use the very first vote in a new Parliament to bring down a government before it has had a chance to prove itself. It would be undemocratic to do so. The decision on which way to vote should be based, in any case, on an impartial assessment of the merits of the issue. That is surely what being an Independent is about. Every vote is a free vote. A party of one is in this sense quite simple to run, without factions and fringes, disputes and distractions and tangled lines of communication. It needs no spin doctors, rebuttal units or focus groups. The going gets tough only in the division lobby. It has been my good fortune to remain on excellent terms with my chief whip, party leader and rank and file, since we are most conveniently the same person. Nor have I followed the example of one of my predecessors, the ex-journalist Vernon Bartlett, who sat as an Independent from 1938 to 1950, and was reputed to have gone into hiding every time that a difficult vote came up.

As a result, I have made mistakes. I don't know exactly what they were, and I hope that they were few and inconsequential. But I do not doubt that I have made them from time to time by voting in haste, in error or in insufficient knowledge of the issue before the House. I can even take a certain pride in them, because at least they were *my* mistakes and no one else's, and not imposed on me by a party's three-line whip. I waited and watched, I followed the advice to bide my time, and sometimes in the early days I did not vote at all. The University of Hull's Centre for Legislative Studies, which takes an interest in these things, observed that 'The most striking thing about the way that Martin Bell votes is that more often than not he doesn't.' But with the passage of time confidence improved, and so did the voting record. It averaged 28 per cent in the first 200 divisions, grew to 36 per cent in the next 180, reached 45 per cent in the second session, and rose to 56 per cent in the third.[2] Neil Hamilton's score, for those who are interested, was 74 per cent.

On one occasion I even voted both for and against the same motion. MPs usually do this to cancel out the vote they have just cast, when they have lingered too long in Annie's Bar and strayed into the wrong division lobby by mistake. I once saw two MPs do it because they were arguing so much with each other that they didn't see where they were going or the company they were keeping. I did it deliberately. The Liberal Democrats had initiated a debate on parliamentary democracy – an important issue in a rubber stamp assembly which, as Tony Benn observed, had become a queue for office or for appearances on the BBC's *Today* programme. But the debate was a waste of time – a gruesome three-hour slanging match between the Lib Dems and the Conservatives, each accusing the other of being a weak and ineffective opposition. Maybe they were both right. I was so dismayed that I wished to abstain, but the voting system made no distinction between an abstention and an absence. So I registered a principled and constructive abstention, by completing the full circuit of the 'aye' and 'no' lobbies and having my name recorded in both. This was good for the voting record, and it considerably baffled the academics in Hull.

Being an Independent means a great deal more than simply not having a party. It is, or should be, about practising a different kind of politics – a kinder and gentler and more considerate politics, closer to the public and without the disparagement and ill will that are disfiguring features of the regular party battlefield. In this respect my road to Damascus was the battle of Knutsford Heath. I saw then, and believe to this day, that people are tired of the culture of belligerence, the greasepaint and sawdust of the two-and-a-half-ring circus, and the artificial antagonisms which are among the reasons for the parties' ill repute. I brought this message to the Independent group of councillors at their annual conference in Harrogate: if you are attacked, never retaliate; the mud-slingers will discover soon enough that they are excavating the ground from under their feet, and the prevailing wind will blow it back in their faces. Occasionally and in general terms I endorsed Independent candidates for local councils. I then received outraged letters from their opponents, claiming that the Independents were sailing under flags of convenience like Liberian tankers, and were really party members in disguise. I replied as courteously as possible that, even if this were true, the shedding of the party label was the first step to a political state of grace. Politics is about all our futures, and our children's. It is too important to be left to the politicians. And of the tens of thousands of letters I received since becoming an MP, not one of them asked, 'Can we please have our three-party politics back?'

I remembered the words of my father Adrian Bell, an Independent-minded man if ever there was one. When asked by the political parties for his vote in 1974, he replied, 'I am on the side of those who cultivate their gardens.' An Independent serves the people and not the party; and is thus, in terms of the uses of time and energy, demonstrably more efficient than a party MP. There are no constituency executives to be reported to, no by-election voters to be canvassed, no visiting grandees to be welcomed, no agents to be recruited and remunerated, no rank and file members to be charmed or placated, no patrons' clubs to be addressed, no wine and cheese parties to be attended, no self-promoting newsletters to be written, and no financial quotas to be met either locally or nationally for the fund-hungry party machine.

I spent a night as Paddy Ashdown's guest at his home in Norton sub Hamdon near Yeovil. I knew I had arrived at the right address because it sounded like the Royal Marines' assault course: Paddy's idea of keeping fit was to pound up and down his staircase as if to destroy it. We were supporting Hope and Homes for Children, an outstanding charity of which we are both patrons; and I was astonished by the attention that even he, then a party leader on a 12,000 vote majority, had to pay to the nuts and bolts of his constituency operation. The life of Liberal Democrats especially is a never-ending election campaign. And I hardly saw a happier MP than Peter Temple-Morris, with a huge box of Christmas cards on his shoulder in December 1997. He had just lost the Conservative whip, and no longer had to sign and dispatch 200 of them to his former party workers in Leominster. There are times when the parties' self-absorption reminds me of the United Nations at the nadir of its fortunes in the Bosnian war: they exist for no other purpose than to sustain themselves, to protect themselves, to promote themselves and to ensure their own survival. In toiling so tirelessly to feed their machines, they tend to lose sight of the larger dimension of what on earth they are for and why we need them. And even their own supporters are troubled by doubt. When the government was trying to privatize the air traffic control system, one of its senior back-benchers remarked rather sadly, 'I don't know how much longer I can go on voting for things I don't believe in.'

Sadder still is the mind-set of MPs so avid for advancement that they will even ask counterfeit questions. Someone slipped me a list of such questions suggested by a parliamentary private secretary, a minister's bag-carrier on the bottom rung of the ladder of promotion. The accompanying memo said, 'This Thursday is DTI tabling day and I would be grateful if you would consider tabling one of the questions from the list below.' There were twenty-four of these toadying questions on policy areas to which the DTI sought to draw attention – but nothing, for instance, on the ailing Rover car company.

Others may disagree, but it seems to me a waste of time and space on the Order Paper, that ministers go to the dispatch box to answer questions which they not only know in advance, but which have actually been composed in their own offices. At such times the House of Commons resembles not so much the free parliament of a free people as a ventriloquist's palace of varieties. When it does not, but remains true to itself, it is because of our instincts and traditions. I was honoured, when Madam Speaker retired in October 2000, to be asked by three of the candidates seeking to succeed her to propose their nominations. The one I spoke for was Richard Shepherd MP, an old-fashioned libertarian Tory who these days would probably not even reach a candidates' short list.

The worst thing that the parties do is to solicit large sums of money from those who might seek favours in return. The second worst thing is to incubate careerism. They recruit young people at university or even earlier, who have no experience of life outside politics and whose only qualification is their ambition. The ancient universities must also take a share of the blame. The Oxford and Cambridge union societies are presented to impressionable undergraduates as thresholds and climbing frames for a career in the House of Commons. The presidents of the Cambridge Union during my time in the early 1960s included John Gummer, Leon Brittan and Kenneth Clarke, all of whom duly went on to serve as Conservative MPs, privy councillors and cabinet ministers. I wondered whether anything disagreeable had ever happened to them. The gilt-edged Oxbridge escalator bore them effortlessly upward.

Surveying the green leather benches today, especially when William Hague is in debating-society and point-scoring form, I have the impression that the process has somehow been reversed and that the House of Commons is modelling itself on the union societies. It is that unreal. What is missing is a sense of what the politicians believe in, if indeed they believe in anything beyond their own prospects and those of the locomotive parties which propel them into office. That is why, like Michael Portillo after his defeat in 1997, or Peter Mandelson after his home loan scandal, they find it so breathtakingly easy to reinvent themselves. Overnight, yesterday's man is transformed into tomorrow's. Nor is it clear, at a time of ideological convergence, what is the parties' *raison d'être* except to take power or to keep it.

The extreme expression of this is the party conference. These annual rituals no longer have any deliberative or policy-making function. They are political holiday camps and trade fairs. Mr Jeremy Paxman of the BBC, who has been around them for long enough to know, describes them as frauds on the public. They exist for no other purpose than to raise money, to enthuse and inspire a party's supporters, to disparage its opponents, to provide a platform for its leader and to secure unpaid publicity for it in the press and on television. Who needs to go to the expense of posters and billboards if the TV news can do the same thing for you at no cost at all? The party conferences are the political equivalent of Sir Richard Branson's hot air balloons, great advertising signs in the sky whose single function is to promote the man's commercial enterprises. With the conferences, as with the balloons, the press are a willing part of the conspiracy – accomplices in the great illusion that some larger and grander purpose is being served. A seaside holiday completes and seals the bargain.

Not to be outdone by the big battalions, the Tatton Independent Party held its own annual conferences. The seaside wasn't really an option because of the constituency's rather conspicuous lack of a coast. The chosen venue in 1997 and 1998 was a marquee on the farm of two good friends, Mike and June Clayton in Mere. Then, when they moved north in 1999, we switched to the magnificently restored ballroom of the Royal George Hotel in Knutsford. The costs were defrayed by newspaper articles, duly declared in the Register of Members' Interests, and the event was, in each case, much more party than conference – the model of our different kind of politics. There were no composite resolutions moved, no block votes, no lobbyists in attendance, no policy speeches of any kind, no contentious fringe meetings – and an absolute ban on standing ovations for the leader. I did give a very short speech to the hundred delegates, my friends and supporters of all parties or no party at all (at least one of them, Councillor Bert Grange, the mayor of Knutsford, was believed on good authority to have backed Neil Hamilton), to thank them for keeping alive the spirit of Tatton, and to celebrate the blessed and continuing holiday from party politics. Honesty compels me to record that there was one heckler at the third of these conferences – my four-month old grandson Max, who was missing his lunch.

Keeping the company of Independent MPs is like walking with dinosaurs. As the dinosaur in question, I know how it feels to belong to a species thought to be extinct. It is a relief to be declared extant, if endangered. Clearly I am an interested party, or rather non-party, in hoping for the survival of the species. It may just possibly have a future. I gave a short speech in Stoke-on-Trent in support of the Independents. Stoke-on-Trent had been a Labour Party fiefdom for ever, or at least within living memory. The Independents put up nine candidates for the council and won nine seats. If they could have found more candidates, they would have won more seats. The climate of the times was changing, and political allegiances were a great deal looser than they used to be. Sensing this, the parties acted – or perhaps a better word would be conspired – to protect themselves through the Registration of Political Parties Act 1998. I was late in seeing its significance and in protesting about it – a mistake which I should not have made and freely admit. As soon as the bill received the royal assent, I received a letter from the Registrar of Political Parties in Cardiff (similar letters went to Mr Blair, Mr Hague and Mr Ashdown) asking if I wished, for a mere £150, to register my political party, and to choose and register a party emblem with it. There was, however, a catch. It could not be called the Independent Party. I had stood as an Independent, I sat in Parliament as an Independent, but I was not allowed to register as an Independent. Nor could there be an Independent Conservative Party, an Independent Labour Party (despite that party's historical existence) or an Independent Liberal Democrat Party. Independent is the most coveted label in politics, and I think I understand why. It is the most attractive to the voters, and the most subversive of the established order.

One day in April 2000, rather to my surprise, I was asked to play the Bridgewater Hall in Manchester, at the centenary of the birth of Aaron Copland. To be honest, I did not so much play it as turn up at it. The BBC Philharmonic Orchestra provided the music, and I who am musically illiterate the narration, for the American composer's extraordinary and eloquent *Portrait of Abraham Lincoln*. Most of the words were Lincoln's own, including these on the eve of the American civil war: 'As our case is new, so we must think anew and act anew. We must disenthral ourselves.' We could use a bit of disenthralment ourselves. It is an idea as appropriate to our time as to his, if less dramatically so, and has a political application.

There are some 2,000 Independent councillors in local government. Because by law they are not allowed to band together under the banner of the Independent Party, they do not qualify, as do the regular parties, for political broadcasts just before the municipal elections. Is that altogether equitable? Or is it a case of the parties ganging up to protect themselves and their electoral monopoly? From my travels around the country I have the sense that a growing number of people are wondering how democratic our democracy really is.

It is not as democratic as we would wish it to be. Nor is it as democratic as it appears to be. A new model parliament actually exists, in the parallel chamber established for adjournment debates in the former Grand Committee Room in Westminster Hall. Both carpentry and compromise went into this project, in which government and opposition no longer confront each other at two swords' lengths. Instead, as in most democratic assemblies, we sit and debate collaboratively in a hemisphere of seats. I welcomed the rearrangement of the furniture. But still I voted against the second-ary chamber. It is a side show and cave of winds, to which no one but the few participants pays any attention at all. It is the British equivalent of the American custom of reading stuff into the record. We seem to have surrendered a part of our political citadel. The power and influence have ebbed from Westminster and flowed elsewhere – to the judiciary, to Brussels and Strasbourg, to the media and most of all to 10 Downing Street, where the Prime Minister's advisers see focus groups rather than Parliament itself as the democratic institution which really matters. Although this is a system responsive to the whim of the people, it is actually govern-ment by rolling opinion poll. It substitutes followership for leader-ship, and tightens the ruling party's grip on power. Democracy is just the outer casing: within it lie the elements of an autocratic party regime.

Dissatisfaction with party politics is not confined to Britain. Stirrings of rebellion have shaken the status quo in the United States, with the emergence of citizen candidates in local politics, and the election of a complete outsider as governor of Minnesota in 1998. Jesse 'The Body' Ventura was no ordinary outsider, but a former navy commando and professional wrestler whose flamboy-ant appearance in the ring led his opponents to make the serious mistake of underestimating him. The lesson of that was simple: never think less of a man who wears a pink feather boa and star-spangled tights. He was drawn into politics by the issue of corruption at the town hall level, and dismissed as a stunt or joke candidate when he challenged Democrats and Republicans for the governorship. I knew the feeling: 'The trouble about political jokes,' said Neil Hamilton, 'is that too often they get elected.' He may have been referring to someone he knew.

Mr Ventura's only mistake was to stand not as an Independent but as the candidate of the Reform Party, the old Ross Perot vehicle which attracted some characters even stranger than Mr Perot himself. The ex-wrestler spent $600,000 on the campaign, mostly in matching funds through a loophole in the election law that the regular parties must have wished they had closed, and his opponents spent $13 million between them. It made no difference. He inspired the enthusiasm of people with little previous interest in politics, especially the young; he challenged the power of the party machines and coasted to victory in a three-way contest with 38 per cent of the vote. 'You don't have to be a career politician to serve in public office,' he wrote. 'You can stand on your own two feet and speak your mind, because if people like where you're coming from they will vote you in. The will of the people is still the most powerful voice in government.'[3]

So far from Governor Ventura not being up to the job, as his opponents predicted, he was both successful and popular. His experiences in professional wrestling's school of hard knocks were anything but a handicap for a career in politics. He is a more physical character than I am, and would no doubt have dealt with the ambush on Knutsford Heath with a double head-lock. 'Toughing it out in the ring and dealing with all the back-stabbing and betrayal and infighting – what better training is there for public office?'[4] And in taking on the Republicans and Democrats, he did his country as well as his state a favour. Some of his opinions were completely off the wall, and an easy target for Washington's superior columnists. But it made no difference. The *Washington Post*'s opinions went unheeded in the twin cities of Minneapolis and Saint Paul.

The insurgent campaign of Senator John McCain in the Republican presidential primaries was the same phenomenon on a national scale. Fifteen per cent of Americans now register not as Democrats or Republicans but as Independents; and it was the Independents and new voters who helped bring about the senator's upset victories in New Hampshire and Michigan. They were attracted by his record as a man of honour and an anti-Clinton candidate (no one could be less of a draft-dodger than one who had spent five years in a North Vietnamese prison camp), and by a campaign that had an independent cause as the central plank in its platform. This was the scandal of election spending and the need to put elective office beyond the reach of wealthy people to procure it. McCain's opponent, George W. Bush, had raised $70 million – the biggest war chest in American political history – and was spending it at the rate of $400,000 a day. It bought him the nomination and then the presidency.

Both McCain and Ventura shook up the established order and reminded the politicians of the democratic truth that power lies not with the parties but with the people. British politics could benefit from such a reminder from time to time. The mainstream fringe has something original to offer.

Americans follow our politics closely, because it was the ancestor of theirs; and their scrutiny of the executive seems to work rather better than ours does, although their campaign financing is even more scandalous. A former congressman wrote to me from Florida, concerned about what he had seen of our Parliament on cable TV, where Prime Minister's Question Time competes with other soap operas: 'Do everything you can to check the executive. Damn the torpedoes! Your course will be rewarded by history.'

I am no McCain or Ventura, and am not seeking to break a system which has served our country reasonably well. Representative government needs parties to give it purpose and to make it work. But they are not the be-all and end-all of democracy, and are subject to distortion from within by elements more concerned with power than with process. A case in point in the Labour Party was the electoral college system used to select candidates in the elections for the Welsh Assembly and for Mayor of London: a democratic poll of the party's membership would have yielded different results. Rhodri Morgan and Ken Livingstone, the people's choices in Wales and London, had every right to feel aggrieved. The stitch-up of Livingstone in his contest against Frank Dobson was a contempt of democracy of a crudity not even attempted in North Korea. Only in the people's republic of a Labour Party electoral college could the loser receive 55,000 more votes than the winner. In defending the system, the title of Machine Politician of the Millennium was won beyond dispute by the Home Office Minister Paul Boateng:

'Politics,' he said, 'is about making sure you have the right processes to arrive at the result that enables you to do a job of work.'[5]

Ken Livingstone thrived on persecution like the early Church. And the devices his party used to block him were those that propelled him to victory. I was neutral in the contest, and even refereed one of the candidates' debates. At one point the Labour Party made it known to me, through an intermediary, that they would have liked me to accuse Mr Livingstone of financial impropriety: he had been in a spot of bother with our Commons committee on a matter of undeclared fees for public speaking. I was unimpressed. The Labour Party's procedures had been undemocratic, and I saw no reason to dig them out of a hole of their own making. Besides, Ken was now officially an Independent MP. Since there were two of us, I suggested to him that we should have a leadership contest complete with a rigged electoral college. That was how real political parties did business.

'But what if we don't agree on everything?' he asked.

'That's the whole point of being an Independent,' I answered.

To oppose the controlling tendency, a governing party especially needs within its tent its own champions of democracy, whether it likes them or not (and it tends to find them irritating). The Labour Party is fortunate to have such people, like Bob Marshall-Andrews MP, who describes the device of the electoral college as 'almost always an electoral fraud'.[6] A similar case can be made for one or two (or perhaps even more) Independents outside the party system, to detect anti-democratic toxins in the atmosphere and sound the alarm. It is the function of the canary in the coal mine.

The parties are as indispensable as they think they are, but not as popular. The more rigidly they enforce their discipline, the harder it is for people of self-respect and an independent spirit to operate within them, or even to vote for them. The voting system adopted for the European elections in 1999, for instance, was a party list system which would have done credit to the rule book of the old Bulgarian Communist Party. The people responded, as they had every right to, by staying at home. The 30 per cent turn-out – less than 2 per cent in one ward in Sunderland – was a resounding victory for the Apathy Party. 'In Wales,' wrote Paul Flynn MP, 'bruised, insulted party workers refused to campaign for candidates they had not chosen.'[7] There is a precarious future in such a system, not only for Independents, but for independent-minded MPs like Mr Flynn within a party. They will find no place on a party list, and appear to be an endangered species even in Westminster. There is only too much future, alas, for the ranks of nodding and obsequious back-benchers – the driftwood of politics whose only instinct is to go with the flow. Even the whips despise them.

The obsequiousness of one side provokes the antic behaviour of the other. So it happened in January 2000, when Conservative back-benchers initiated the longest filibuster for more than ten years, on a relatively minor constitutional issue. The debate on the Disqualifications Bill started on Tuesday afternoon and lasted until Wednesday evening without an adjournment. So Wednesday was declared to be Tuesday in the Commons, although it was allowed to be Wednesday in the Lords. It was as if the International Date Line ran through the Central Lobby. When challenged on this nonsense, the Deputy Speaker ruled, 'What goes on outside the Chamber has nothing to do with us.' Michael Fabricant, MP for Lichfield, said of one of the clauses being debated, 'It neither matters nor does not matter.'[8] Either remark could have served as the millennial Parliament's epitaph.

'You do know, don't you,' remarked a rueful Austin Mitchell MP one day, 'that the Parliament you are sitting in is the most depressing there ever was?' He may well have been right, but I will probably know no others to judge it by.

If the New Labour government disappoints, either in its first or second term, in my view it will not be because of a lack of competence, because it is generally competent; or because of a lack of honesty, because it is generally honest; but because of what is best described as its *democratic deficit*. The closed list voting system, the use of electoral colleges for candidate selection, the Registration of Political Parties Act, the intolerance of dissent and the steamrollering of its own back-benchers are all an expression of this, its darker side. It feels threatened by whatever it cannot control. This is a truth evident not only to me but to such free spirits on its own side as Mr Marshall-Andrews: 'This Labour Administration has many virtues but one fatal tragic flaw. All governments ultimately fall on their own swords and the weapon that hangs in the scabbard of New Labour was forged in the obsession with political control at any price.'[9]

The parties' discipline is self-defeating. The tighter it becomes, the greater will be the people's impatience with it, and the incentive for citizen candidates outside the system to break the mould. They will be democrats. They may not be great parliamentarians, ambitious for office and accomplished at the dispatch box, but they will have had a life outside the feverish precincts of Westminster. They will be people with a record of achievement in another world which has nothing to do with politics. They will care little about feuds and factions. They will not play the party game, but will treat their opponents and rivals with courtesy. They will vote without regard to personal advancement. They will aim to make a difference rather than to fill a space, and to leave their mark upon the sands of time. They will not be careerists numbered, in Theodore Roosevelt's phrase, 'among those cold and timid souls who know neither victory or defeat'. And if they fail, they will fail while daring greatly.

Let me state my conviction, finally, that 29,354 of the electors of Tatton did not fail when they voted as they did on that remarkable May Day in 1997. We must be careful not to claim too much for their insurrection, but it surely resounded far beyond the constituency, and both strengthened and cleansed our parliamentary democracy. They applied an independent corrective to a specific and damaging failure of party politics. I hope that, when the history of our times comes to be written, what they accomplished on that day will have an enduring place in it – perhaps not as a chapter but as a footnote, and a benign one. They should be proud of it. They did what they meant to. Their best efforts did not go amiss.

As for my own part in it, I was by chance among those present and found it a considerable privilege as well as an ordeal. There are things in life that you may not enjoy doing, but you will enjoy having done. Campaigning in Tatton in that turbulent spring of 1997 was one of them. I have not led an uneventful life, indeed in some respects I should have liked it to have been quieter than it was, but representing the constituency in Parliament has been professionally the best thing that ever happened to me. Sometimes down south I am asked what it is like. 'Like Surrey,' I always answer, 'but with real people.'

I was lucky to know them and luckier still to represent them. Their good sense, and that of millions of others like them, is the best guarantee the country has of honesty and democracy.

May it happen for you.

17. 'Ethics Man'

Time doesn't just pass in politics. It accelerates. The same thing had happened in the BBC. One day it seemed I was one of the Young Turks, and the next I was the last of the old school of foreign correspondents, closing on retirement with a sense of the years between having vanished almost without trace, or at least with insufficient achievement for all that risk. So it was with my political career, which I dealt with one day at a time. It seemed to be over almost before it began. But others were more far-sighted. As the 1997 Parliament was entering its third year they were already looking ahead to the possibility of Independent representation in the Parliament of 2001. Since my one-term pledge in Tatton was well enough known, they wrote to me eloquently urging me to stand in other constituencies.

It would be a manoeuvre perhaps best described as the reverse chicken run, and as far as I knew it had never before been attempted. The straightforward chicken run is the last resort of a desperate politician. It is what happens when an MP in a marginal constituency, fearing defeat at the next election, moves to a safer and usually neighbouring seat. It is neither daring nor dignified, and wins no friends in the seat being abandoned, but it protects against oblivion. The reverse chicken run, by contrast, would mean leaving a seat which I had a very good chance of winning for a far harder prospect somewhere else. George Osborne remarked that, if I were to try again for Tatton, it would be a 'messy election'. My own view was that mess was beside the point. It would have been quite a contest, a clash of ideas as well as personalities, and I might have prevailed.

I came upon William Hague one day in the corridor outside the House of Commons Library. 'Found yourself a seat yet?' he asked.

'I'm not really looking,' I told him, 'but I've had a few offers, and in fact I have a whole file marked "Independent possibilities".'

'What about Coventry North West?' Coventry North West was Geoffrey Robinson's seat.

'I haven't had a single letter from Coventry.' Neither had I received one from Hartlepool, which was Peter Mandelson's.

'I'm sure it could be arranged.'

Other senior Conservatives, including Ann Widdecombe and Michael Ancram, were of the same opinion. Ann was quite forceful about it and not especially polite. Michael glared at me across the floor of the House. Central Office sent an emissary to my new office in Portcullis House to sound me out. But I am a democrat, and the silences from Coventry and Hartlepool were more convincing than all of their persuasions.

The invitations that I did receive were in equal measure from Conservative and Labour constituencies, as well as one Liberal Democrat. Among the Tories' seats were Rutland and South Norfolk. The Labour places included Harwich and Stoke-on-Trent, which boasted flourishing Independent groups challenging the ruling party's domination. And a free spirit wrote to me from the village of Redmarley d'Abitôt in the Forest of Dean, 'If you would consider standing for us, you would be assured of a very warm welcome and a great many votes. Please, we need you.' Much as I would like to have represented a place with a circumflex accent, it did not by itself seem a sufficient reason to run the Independent flag up the mast and have it shot to pieces by the bombardiers of party politics.

The most challenging offer by far was from Brentwood and Ongar in Essex. A high school student, Ollie Cochran, first wrote to me about it in 1998. Then, a year later, I met Tony Donnelly, Chairman of its Independent Conservatives. He and his group had become alienated from the Conservative Association after their bid to deselect the sitting MP, Eric Pickles, was blocked by Central Office in 1995. Mr Pickles, the former leader of the Tories on Bradford Council, was a Thatcher favourite imposed on Brentwood in 1992, and a hard-working politician but not everyone's idea of a deeply loved constituency MP. A former colleague in Bradford described him as having the temperament of a warlord. None of the infighting was in itself remarkable. It happens all the time in the turbulent world of constituency politics. It is not unusual for MPs to be given more grief locally by their own parties than by their opposition.

What was remarkable was that early in 1998 the Conservative Association, which had been haemorrhaging members, made up some of the loss by recruiting from the congregation of the Peniel Pentecostal Church. This was an evangelical enterprise which had grown out of a bible study group founded by Michael Reid, a former policeman and insurance salesman who was consecrated a Bishop by the late Archbishop Benson Idahosa of Benin City in Nigeria. Mr Reid supported Mr Pickles and the Conservative Association, and urged his followers to do likewise. One hundred and nineteen members of his church joined its Pilgrims Hatch branch between New Year and the annual general meeting in March. They voted out the officers and installed their own. This was the kind of entryism that was strictly against the rules, and had afflicted the Labour Party in the 1980s. Central Office investigated it and found nothing amiss, but without questioning the principal Independent Conservatives on the grounds that they were no longer members of the Party. It was of course a circular argument. They were no longer members of the party *because of the dispute* that the Central Office officials were supposed to be investigating. They could have saved themselves a lot of bother by making a proper job of it.

Beyond these issues of democracy were other shadows cast by the Peniel Pentecostal Church which, if they were found to have substance, would disqualify it from the Evangelical Alliance and from Brentwood's Churches Together, which had been founded at least in part to reach out to Bishop Reid's church and to curb its sectarian tendencies. He was on record as saying that the unemployed should starve, that Moslems were 'vile heathens' and homosexuals were 'filthy perverts'. Even to mention the further allegations was to alert his lawyers to new and lucrative seams of litigation. Brentwood had many more writs flying about in it than you would expect to find in a community at ease with itself. Local journalists felt intimidated. So did some of the clergy. More than 200 people wrote to me asking me to stand. One of them called it a distressed constituency.

My name was first linked with Brentwood and Ongar in a press report in September 2000. I received an immediate call from Bishop Reid requesting a meeting. Better my ground than his, I thought; and I was in no rush. So we met after some strategic delay in the Strangers' Dining Room of the House of Commons. 'Know thine enemy,' was his idea of small talk as we sat down to lunch.

It was one of the most difficult encounters of my life. Outside the Balkan war zones I had seldom met anyone with such a talent for thinking and speaking ill of others. The conversation was wide-ranging, but he kept steering it round to homosexuals and paedophiles – two groups of people who don't cross my personal radar screen for weeks on end. Whatever kind of Christianity this was, it wasn't my kind. It was long on Scripture and short on charity. The Bishop, like the MP, seemed to me to have something of the warlord about him. He provoked a Biblical recollection of my own, *Man is born unto trouble, as the sparks fly upward* (Job v. 7). I remember asking myself why, at a pensionable age, I was doing this again. And why was I destined to deal with such people in both my lives, from Belgrade to Brentwood and from Mostar to Ongar?

I remembered the lessons of Knutsford Heath. In announcing my prospective candidature this time I steered clear of open spaces and common land. I held a press conference on 8 December 2000 in a hotel at the junction of the M25 and A12 in Essex. (The secret agenda was to put the M6's permanent car park, junctions 6 to 10 outside Birmingham, behind me for good.) The journalists asked me, as journalists tend to, whether I was confident of victory. 'Not at all,' I replied, 'I have absolutely no such confidence.'

Since I practised a kind of counter-politics, I encouraged them to write me off as a no-hope candidate. They duly obliged. 'He is bound to lose,' declared the *Independent*.[1] 'His chances are less than zero,' said the *Mail on Sunday*.[2] And Jim Hancock, the BBC's veteran political editor in Manchester, predicted that my parliamentary episode would come to a messy end. This was fine by me.

The idea of a romantic defeat is not recognized by the professional watchers of the political world, with its culture of winner-takes-all. It is a useful rule, in the insurgent campaign of an Independent, to start with low expectations and bad jokes. Perhaps it was not such a bad joke after all. Almost without exception the press reports of that first press conference described me as 'Ethics Man'.

One of those present on that day was John Sweeney of the *Observer*, who has appeared in this chronicle before. He was the scourge of the Hamiltons in the Tatton campaign of 1997 and a man with an unusual sense (for a reporter) of the distinction between right and wrong. What to others was just a news story was to him the bugle call to a crusade. After three weeks of research he produced an excoriating two-page report under the headline 'Sects, power and miracles in the Bible belt of Essex'. It had been modified by the seven lawyers across whose desks it had passed; but it still raised serious questions about the Bishop and his miracles, and about the influence of his Church on family life in the community and on the politics of the constituency. Sweeney believed, as I did, that the underlying issues were even more important in Essex than they had been in Tatton. Neil Hamilton in the last analysis was a middle-ranking politician on the make. Brentwood was different. Witnesses testified to a climate of fear and intimidation. A woman wrote to me from Lancashire who had personal and painful experience of it. She felt that she had been in the presence of something uniquely disturbing.

Then the campaign took a curious turn. Frank Bruno entered the ring. The former heavyweight boxing champion, who lived in Stondon Massey near Brentwood, followed my announcement with one of his own, that he was considering standing as the official Conservative candidate. This was news to Eric Pickles, who already *was* the official Conservative. Mr Bruno, who was appearing in the pantomine *Goldilocks* in Milton Keynes at the time, came up with the arresting slogan 'Don't be a plank, vote for Frank'. As a political programme it lacked definition but promised an original campaign. There was no way of knowing if he was serious. It turned out that he wasn't.

One effect of his intervention was to blow my cover as the no-hope outsider. The bookies started laying odds. The incumbent MP remained the favourite. I was quoted at 3/1. Frank was 66/1. 3/1 was a good price for an unfavoured newcomer. I wondered for how long Mr Pickles would be able to stand by his promise made to me in December of dealing with the challenge by ignoring it.

An unexpected diversion occurred when Peter Mandelson fell from grace for a second time, in January 2001. My mailbag overflowed with letters urging me to abandon Essex and stand against him in Hartlepool. It was an intriguing challenge, and I might have accepted it had it been put to me two months earlier. But none of the letters came from Hartlepool except one from the well-qualified Conservative candidate, Gus Robinson, who implored me most courteously to stay away. I eventually endorsed him, together with Paul Keetch the Liberal Democrat in Hereford, and Hilton Dawson the Labour MP in Lancaster. Both Keetch and Dawson survived with wafer-thin majorities.

I also received invitations to stand in Leicester East against Keith Vaz, the Minister for Europe, who had courted disgrace by refusing to co-operate fully with the Parliamentary Commissioner for Standards. I was tempted, but again the opportunity came too late. I was already committed to my new friends in Brentwood and Ongar.

The Essex constituency had a Tatton-style buzz to it. A steering group was formed without my instigation, under the banner of 'Friends of Bell'. Its twenty members ranged across the political spectrum from deep red, through tinges of green and yellow, to true blue. They worked together with missionary zeal and enthusiasm, and I thought of them affectionately as the Crazy Gang. On a damp night in February they organized an exploratory public meeting at a school hall in Ingatestone. It was not especially well advertised. They hoped for a turnout of 100; 300 showed up. This served notice to the Pickles Conservatives that we were serious, and to the Bishop that he had competition. The atmosphere was, in its own way, evangelical. Paul Vallely wrote in the *Independent*, 'Mr Pickles' 9,690 vote majority is looking anything but secure.'[3] An investment banker friend added, 'Were I a betting man, I would feel that an even-money punt would be irresistible. At 3/1 I would be re-mortgaging the house!'

The Prime Minister went to the Palace on 8 May, and announced the election for 7 June. It was from the start a one-horse race. The Conservative Party was in a state of disarray close to meltdown. The polls showed an impregnable Labour lead, but also a wider disaffection with party politics. It was a good time to be offering an alternative electoral style, which the *Brentwood Gazette* described as 'alluring'. The *Gazette*, although a Toryish newspaper, stood to gain from a high-profile contest. So did the town itself.

I opened the campaign at a crowded press conference in the Brentwood Theatre on 14 May, the day of the dissolution of Parliament. As before, I set a ceiling of £100 on campaign contributions – later raised to £300 because of threats of legal action. The money and the volunteers started flowing in immediately to our office in Brentwood and our shop on the High Street in Ongar. At the same early stage the Tatton campaign had been a shambles in a hotel cellar. We were better organized now, but needed to be. No Independent had successfully taken on the established parties for half a century – with the possible exception of Dick Taverne, standing under the banner of Democratic Labour in the Lincoln by-election in 1973.

The press for the most part greeted the enterprise with a drizzle of sceptical comment; what was I doing, they wondered, involving myself in a Conservative club brawl? They skimmed the surface of the issue and moved on. Only those who had lived or worked in Brentwood understood the complexity and depth of it. They reacted differently. Most of them welcomed me warmly, although a few did not. They took posters and stickers and signed on to join the campaign. One man wound down his car window and called me a 'top notch geezer'. I had never been called that before. I felt at that stage that I would either win or lose by a small margin. It would take a lot of hard work, a bit of luck, a general rejection of status quo politics – and a higher 'geezer rating' than Eric Pickles.

Help also came from outside. Some of my former supporters, the forces of democracy in Tatton, insisted on coming down to Brentwood and Ongar. I never invited them, but wouldn't have stopped them either. There were endorsements from John Le Carré, Jeremy Irons, John Fortune, the Earl of Iveagh, Lord Chalfont and Alex Salmond, among others. Contributions arrived from Bradford; Mr Pickles was not universally admired in his former fiefdom. And an inmate of Frankland Prison in Durham, whose family I had helped in Tatton, offered to stuff envelopes for me if I would send them to his prison. As in Tatton, there was a dynamic to it – like fighting a national by-election.

There was also a potentially fatal handicap. The political narrative was harder to establish. Eric Pickles was no Neil Hamilton. He was an average, or even above average, politician whose handling of constituency matters was, however, not beyond reproach. There was a perception of certain conflicts of interest, and his relationship with the Peniel Church was only one of them. Another was the sale of the Epping to Ongar Railway to Pilot Developments, a property company which stood to make a small fortune – fifteen times the purchase price – by selling the railway yard as building land. The promise to revive the rail link was never fulfilled. Many of Mr Pickles's constituents were suspicious, and some were outraged, by the most controversial property deal during his nine years as their MP. None of this would have damaged him, except that one of the company's directors at the time of the sale was Mr Willy White, his close personal friend and Chairman of the Brentwood and Ongar Conservative Association. Mr Pickles properly acknowledged these links, and claimed he had not been influenced by them.

There were reasonable questions to be asked about this, and

about his relationship with the Peniel Pentecostal Church. He drew support both financially and politically from the church community, which had been instructed to join the Conservative Party. He might have difficulty being perceived as neutral in any future constituency issue involving the Church and its Bishop; and that there would be such issues was as certain as tomorrow's traffic jams and next year's tax demands.

The role of Bishop Michael Reid was the iceberg issue of the whole campaign – not much visible above the surface, but lurking with menace beneath it. Many people in Pilgrim's Hatch, where the Church was situated, were in a state of deep anxiety about it. They included a few who had managed to escape and restart their lives outside it. Brian and Elizabeth Armstrong bravely came forward during the campaign and spoke of the systematic enrolment of the Church's congregation in party politics: 'There was a kind of dictatorship telling us we must join the Conservative Party.' Ironically, Mr Armstrong was a natural Tory who would have joined the party if he hadn't been ordered to.

The Bishop had taken a temporary vow of silence, but he could not silence the internet. A Brentwood exile in New York sent me an interview, from a religious website, which was couched in distinctly unfriendly terms. It was headed 'Defrocking the Man in the White Suit'. The Bishop called me 'a devious individual' and even a kind of fascist: 'Listening to Martin Bell and his cronies you'd think we'd all need to wear a yellow star . . . It smacks of one of the most spiteful, hateful things that ever hit this century; it's called Nazism.'

I had been called many things in my sixty-two years, but never before a Nazi. I drew the Bishop's rant to the attention of the *Brentwood Gazette*. I suggested that at least a retraction was in order, and that Mr Pickles – who was not an extremist – might like to disown the support of someone who was. The *Gazette* printed not a word of it. Nor did it mention the compelling testimony of the Church's most recent defectors. As for the people of Pilgrim's Hatch, their newspaper of record left them without a voice – as if it had decided to join the Bishop in a timely conversion to Trappism. Its only reference to the Church, at this critical phase of the campaign, was a story about the Peniel Academy's winning table tennis team. For the first time in my life I understood the peculiar passion of conspiracy theorists everywhere. Give me a couple more weeks of this, and I'd be a paid-up member of the green ink brigade. I was saddened but not greatly surprised, since I had been this way before. The *Knutsford Guardian* had won itself no medals for valour either.

One thing the *Gazette* couldn't wish away was the result of its own opinion poll, commissioned the week before. It put Eric Pickles at 45.3 per cent, myself at 42.9 per cent, the Liberal Democrat David Kendall at 6.8 per cent and the Labour candidate, Diana Johnson, at 5.0 per cent. The poll was damaging to the minor parties; but it broadly reflected our own canvass returns, and to be within three points of Mr Pickles was no mean achievement from a standing start in just seven days of campaigning. The *News of the World* headlined: 'BELL ON BRINK OF "SLEAZE" WIN No. 2'.[4]

Under pressure the *Gazette* relented. It published the 'Nazi' allegation a week later, but balanced this out with an interview with Bishop Reid which filled the editorial page on the week before polling day. I wondered what had earned him the right to such a platform, except his unprecedented intervention in party politics. The Roman Catholic Bishop of Brentwood and the Anglican Bishop of Chelmsford, whose authority was unquestioned, were offered no such generous space in the newspaper's pages. Their views would have been a contribution to the democratic debate. Bishop Reid's were not. He was partisan and polemical in a way which I actually welcomed. The Bishop was the Christine Hamilton of the Brentwood campaign. He could no longer keep silent, and every time he sounded off he won me more votes. There is an element of serendipity in politics, and a candidate can be as lucky in his enemies as in his friends. I was only sorry that the *Gazette* didn't publish the full transcript of its interview, in which he described me as a 'whited sepulchre'. The last person who had called me that was Neil Hamilton . . . and look what happened to him.

The Bishop also replicated the Hamilton campaign in resorting to lawyers' letters to try to stop us. At that point I revived the form of words I had used about Neil Hamilton: I described him as a difficult man to admire. So much of honest politics is common sense, or should be, that it made me wonder why Mr Pickles should still accept the support of someone who had done him so much damage. Without the Bishop and his Church I would have been campaigning elsewhere, probably in Leicester East, or not at all.

The Tories were rattled. Our website took 12,000 hits in one week, including 123 from Conservative Central Office. In the streets and on the doorsteps the tide was turning, although perhaps not far or fast enough. The canvass returns improved dramatically. The posters flourished. Tactical voters and first-time voters turned to us in droves. At public meetings Eric Pickles was shouted down by his former supporters. The most powerful force in any election, word of mouth, was working in our favour. Antonio Fargas – Huggy Bear of *Starsky and Hutch* – joined the campaign and coined a slogan for it: 'The word on the street is Bell'. The street in question was Brentwood High Street. David Soul was alongside him. All that we lacked was Starsky: the stars of the 70s were working their magic for us.

We were possessed by an exhilaration. We thought that we had within our reach one of the most spectacular victories of the 2001 General Election. And yet . . . a still small voice inside me warned that we could be deluding ourselves. The contest turned on the links between Bishop Reid and Eric Pickles – links which Mr Pickles denied. There were links, of course, both political and financial. The two men even shared the same publicist. But the denials could be enough to persuade wavering Tories to vote tribally on the day. We needed a political earthquake and three quarters of an earthquake would not be enough.

At midnight on 7 June, two hours after the polls closed, I arrived at the Brentwood Leisure Centre, surrounded by a great crowd of supporters. Tony Donnelly and his son Richard were already inside, and were trying hard not to look shattered. 'I'm not over the moon,' said Tony. From the first ballot boxes to be opened they had seen that we were running Pickles close, but not quite close enough. Liberal Democrat and Labour supporters had switched to us in their thousands, but enough of them had stayed loyal to their parties to hand the seat to the Tories. Eric Pickles had 16,558 votes. I had 13,737. Some of those Liberal Democrat and Labour voters must have wondered afterwards whether it was really the result that they wanted. From a standing start, and against all parties, I had cut the Conservative majority by more than 6,000. 'You should have won,' said Diana Johnson, the Labour candidate. But Eric Pickles was still the MP, and for the first time in my life I was unemployed.

There was an immediate consolation in the election of another Independent in Wyre Forest (Kidderminster). During the campaign I had travelled there with John Fortune to speak for Dr Richard Taylor, the retired consultant who was the candidate of the Kidderminster Health Concern Party. The issue which had provoked an insurrection was the government's downgrading of the town's once excellent hospital. In the greatest upset of the night, Dr Taylor defeated the sitting MP and junior minister David Lock by more than 17,000 votes. It was the biggest Opposition majority of the entire General Election. I offered the new MP my computer, my office and my wonderful secretary – as well as advice about how to survive outside the party system. He was no more a professional politician than I was; but he was the keeper of the Independent flame, and would have to live – as I once had – with the consequences of victory.

Life for a loser is altogether easier. The more I looked at my future, the brighter it seemed. No longer would I have to attend the parliamentary puppet show and listen to Members hungry for preferment congratulating their Right Honourable Friends. No longer would I acquiesce in committee room compromises. No longer would I play the part of super-councillor, and intervene in neighbours' disputes and planning disputes. No longer would I tangle with the bureaucracy of the Child Support Agency. No longer would I be obliged to answer the tide of green ink mail when the moon was full.

I walked out of the Leisure Centre into the soft light of dawn on 8 June. I was followed by the most remarkable team of people I had ever worked with. They were trying not to be downcast. I was close to tears yet also somehow euphoric. The enterprise had justified itself. David Butler, the historian of general elections, wrote to me, 'Your 32 per cent was, apart from Wyre Forest, the most impressive performance of 2001.'

No regrets. The adventure was over, at least for the time being – and probably for good.

Notes

1 *The Death of News*
1. BBC Radio 4, *The News Is Our Currency*, May 1997
2. Eli Wiesel, speech at the opening of the Washington Holocaust Memorial, April 1993

2 *The Edge of Madness*
1. A. P. Herbert, *Independent Member*, Methuen, 1950, p. 28

3 *Planet Tatton*
1. Samuel Johnson, *Diaries, Prayers, and Annals*, Yale University Press, 1958
2. An involuntary misquotation from Chesterton's 'The Secret People', *The Collected Poems of G. K. Chesterton*, Methuen, 1954, p. 173
3. Václav Havel, New Year speech, Prague, 1 January 1990
4. S. Pugh, 'Sometimes', *Poems on the Underground*, Cassell, 1999

4 *Where Do I Hang My Sword?*
1. Committee on Standards and Privileges, First Report, 2 July 1997, p.129
2. Committee on Standards and Privileges, Eighth Report, 5 November 1997, p. viii

5 *The People's Stooge*
1. A. P. Herbert, *Independent Member*, Methuen, 1950
2. Ibid.
3. Ibid.
4. Isaiah Berlin, *First and Last*, Granta Books, 1999, p. 77

8 *Minefields*
1. *Daily Telegraph*, 27 June 1998
2. *The Tablet*, 13 September 1997

9 *Loose Cannons*
1. Hansard, 17 December 1998
2. Ibid.
3. Tony Benn's assertion was based on a disputed analysis of a Truman policy statement in November 1950
4. Hansard, 17 December 1998
5. Ibid.
6. Ibid.

10 *Soldier's Story*
1. Hansard, 13 December 1997
2. Ibid., 14 July 1999

11 *Kosovo*
1. A. Loyd, *My War Gone By, I Miss It So*, Doubleday, 1999, p. 303
2. *Mail on Sunday*, 4 April 1999
3. Hansard, 28 March 1999
4. Ibid., 10 May 1999
5. *Daily Telegraph*, 11 June 1999
6. M. Stankovic, *Trusted Mole*, HarperCollins, 2000, p. 85
7. Speech at RUSI, 9 July 1999

12 *Happenings*
1. Hansard, 21 July 1999
2. *Manchester Evening News*, 15 June 1999

13 *New Labour, New Sleaze?*
1. Evidence to the Neill Committee, 12 July 1999
2. Standards and Privileges Committee, Nineteenth Report, 10 November 1998, p. vi

3. Standards and Privileges Committee, Ninth Report, 30 June 1999, p. xiii

4. Ibid., p. 17

5. Ibid., p. 14

6. Quoted by Catherine Bennett, *Guardian*, 14 October 1999

7. Evidence to the Neill Committee, 13 May 1998

8. Government Proposals on the Funding of Political Parties, July 1999, p. 53

14 The Pledge

1. Julian Critchley, *A Bag of Boiled Sweets*, Faber and Faber, 1995, p. 191

15 Unfinished Business

1. *The Times*, 22 December 1999

2. Manifesto Magazine, May 1998

16 Standing Alone

1. Enoch Powell (ed. R. Collings), *Reflections*, Bellew, 1992, pp. 118–19.

2. Interview by Philip Cowley, Deputy Director of the Centre for Legislative Studies, June 1999

3. Jesse Ventura, *I Ain't Got Time To Bleed*, Villard Books, 1999, p. 145

4. Ibid., p. 122

5. BBC 1, *Panorama*, 13 December 1999

6. Bob Marshall-Andrews MP, Foreword to *Dragons Led By Poodles*, Politico's, 1999, p. 3

7. Paul Flynn MP, *Dragons Led By Poodles*, p. 153

8. Hansard, 28 January 2000

9. Bob Marshall-Andrews MP, Foreword to *Dragons Led By Poodles*, p. 4

17 'Ethics Man'

1. *Independent*, 9 December 2000

2. *Mail on Sunday*, 11 December 2000

3. *Independent*, 20 February 2001

4. *News of the World*, 27 May 2001

Index